Contemporary Cases in Sport

Volume 1

Also available online

All the cases within *Contemporary Cases in Sport Volume 1* are available for individual download from the Contemporary Cases Online website at:

www.goodfellowpublishers.com

Ideal for student and seminar use, the online cases are packed with hyperlinks to original sources, further readings and websites. Readers can immediately follow these links to obtain further information about the specific concepts, terms, issues and organisations identified in each case.

Cases can also be purchased in a 'pick-and-mix' fashion to suit course content or research requirements.

Also in this series

Contemporary Cases in Tourism: Volume 1

Hardback: £65.00

ISBN: 9781906884536

All of its 10 cases are also available for individual download from the Contemporary Cases Online website at:

www.goodfellowpublishers.com

Contemporary Cases in

Tourism Heritage Hospitality Leisure Retail Events Sport

Series editors: Brian Garrod (Aberystwyth University) and Alan Fyall (University of Central Florida)

Contemporary Cases in Sport

Volume 1

Edited by
Brian Garrod
Alan Fyall

 Goodfellow Publishers Ltd

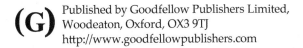 Published by Goodfellow Publishers Limited,
Woodeaton, Oxford, OX3 9TJ
http://www.goodfellowpublishers.com

British Library Cataloguing in Publication Data: a catalogue record for
this title is available from the British Library.

Library of Congress Catalog Card Number: on file.

ISBN: 978-1-908999-21-4

Copyright © Goodfellow Publishers Ltd 2013

 Design and typesetting by P.K. McBride, www.macbride.org.uk

Printed by Baker & Taylor, www.baker-taylor.com

Cover design by Cylinder, www.cylindermedia.com

Contents

Contributors

Margaret Deery, Curtin University, Australia

Tim Breitbarth, Bournemouth University, United Kingdom

Liz Fredline, Griffith University, Australia

Sean Gammon, University of Central Lancashire, United Kingdom

Tom Hinch, University of Alberta, Canada

Leo Jago, Bournemouth University, United Kingdom

Katherine King, Bournemouth University, United Kingdom

ShiNa Li, Leeds Metropolitan University, United Kingdom

Amanda Miller, Manchester Metropolitan University, United Kingdom

Gregory Ramshaw, Clemson University, United States of America

Nancy Stevenson, University of Westminster, United Kingdom

Xi Wang, China Meteorological Administration, China Foreign Affairs University, China

Richard Keith Wright, Auckland University of Technology, New Zealand

About the Editors

Dr Brian Garrod is Reader in Tourism Management at Aberystwyth University. His interests span all aspects of tourism and recreation but his particular areas of specialism are in sustainable tourism, ecotourism and heritage tourism. He is also fascinated by the role of photography in tourism. He has published widely, including several text books with Alan Fyall. He has worked as a consultant to the United Nations World Tourism Organization (UNWTO), the Organisation for Economic Cooperation and Development (OECD) and the Welsh Assembly Government (WAG). He is Co-Editor of Elsevier's *Journal of Destination Marketing & Management*, Book Reviews Editor of the *Journal of Heritage Tourism* and a member of the editorial boards of the *Journal of Ecotourism*, the *International Journal of Tourism Research* and *Tourism in Marine Environments*. He lives deep in the Welsh countryside with his wife and three children, and in his spare time he enjoys rocking out on his bass guitar.

Dr Alan Fyall is Professor at the Rosen College of Hospitality Management, University of Central Florida. Prior to arriving in the USA, Alan was Professor of Tourism and Deputy Dean, Research & Enterprise in the School of Tourism, Bournemouth University, UK. He has published widely in his fields of expertise and is the author of over 100 articles, book chapters and conference papers, as well as 14 books including *Tourism Principles & Practice*, one of the leading international textbooks on the subject published by Pearson. Alan has organised a number of international conferences and workshops for academic, professional and governmental audiences and is frequently invited to deliver key note addresses. He is Co-Editor of Elsevier's *Journal of Destination Marketing & Management*, while he also sits on the editorial boards of *Annals of Tourism Research*, *Journal of Heritage Tourism*, *International Journal of Tourism Research*, *Anatolia* and *Regional Statistics*. Alan is also a visiting professor at the universities of Ulster and Edinburgh Napier in the UK and the Université d'Angers in France. Alan's current research interests lie in destination management and emerging destination management structures, and the impact of generational change on patterns of buying behaviour in the context of attractions and destinations. Alan is a former member of the Bournemouth Tourism Management Board and has conducted numerous consulting and applied research projects for clients across the UK and overseas, including the European Union, Commonwealth Secretariat, Grant Thornton and Malaysian Ministry of Tourism. Alan lives in Florida with his wife and two children and spends as much time outdoors as possible.

Acknowledgements

The editors would like to thank all contributors to this volume for their perseverance with the reviewing process and for their patience in accommodating Prof Alan Fyall's move to the United States.

Special thanks are also due to Dr Richard Shipway, Bourenmouth University, UK, as many of the contributions to this volume originated from his ESRC *'International Networking and Training Opportunities'* research grant linked to sport tourism and international sports events, that supported early career researchers with an interest in research on the impacts and legacies of sports events.

Finally, sincere thanks are due to Tim Goodfellow and Sally North of Goodfellow Publishers Limited, for their continued support and encouragement.

1

The Case Study Approach

Academic Pariah or Wrongly Maligned?

Brian Garrod and Alan Fyall

Introduction

The case study approach has often been marked out as an academic pariah, depicted at best as a highly inferior method of advancing human knowledge about a subject (Xiao and Smith, 2006), at worse as a refuge of academic charlatans "whose disciplinary origins do not include the tools necessary to analyze and theorize the complex cultural and social processes" associated with tourism (Franklin and Crang, 2001: 5). Xiao and Smith (2006) further note that case studies have been described as atheoretical, ungeneralisable, fundamentally intuitive, primitive and unmanageable. Much of this denigration of the case study approach has actually come from within the social sciences, with those hailing from disciplines with a quantitative tradition tending to be among its most vociferous critics.

Such arguments, which can probably be attributed as much to academic snobbery as they can to a clear understanding of the principles of research methodology, have tended to suppress the use of the case study approach in tourism research. Many academics have avoided case study research because they fear that it will not be accepted by peers, let alone published in the learned journals. Even so, Xiao and Smith (2006) identified a total of 78 articles based on case studies published between 2000 and 2004 in the *Journal of Travel Research*, *Annals of Tourism Research*, *Tourism Analysis* and *Tourism Management*, representing nearly 10% of the total number of articles published in those four journals over that time period. This represents not an insubstantial proportion of the research that tourism academics have been publishing.

Setting aside for the moment arguments concerning the value of the case study approach in the context of research, it will be evident to readers who regularly work in the classroom that students, at all levels of ability and from all backgrounds, appreciate the opportunity to learn through case studies.

When asked why they like case studies, students often reply that they help them to consolidate what they are learning and to apply it to the 'real world' they see around them. Are we then to believe that our students must be misguided in their desire to learn through case studies? Perhaps they have failed to appreciate that case studies really have no intellectual value and hence deserve no place in the classroom? Their craving for case studies must simply be a phase they are going through; all we really need to do is to wait patiently for them to grow out of it?

We believe otherwise. The intention of this series of books is to demonstrate that not only do case studies merit a place in the classroom but that they can be extremely effective pedagogical tools. Indeed, no scheme of work should be without one or more in-depth case studies to help students to appreciate more fully the conceptual and theoretical material we are delivering to them. We believe that students are not fundamentally mistaken in their liking of the case study approach. When students are continually fed a diet of dry theory, it is only natural that they will show cravings for the occasional juicy case study to help them to swallow down their meals. Rather than being something to avoid at all costs, case studies can be a positive asset in our teaching.

The major problem faced by potential users of case studies in the classroom is, however, that case studies can take an inordinate amount of time and effort to write. The purpose of a case study should be to communicate facts, not broad concepts or general principles, so that students can situate their learning in a particular context, thereby developing their understanding of how concepts and theories can be applied to the world outside their classroom window. But the facts specific to a particular case are often hard to track down. Writing an effective case study also requires that the author appreciates not only what the readers are supposed to learn from the case but how they are supposed to learn it. Writers of cases will need to anticipate the learning process in order that by reading the text of the case, examining the accompanying material, discussing issues raised in the case with each other, answering the questions at the end and reflecting on what it all means, readers will be able to develop a deeper understanding of what the case is all about. If writing good case studies was easy, then presumably there would be a lot more of them freely available for educators to introduce directly into their courses.

Sadly this is not the case. Until the publication of this book series, there have been very few sets of ready-made case studies for the educator to call upon that are relevant to the needs of students, instructive and contemporary. Part of the problem is that much material that is labelled as a case study turns out not to be especially useful in the classroom. Many of the so-called case studies included in textbooks simply take the form of extended examples: perhaps a few hundred words to illustrate a particular point the author wishes to emphasise. This kind of case study tends not to be sufficiently extensive or in-depth for students to get a very good grasp of the background to the subject, the forces coming to bear on a particular problem, the actors involved, the potential range of solutions, the constraints presently faced or the implications of any of this. Students therefore tend to struggle to use such case studies to develop their understanding of the subject they relate to. They are, to be blunt, often of strictly limited value as pedagogical tools.

Case studies can also quickly go out of date: economic conditions alter, government policy contexts change, new actors enter while others exit, and existing problems are overcome (or accommodated) while new problems emerge to take their place. Young people do not have long memories; nor do they relate well to case studies set in the context of the world they lived in when they were children, maybe even before they were born. As such, there is always room for new cases to be developed for use in the classroom: contemporary cases that relate to the problems of today in the context of today. It is often possible for existing cases that have become outdated to be modernised. Cases that consider very recent issues and subjects will usually, however, have to be written from scratch. Keeping one's case studies fresh is always going to be a problem for the instructor wishing to use them in his or her schemes of work.

The purpose of the *Contemporary Cases* series is to rehabilitate the case study approach and instate it on the educational map by establishing a ready resource of in-depth, high-quality, up-to-date case studies for instructors to use in their teaching. Each volume will focus on one of the subject areas covered by the series as a whole – events, heritage, hospitality, leisure, tourism, retail and sport – and provide a number of detailed, in-depth case studies that can be inserted, more or less directly, in the scheme of work of a module covering these subjects. At the end of each chapter will be a number of self-test questions for students to consider. These are designed to encourage students to reflect on the case, mentally wrestle with the issues it covers, apply their prior learning to the case and draw appropriate lessons from it. Each case study chapter will also include some suggestions for further reading and websites related to the material presented in the case study.

Each case study will also be made available electronically via the *Contemporary Cases Online* (CCO) website. The benefit of purchasing the case studies in this way is that the electronic version will include a large number of hyperlinks to websites. Readers with a web browser will be able to follow these links to obtain further information about the specific concepts, terms, issues and organisations identified in each case. The CCO website will also include an instructor's pack for each case study for separate purchase. These will include a number of essay questions based on the case, ideas for specific themes that can be developed from the case material, links to further teaching resources and a number of questions that can be used in an examination, along with guideline answers. The instructor's pack will also include a slideshow presentation that can be used in the class to remind students of the themes considered in the case and look at any photographs or diagrams accompanying the case in full colour.

It is the intention of the series editors that, wherever possible, the material published on the web will be regularly updated. This will help to ensure that the cases remain contemporary, relevant, vibrant and easy for students to relate to.

What is a case study?

Stake (1995: xi) provides a basic definition of the case study approach, that being:

> "the study of the complexity and particularity of a single case, coming to understand its activity within important circumstances".

The purpose of a case study, then, is to attempt to develop a nuanced understanding of what is happening at a specific point of time in a specific context, and why it is happening. As such, a case study will attempt to answer questions such as what are the processes of change, what are the external and internal factors that influence those processes, and what the changes might imply for those implicated in them, be it directly or indirectly, actively or passively.

Stake goes on to identify three types of case study: *intrinsic*, *instrumental* and *collective*.

♦   The first type, the intrinsic case study, is intended simply to study a particular case, with no attempt to learn about other cases or draw wider lessons.

♦   Second is the instrumental case study, the purpose of which is to learn wider lessons for the study of the subject, issue, organisation or problem at hand. The intention is that by studying one case in depth we will get a clearer picture of what is going on in the broader context. In view of this aim, it is sometimes better to choose to study an atypical one rather than a typical one. Indeed, an atypical case study may allow us to draw more relevant lessons than a typical one. For example, holiday companies expect, or at least hope, that their holidays will usually be delivered successfully from the holidaymaker's point of view. Sometimes, however, things will go wrong. Arguably there are more valuable lessons to be learned from the minority of cases where the holiday has been unsatisfactory than from the majority of cases where it has proceeded successfully.

♦ The third type of case study, according to Stake, is the collective case study. This is part of a set of case studies related to a particular context or problem, the cases being selected in such a way as to enable comparisons and contrasts to be drawn across them. In this way a broader and more detailed picture can be built up of the subject as a whole.

Perhaps the best-know definition of the case study approach, however, is that of Yin (1994: 13), who defines a case study as the:

> "investigation of a contemporary phenomenon within its real-life context, especially when the boundaries between phenomenon and context are not clearly evident, and that relies on multiple sources of evidence, with data needing to converge in a triangulating fashion".

For Yin, then, the emphasis is on investigating a phenomenon that is so deeply embedded in its context that it is hard to distinguish one from the other. To divorce the problem from its context would be to risk, almost guarantee, that the problem will be misunderstood. In order to learn about the problem, and hopefully develop solutions to it, we need to study it in the specific context in which it is situated. Abstracted study of the problem that is divorced from its context will not yield meaningful or effective answers. The definition suggested by Yin also emphasises the need to draw upon multiple sources of information, bringing them together in the context of the case study through a process of triangulation (Decrop, 1999; Oppermann, 2000). This enables the researcher to examine the issue or problem at hand from a number of different perspectives, yielding insights that they would not be possible to gain by examining the situation from a single viewpoint. In this way, case studies paint a rich picture of the subject, enabling readers to appreciate more fully what is going on and why.

Yin (2003) then goes on to identify six different kinds of case study that fit within his definition. First, any case can be a *single case study* or a *multiple case study*, depending on whether it focuses on just one instance of the phenomenon or on several instances. Either way, the purpose is to draw out wider lessons about the subject. Secondly, any case, whether single or multiple, can be an *exploratory*, *descriptive* or *explanatory case study*. The first of these, exploratory case studies, are intended to help to define questions and hypothesis about the phenomenon being studied. These questions can then be effectively addressed by other kinds of case study (descriptive or explanatory) or through alternative research methods if they are deemed better suited to the task. The purpose of the second type, the descriptive case study, is to describe the phenomenon at hand, perhaps in greater detail than has been achieved before or perhaps focusing on some aspect of the phenomenon that has hitherto been overlooked. The third type, the explanatory case study, attempts to identify cause-and-effect relationships, explaining how and perhaps why things happened in the way that they did.

The purpose of single case studies will often be *deductive*: to see how well a concept or theory can be applied to a real-world situation, or to investigate how a concept or theory might be modified to fit a particular context. The purpose of multiple case studies, meanwhile, will often be *inductive*: to compare, contrast and identify patterns and regularities within and between cases, thereby enabling a broader understanding of the subject to be achieved (Xiao and Smith, 2006).

While single case studies are often criticised on methodological grounds, Yin (2003) provides a number of styles of single case study which he considers to be potentially useful: the *critical case study*, which tries to bring out the pros and cons of a particular case (for example, to consider the critical incidents in a process); the *extreme/unique case study*, which attempts to bring out lessons by considering what happens at the extremes of the phenomenon; the *representative/typical case study*, which attempts to explain what 'normally' happens in a particular context; the *revelatory case study*, which attempts to challenge and reshape the reader's preconceptions; and the *longitudinal case study*, which provides a series of snapshots of the case over a period of time, often encouraging readers to decide what they would do to solve a problem and to discover whether that solution would indeed have worked. This latter kind of case study is actually very similar to a simulation exercise, which may be based around some form of decision tree so that users can go back and explore the implications of alternative decisions they could have made.

The benefits of using case studies in the classroom

While the case study approach is often maligned by academics, it also has a number of fierce proponents. The latter tend to advocate the use of case studies in the classroom for the following reasons:

♦ Case studies can help students to see for themselves how theory links to practice, encourage them to think more deeply about the subject at hand and persuade them to consider more carefully the implications of what they have learned.

♦ The multi-source nature of case studies enables alternative viewpoints of various stakeholders to be illustrated, as well as demonstrating the interaction among and between the different actors and variables concerned.

♦ The open-ended character of case studies helps to show students that there is very often no 'right' or 'wrong' answer to a problem. As such, case studies reflect the true nature of knowledge-building, which is frequently contextual, situated, complex and ambiguous.

♦ Case studies can stimulate students' interest and get them thinking seriously about the issues concerned. This promotes active rather than passive learning. It also emphasises free-thinking and exploration as opposed to prescription or prediction.

♦ It is possible to simulate the passage of time through longitudinal case studies, which allows students to see the consequences of decisions made by actors in the case or by themselves (a form of simulation game).

♦ Working with case studies helps students to develop and apply various transferable skills, including problem-solving, critical thinking, inter-personal communication and team-working.

♦ The 'real-world' nature of case studies helps students to link their learning to their personal goals, helping them to see the relevance of what they are learning and thus harnessing their enthusiasm to learn.

♦ Using case studies can encourage greater, two-way interaction among students, and between the students and the instructor.

The chapters that follow in this book embody the various authors' attempts to capture such benefits. The editors sincerely hope that readers will adopt some of these cases for use in their classrooms and would be very interested to receive users' feedback. Whether you have had positive or negative experiences of using these cases, please do let us know.

Brian Garrod (bgg@aber.ac.uk)

Alan Fyall (alan.fyall@ucf.edu)

January 2013

References

Decrop A. 1999. Triangulation in qualitative tourism research. *Tourism Management* **20** (1): 157-161.

Franklin A, Crang M. 2001. The trouble with tourism and travel theory. *Tourist Studies* **1** (1): 5-22.

Oppermann M. 2000. Triangulation: A methodological discussion. *International Journal of Tourism Research* **2** (2): 141-145.

Stake RE. 1995. *The Art of Case Study Research*. Thousand Oaks, London and New Delhi: Sage.

Xiao H, Smith S L J. 2006. Case studies in tourism research: A state-of-the-art analysis, *Tourism Management* **27** (5): 738-749.

Yin R K. 1994. *Case Study Research: Design and Methods*, 2nd Edition. Thousand Oaks: Sage.

Yin R K. 2003. *Case Study Research: Design and Methods*, 3rd Edition. Thousand Oaks: Sage.

2

Writing Case Studies

Reaction and Reflection, Rigour and Relevance

Alan Fyall and Brian Garrod

Introduction: Reaction and reflections on case authorship

One of the catalysts for the creation of the *Contemporary Cases* series was the sense of frustration the editors had with the paucity of high-quality case study materials in the tourism, heritage, hospitality, leisure, retail, events and sport subject areas. This frustration was only heightened by the recognition that the student learning experience could be improved so much through the use of carefully designed, well-written, in-depth case studies. Most of the case studies in existence seemed to be too short, too shallow, too bland or too out-of-date to be of real use in university teaching. What was needed was a series of cases with more ambition, that educators could adopt and use in their classes almost straight away, and which students would find relevant, instructive and – perhaps most importantly of all – stimulating. The scarcity of such case materials raised a number of questions in the editors' minds, including why there seemed to be so few fully developed case studies in publication, why academics are not more widely engaged in writing such cases for their own use and, more fundamentally, what constitutes a 'successful' case study?

Students at all levels seem to appreciate and benefit from learning through the use of case studies and tutors always seem to be on the look-out for contemporary case material to use in their classes. This demand on the part of tutors is in fact one of the key messages communicated by publishers when they negotiate book contracts with aspiring authors: the promise to include copious amounts of 'high-quality case material' is almost a standard prerequisite for winning a book contract. It is therefore a perpetual source of astonishment, as well as disappointment, that there are so few published works that actually deliver on this promise. To put it bluntly, there is a very real and expressed need for high-quality case material, yet the academic community – at least in the fields of tourism, heritage, hospitality, leisure, retail, events and sport – does not seem to be delivering the materials required to meet this need.

The aim of this series of case studies is to help address this paucity of high-quality case material. In doing so, it aspires to 'raise the bar' in terms of the quality of case-study writing. It also seeks to stimulate higher levels of engagement in the use of the case studies, both by students and tutors, by providing a body of materials that are challenging, thought-provoking and instructive. This, in the view of the editors, is best achieved by making the case studies rich in terms of visual materials, numerical data, references, hyperlinks to sources and further reading, and so on. In this way, readers can immerse themselves in the case study and almost feel that they are there, in context, learning from real life rather than out of books.

While it is still undoubtedly too early to judge the success of this approach, the first volume in the series, which is on the subject of tourism, has so far been well received. For example, Sigala (2012: 299) comments that the book does much to highlight case studies as a "valuable educational tool to enrich instruction", through its integration of "theoretical concepts with practical evidence gathered through a wide spectrum of international case studies". While this is clearly only an early vote of confidence in the approach adopted, the editors hope that it marks the beginning of a genuine and continuing effort to raise the overall quality of case studies in the fields of study covered by the series. The intention of this second volume, which comprises cases examining a range of contemporary issues in sport, is to consolidate the start that has been made. The third volume, comprising cases in heritage, is already in production.

Case studies have a number of benefits as a pedagogical vehicle: they can serve to help transfer knowledge, develop critical-thinking skills, explain theory by applying it, provide a route-map for tutors and students to grasp complex issues, and – perhaps more importantly – enable students to engage more fully in the learning experience. This last point is particularly pertinent in view of one of the stated aspirations of this series of case studies, which is to rehabilitate the case study, bringing it back into mainstream education and helping to put students back into "active learning mode" (Lane, 2007). Rather than to articulate the potential benefits of case studies, both for tutors and students, however, or to debate the use of the case-study method of research, the purpose of this chapter is to bring together a number of important lessons for case authorship.

One question that arises is why students cannot simply make use of journal articles. After all, as academics we read these all the time, to keep up to date with the state of knowledge in our subject area and to gain insights into cutting-edge ideas. Given the exponential growth in the number of downloads from scientific journals seen over recent years there is no doubt that students are increasingly accessing such material. This is, in and of itself, surely a good thing. Its effectiveness as a teaching strategy might, however, be questionable. Many students view peer-reviewed journal articles as being inaccessible, turgid, abstract and irrelevant, involving overly complicated methodologies and incomprehensible research paradigms. The increasing significance of research evaluation exercises, such as the Research Excellence Framework in the UK, is arguably driving a particular pattern of authorship behaviour among academics, which is only serving to increase even further the gap between academic research papers and their relevance to the educa tion of our students (Turner, Wuetherick and Healey, 2008). Furthermore, in the age of 'copy and paste', it is all too tempting for students simply to skim-read material they find disengaging and difficult to read, select only those sections or paragraphs of perceived relevance, and copy them straight into their essays. The ability to copy references from the end of journal papers and paste them into their own bibliographies is a particularly worrying feature of the digital age of education.

Journal articles need to be underpinned by sound research and the educational case study is really no different in this respect. The main difference between the way in which case studies and journal papers need to be written is the intended audience. Those attempting to write case studies have to understand their students' needs in the process of learning as well as possessing an expert grasp of the research upon which it is based. As such, case-study authors ideally need to be both highly experienced researchers and passionate educators. This will enable them to communicate the research they have undertaken for the case in a style that is accessible, stimulating and engaging, with a strong narrative running through the entire piece. The process of writing case studies should involve analysis, evaluation and interpretation, along with the synthesis of information and ideas (Lane, 2007). In this way, the case study can (and should) enrich both academic research and teaching.

Interestingly, despite the growth in recent decades in higher education across many parts of the world, the number of academics with a sufficiently strong interest in both research and education would seem to be limited. The problem is perhaps not so much that academics do not like writing case material, more that the rewards do not seem as great or as tangible as those associated with writing academic research articles, which clearly carry more weight in the recruitment, promotion and tenure processes worldwide. Although many academics politely cite 'lack of time' as a reason not to accept invitations to submit case studies to collections such as this one, this is most probably a smokescreen for pedagogical outputs not being as high in the pecking order of departmental strategies, where the reward systems are heavily weighted in favour of the quantity and/or quality of research papers published. This system-wide bias is unfortunate, in that the development of research-informed but education-oriented, student-friendly case study material is of so much value to the educational learning environment. This is a real shame, as writing case studies can be hugely rewarding, especially when the author sees first-hand the positive reaction from students and the enhancement of their learning that a good case study can deliver.

The following section now builds on these reactions and reflections, beginning with an overview of the key criteria involved in successful case-study writing.

Rigour and relevance: The essentials of successful case writing

The potential benefits of using a good case study in class are clear, as is evident in the previous chapter (see also Garrod and Fyall, 2011a). What is less clear however, is what makes a good case study. Based on the reaction to and reflections on the first volume (Garrod and Fyall, 2011b), this section presents the criteria for a successful case study. A good case study should be:

♦ **Introduced by a clearly articulated set of learning outcomes** – where each learning outcome is introduced and discussed through the case narrative. Irrespective of what type of case is being written, it is imperative that learners are clear about what it is they are expected to understand and learn, their role in examining and using the case, and how they are expected to learn from it. Writing clear and logical learning outcomes necessitates a thorough knowledge of learners and their learning modes. This is why the earlier point was made that authors really need to be both dedicated researchers and passionate educators, who demonstrate empathy not only with research processes but also with the processes involved in learning. It is also important for learning outcomes to articulate a clear sense of purpose of the case study, the chronological order of the case material and the logic of the narrative flow. Ultimately, all case studies should place the application of knowledge in a real-world setting and encourage learning through a consideration of practice.

♦ **Embedded within their particular case context** – whereby the context, or the individual instance, is the core focus of the case study. While it is usually quite easy to see what this means in practice, case study authors do not always grasp what this means for the subject matter in which they have expertise. As a rule, it is normally easier to select the particular concept or theory, and then to chose a particular context or individual instances as the case. In reality, however, most authors work the other way around. As an example, if one was contemplating writing a case study on visitor management, a case study author would select a suitable case context, such as Skara Brae Prehistoric Village (Leask and Garrod, 2011). This would then be used to help readers to learn about the visitor management theory and practices. Similarly, Knott, Fyall and Jones (2011) used the specific case of the hosting of the 2010 FIFA Soccer World Cup by South Africa to examine the broader relationship between sport, tourism and mega-events, particularly in terms of the issues of legacy and nation branding. What is special about case studies is that there is no need to disentangle the phenomenon from its context, as would normally be necessary using the traditional learning approach. In a good case study, they are one and the same thing.

♦ **A one-stop knowledge shop** – where all the material required for a good understanding of the phenomenon in its specific context is included within the case. It is simply too easy nowadays to direct students to an Internet search engine without fully considering the consequences of students obtaining poor, superficial and descriptive information, which although on the surface may look good illustrative material, lacks the academic rigour necessary for deep learning. Ad hoc research reports, news clippings and glorified gossip are readily accessible. Less so are rich case studies that truly facilitate learning. It is also worth noting that traditional textbooks and journals are primarily paper-based, making them linear and one dimensional. This is in part driven by publication costs and copyright fees. However it is not necessary for case studies to be so limited. In fact, the approach taken with this series of case studies is to encourage imagination, creativity and innovation in case writing. In particular, the case studies in this series all include the use of hyperlinks to make teaching and learning more engaging, allowing readers to dig down beneath the surface of the case and examine the source documents upon which it is based. This means that a wealth of information necessary for understanding the learning outcomes is either contained within or hyperlinked to the case. Both the electronic and hard-copy versions of the cases in this series enable this, the former through live hyperlinks in the actual text and the latter through the use of a QR code at the end of the case.

- **Underpinned by multiple sources of evidence** – so that the reader has all the material and evidence necessary to understand the learning outcomes of the case. Triangulation is a key component of case study methodology and, as such, is a critical feature of any case material for it to have academic credibility (Yin, 2009; Woodside, 2010). It also helps underpin the objectivity of the case study, bring theory to life with real examples, real material and real evidence, and encourages readers to build their knowledge based on a variety of different sources of evidence. Readers will thereby have a breadth of material made available to them, which they have been directed to by the author. This helps to ensure that the reader bases their understanding on high-quality materials, as opposed to the often superficial and biased material that can be downloaded from the Web. When beginning to write the case, therefore, it is imperative that the author clarifies what information is necessary for inclusion, so as to ensure that all dimensions and perspectives are covered, including key themes, theories and concepts.

- **Visually engaging** – with tables, figures, photographs and boxed material bringing the case to life and making it both visually appealing and contemporary. One under-used approach is the use of spider diagrams (see Figure 1), word bubbles, cartoons or storyboards. These can help bring drier material to life for both tutors and students. In the first volume of this series, the case on sport tourism by Hudson (2011) is a good example, being visually appealing with its integration of boxed press releases, offline and online marketing collateral, a customer satisfaction survey form, maps, secondary research data, and diagrams of conceptual models. While some authors may worry about including 'too much' non-text material, it has to be borne in mind that many readers will learn as much from the non-text material as they do the text, particularly those who have a predominantly visual learning style. As such, it is almost always better to have too much than too little such material, provided of course that all the material relates specifically to the learning outcomes of the case

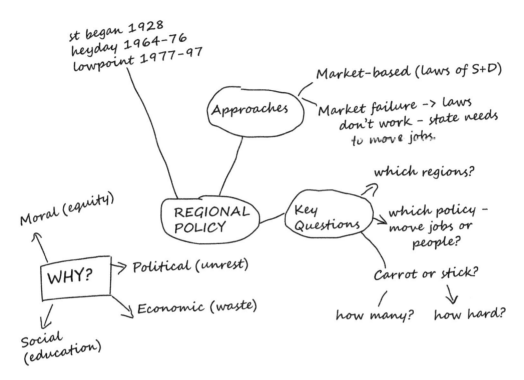

Figure 1: Spider diagram

- **Challenging and controversial** – in order to truly stimulate students' minds and engage them in critical debate with their peers and tutors. Case learning is driven by both intellectual and practical questions. This means that studying the case can help readers to form connections between academic theory and concepts on the one hand and practical ways and means to solve real problems on the other. There is a fine art to this and in this respect the peer review process is of critical importance. Both authors and editors also need to exercise great patience as the case writing passes through numerous iterations until the case study is finally ready to be used with students.

- **Contemporary** – as students of today struggle to grasp out-of-date case material, especially that which pre-dates the digital age. Case study material dates ever more quickly in today's dynamic and fast-changing world, so it is imperative to keep case studies current through regular updates. With each update, the author should seek to revise information on the key players, evidence, data, examples and trends featured in the case. Even though it is increasingly difficult to achieve this aim, especially when the speed of change is ever rising, it is essential if the case is to stay relevant to its intended users. The publication of online versions of the case studies in this series is intended to facilitate regular updating (most notably in respect of the hyperlinks). Meanwhile advances in on-demand printing allow more regular updating of 'hard' copies of the case books.

♦ **Rigorous and relevant** – or otherwise the educational worth of case studies will be questionable. To be sufficiently rigorous, every stone needs to be uncovered and every angle explored in the case. Similarly, if the case study is to be relevant to its readership, the material contained within it needs to be reasonably comprehensive, serviceable and appropriate to the needs of the users, as well as to meet as fully as possible the learning objectives set at the beginning of the case study. The material also needs to be multi-faceted and complex, to connect with the key issues identified in the case and to provide a learning experience that encourages and facilitates critical thinking.

What makes a successful case study?

A number of relatively simple techniques can be used to achieve the above. Figure 2 is intended to serve as a framework for the design of case studies. Eight elements are identified as being core in designing a successful case study.

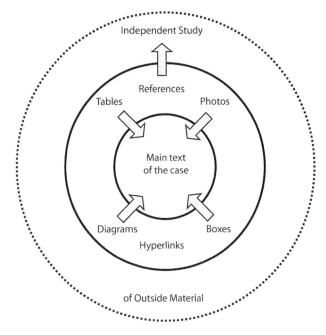

Figure 2: How the elements of a case should fit together

◆ **Main text of the case** – the core narrative is critical to the success of any case study. Although perhaps an obvious point to state, this is easier said than done. To be able to write a good case, authors need to be highly self-critical as well as to have broad shoulders upon which to take constructive criticism from reviewers. From experience, cases will be usually written three or four times, be subject to numerous changes in their structure, including major re-ordering of the material, possibly even being turned upside down, and then be reconfigured yet again to ensure that the learning objectives of the case are met (see Table 1). The case study will require clarity of context, need to offer theoretically informed explanations and engage in a continual interplay between theory and practice. Limited prescription is required with regard to the sense of direction of the case evident on every page. Throughout the writing experience, authors need to put themselves in the shoes of students (rather than their peers) and be prepared to adapt continually in what will be an emergent writing process. Attention to detail is paramount, with a need to grasp, connect and present all the component parts of the case study 'jigsaw'. Ultimately, any case study needs to motivate and engage the reader, contain a high level of description and detail, be problem-based, and bring events and people to life. Although normally chronological in order, this does not necessarily have to be adhered to and a case can be particularly effective when it breaks with expectations. More important is the need to be consistent with the learning objectives established for the case and to ensure that the central idea is clear at all times.

Table 1: Reviewing case studies

1	Will the case produce the intended learning outcomes?
2	Are the problem issue(s) presented in the case related to the learning outcomes?
3	Is the case sufficiently complete, complex and focused?
4	Does the case present a situation, problem, or issue?
5	Dose the case appear to be realistic?
6	Are all the elements of a narrative style used in the case?
7	Are the events and actions in the case sequenced in a logical order?
8	Are the events connected with appropriate transitional signals?
9	Is the content in the case accurate, relevant, and appropriate in terms of subject matter?
10	If there are external resources, are they appropriate?

Source: Lane (2007)

◆   **References** – accurate and up-to-date referencing is of equal
     significance to case studies as it is journal articles. However, the
     volume of references is normally lower, with only key and seminal
     academic studies referenced, along with a greater proportion of
     research reports, policy papers, advisory notes and suchlike: source
     materials that are instrumental in the evidence-based world of case
     writing. It is particularly important to avoid disrupting the flow of the
     narrative, otherwise levels of motivation and engagement will impact
     negatively on the process of case learning. In such cases, footnotes may
     be a good option.

◆   **Photos** – the need to be visually appealing and engaging necessitates
     the inclusion of good-quality images and photographs, with location
     maps an extremely useful tool in demonstrating setting, proximity to
     competitors and related infrastructure (e.g. airports, highways, ports
     and railway stations), and so on.

◆   **Boxes** – the inclusion of 'boxed' material is particularly welcome in
     case studies when there is stand-alone material that can add to, but
     also sit outside of, the core case study. This allows for a more expansive
     case. For example, the inclusion of newspaper articles that develop a
     specific theme or aspect of a case study provides perfect ammunition
     for 'boxes'.

◆   **Hyperlinks** – one of the principal benefits of electronic publication is
     the ability of authors to embed hyperlinks within their case studies
     that take readers directly to 'live' material on the Internet. This feature
     contributes significantly to bringing the case study to life and helps to
     ensure that it is kept up to date (insofar as when the website is updated,
     so is the case study). It also allows case studies to be taken anywhere on
     portable electronic devices; an approach that is already commonplace
     in many primary and secondary schools around the world. The hard
     copy of the case studies that is published in the conventional book,
     meanwhile, still makes use of the internet through the use of QR
     coding. Readers who scan the codes with their smart phone or webcam
     will have the links uploaded to their devices. They can then reach the
     web material by clicking through.

◆   **Diagrams** – the need to include high quality, relevant, well-drawn
     and accurate diagrams is paramount. Diagrams can help learners to
     structure the material, to explore the case more deeply, to facilitate the
     creative interpretation of core case material or to serve as a foundation
     for group discussion.

♦   **Tables and figures** – cases are only as strong as the evidence contained within them, so good quality, up-to-date and relevant statistical and trend data are valuable components of any case.

♦   **Independent study of outside material** – while cases are written as inclusive self-contained vehicles for learning, authors should always offer students opportunities to expand their learning horizons through signposting further reading and additional web-based resources. Independent study can also be encouraged through the provision of self-test material, multiple-choice questions, exam questions and suchlike, as well as providing advice as to how best to learn from the case in question.

Conclusions

With two volumes of case studies published to date, and with one other in the process of publication, the *Contemporary Cases* series aspires to raise the bar for case writing in the fields of tourism, heritage, hospitality, leisure, retail, events and sport. Developed in response to the surprising paucity of high quality case study material in existence, and a genuine desire to enhance the student learning experience, this volume brings to the reader nine quality case studies that are contemporary and accessible yet challenging, thought provoking and, most importantly, instructive. Each case has been carefully written and edited to avoid the inaccessibility of many scholarly articles, with all authors working hard to make the process of learning more enjoyable and engaging for both tutor and student, and encouraging and facilitating a culture of critical thinking by all. It is hoped that each case study in this volume meets the high standards set for the publishing of quality case material while it is also hoped that both this and the previous volume serve as a catalyst to entice academics away from a one-dimension world of publishing to include case study writing in their future portfolio of academic activity. For, not only will the writing of case studies enhance their ability to teach, but the combined discipline and creativity necessary for good case study writing will also make them better researchers and academics.

References

Garrod B, Fyall A. 2011a. The case study approach: Wrongly maligned. In Garrod B, Fyall A (eds) *Contemporary Cases in Tourism: Volume 1*. Oxford: Goodfellow Publishers; ix-xvi.

Garrod B, Fyall A. 2011b. *Contemporary Cases in Tourism: Volume 1*, Oxford: Goodfellow Publishers.

Hudson S. 2011. Bumps for Boomers: Marketing sport tourism to the aging tourist. In Garrod B, Fyall A (eds) *Contemporary Cases in Tourism: Volume 1*. Oxford: Goodfellow Publishers; 165-190.

Knott B, Fyall A, Jones I. 2011. South Africa 2010: Leveraging nation brand benefits from the FIFA World Cup. In Garrod B, Fyall A (eds) *Contemporary Cases in Tourism: Volume 1*. Oxford: Goodfellow Publishers; 33-56.

Lane J. 2007. *Case Writing Guide*. Schreyer Institute for Teaching Excellence, Penn State, University Park, PA 16802.

Leask A, Garrod B. 2011. Visitor management at a world heritage site: Skara Brae prehistoric village. In Garrod B, Fyall A (eds) *Contemporary Cases in Tourism: Volume 1*. Oxford: Goodfellow Publishers; 81-98.

Sigala M. 2012. Book review: Contemporary Cases in Tourism, Volume 1. *Anatolia* **23** (2): 298-299.

Turner N, Wuetherick B, Healey M. 2008. International perspectives on student awareness, experiences and perceptions of research: Implications for academic developers in implementing research-based teaching and learning. *International Journal for Academic Development* **13** (3): 199-211.

Woodside AG. 2010. *Case Study Research: Theory, Methods, Practice*. Bradford: Emerald.

Yin RK. 2009. *Case Study Research: Design and Methods (Volume 5)*. Los Angeles: Sage.

SPORT, POLICY and DEVELOPMENT

3

Ultra-marathons and Tourism Development

The Canadian Death Race in Grande Cache, Alberta

Tom Hinch

Introduction

Sport and travel are inextricably linked. This relationship is captured on the scoreboards found in sport stadiums throughout the world as they tally points in terms of the 'home' team versus the 'visitors': concepts that parallel tourism's 'hosts' and 'guests'.

Athletes are travelers both through choice and out of necessity. The same is true of the many spectators and affiliated parties (e.g. officials, media) at sporting events. While mega-events such as the Olympics and the FIFA World Cup are readily recognized as tourism attractions, the significance of smaller-scale sporting events is often overlooked (Higham, 2005). These lower-profile events can present both opportunities and challenges that merit further consideration.

The purpose of this case study is to illustrate the opportunities and challenges of positioning sport events as tourist attractions in remote resource-based communities through the case of the Canadian Death Race in Grande Cache, Alberta, Canada. The case opens with an examination of ultra-marathons as a sporting trend and an explanation of how these events can function as tourist attractions. The case of the Canadian Death Race is then considered within a sport tourism development framework.

Ultra-marathon races as tourist attractions

Ultra-marathons represent a hybrid of the classic marathon and a new family of sport competitions commonly referred to as adventure races. While the former term refers to running races of 42.195km, usually following routes on roadways in urban environments (e.g. the Boston Marathon), the latter are endurance races that typically range in length from 40 to 700km (Ngiam, 2003). In addition to longer distances, the routes of adventure races are normally found in challenging natural environments. For the purposes of this case study, ultra-marathons are conceptualized as running races that range from 100 to 200km over natural terrain.

There has been tremendous growth in such races over the past 20 years. More than a decade ago, Frontier Adventure Racing (2001) noted a surge in the incidence of adventure races, with the number of such events in Canada increasing six-fold from 1999 to 2000. More recently, Hoffman, Ong and Wang (2010), in their examination of the more narrowly defined activity of 161km ultra-marathons, indicated that the annual number of race finishers increased exponentially from 1997 to 2008, with a reported 53 ultra-marathons in North American in 2008. Similarly, Okayasu, Nogawa and Morais (2010) have noted the growing popularity of ultra-marathons in Japan, with applications to race far exceeding the number of running slots available. Along with their growth as a sport, ultra-marathons are increasingly being recognized as tourist attractions in their own right.

Leiper (1990: 371) defined a tourist attraction as "a system comprising three elements: a tourist or human element, a nucleus or central element, and a marker or informative element. A tourist attraction comes into existence when the three elements are connected". This concept can be translated directly to sport tourism (see Box 1).

Box 1: Elements of a sport tourist attraction

Human

Travelers whose trips are motivated by sport or who are involved in sport while travelling. In the context of sport tourism these include: elite through to recreational athletes, spectators, officials, media, friends and family, and an assortment of others.

Nucleus

The nucleus is where the tourist experience is produced and consumed. It includes any features or characteristics of a place that a traveller contemplates visiting or actually visits. From a sport perspective, it can be conceptualized by the rules, physical competition and ludic (playful) nature as manifested by the activity and its site.

Markers

Markers consist of 'items of information, about any phenomenon that is a potential nuclear element in a tourist attraction' (Leiper 1990: 377). In the context of sport tourism they include a wide range of promotions as well as media activity and even the physical sites where sport occurs.

Source: Based on Leiper (1990)

In the case of ultra-marathons, these elements are present and are, indeed, interconnected. The human element includes the runners, who are serious about their sport (see Stebbins, 2007). As a travel market, ultra-marathons represent a substantial, growing and serious/committed group. Under Reeves's (2000) general classification of sport tourism types (see Table 1), ultra-marathoners would typically fall under the 'dedicated' category. As such, they tend to be willing to negotiate a significant array of potential travel constraints (Jackson, Crawford and Godby, 1993), such as distance, in order to compete in high-quality competitions.

Table 1: Sport tourism types and visitor profiles

Type	Participation	Group Profile	Spending
Incidental	Sense of duty	Family	Minimal
Sporadic	If convenient	Friends and family	Minimal except for one-offs
Occasional	Welcome addition to experience	Often individual, especially business tourists	High on occasion
Regular	Significant part of experience	Group or individual	Considerable
Dedicated	Central to experience	Individuals and groups of like-minded people	Extremely high and consistent
Driven	Sole reason for travel	Elite groups or solitary	Extremely high but funded by others

Source: After Reeves (2000)

While ultra-marathons are not normally positioned as major spectator events due, at least in part, to the remote nature of many of the competitions and the isolated character of the race courses, they do attract significant support teams. Such groups are usually made up of family and friends. Another significant component of the human dimension of ultra-marathons includes the large contingent of volunteers required to deliver this type of event. All of these groups converge for the competition and interact with local residents.

The second component of the attraction is the nucleus, which in this case is ultra-marathon running. Like all sports, ultra-marathon racing can be conceptualized in terms of its essential elements. First, as far as sports go, the rules are fairly basic. It is a timed running race over a set course. Secondly, ultra-marathons are purposely designed to test the competitors' physical and mental endurance, as runners use their gross motor skills and stamina to make their way through challenging terrain. At its base level, competition is manifest in the race of runner against runner, with the time taken to complete the entire course determining the ranking of the participants. Beyond this, multiple layers of competition exist, including that of the runner against the physical challenges of the course and the internal competition of the runners in terms of their previous performance in similar events or within the unique parameters of a particular race. Finally, the activity dimension is characterized by its ludic nature: essentially the joy of running. While the extreme demands of the race are bound to challenge the joy that a runner might feel at any given moment during the race, competitors tend to be motivated by a genuine love for the activity (albeit somewhat masochistic from the perspective of the author); they enter it freely and are driven by intrinsic rewards.

The third or 'marking' component of the ultra-marathons as attractions is manifest in communications about the event. Examples of 'marking' the event include: traditional marketing activities such as promotional web sites, media coverage and social media activity. A particularly interesting aspect of these markers is that some are controlled by the race organizers themselves, while many lie beyond their direct control.

The case of the Canadian Death Race

Grande Cache is a town of just under 4,000 residents nestled against the Rocky Mountains in Alberta, Canada. It was formally established in the early 1970s as part of the development associated with a new coalmine. Since its creation, the local economy has been closely tied to the world markets for natural resources. The town has actively pursued strategies of economic diversification as a way to mitigate the cyclical booms and slumps associated with an economy tied to the volatility of these markets. Tourism is recognized as one of the instruments that can be used for this diversification (Russell, 2009).

Location

Grande Cache is relatively remote even by Canadian standards. It is located 440km to the west of Edmonton: a city of over one million people and the capital of Alberta. Grande Cache is situated near the midway point on Highway 40 between two other resource-based communities: Grande Prairie and Hinton. While this highway primarily provides access for resource extraction activities (e.g. coalmining, pulp and paper, oil and gas), it is also promoted as a scenic route to Alaska and is only a two-hour drive from world-renowned Jasper National Park. Grande Cache is often favorably described in terms of its wilderness setting and small-town feel, as its community profile notes:

"Modern living in Grande Cache is balanced with mountain wilderness, affordability, and a genuine small-town atmosphere. Built on a mountain plateau, the town faces south towards the Continental Divide and the pristine Willmore Wilderness Park. An elevation of 4200 feet gives a panoramic view of 21 mountain peaks and 2 river valleys. Grande Cache offers outstanding outdoor adventure, relaxed lifestyle and unparalleled potential. It is a growing community with a wealth of opportunity in tourism, residential, and resource industry development".

Economy

Key employment sectors in the community include: oil and gas exploration and development, coal production, thermal-electricity generation, forestry and a federal correctional institution. An example of the volatility of these resource industries was the downsizing of one of the coal mines in 1982, which resulted in the immediate layoff of 500 people with another 307 layoffs when the mine eventually ceased operation in 1987. Mass layoffs such as these were reflected in a variable population base that has swung between 4,500 and 3,500 at various times over the past 10 years. At the moment, the resource industries are healthy but the lessons of the past are one of the reasons that tourism development is seen as a priority in the community.

Tourism resources

The Grande Cache community describes its tourism industry as being in growth mode. In terms of private sector initiatives, the community profile lists:

"… Wild Blue Yonder rafting tours, Taste of Wilderness hiking tours, U Bar Trail Rides, Willmore Wilderness Horseback Adventures, and High Country Vacations for horseback trips, and Pacific Western Helicopters, offering sightseeing tours, heli-hiking, skiing, etc. We also have a new sports store offering outdoor recreational rentals, including mountain bikes, canoes, kayaks, camping gear, and more".

These businesses are supported by the natural amenities in the area and by the presence of Willmore Wilderness Park to the south. This park covers an expanse of more than 4,000km² in the northern Rockies and is particularly noteworthy for the fact that motorized vehicles are not allowed in the area. In addition, the town operates an active visitor information/interpretive centre and features a unique 'Passport to the Peaks' program under which visitors can climb any of the 21 peaks surrounding the community and collect 'passport' stamps that are housed in cairn boxes on each peak. The community also plays host to a canoe and kayak festival that celebrates the many waterways found in the area.

Supporting hospitality infrastructure includes seven hotels, motels and inns with over 440 rooms. These are supplemented by an assortment of bed-and-breakfast establishments, lodges, cabins, and campgrounds. Food and beverage amenities include 10 full-service restaurants, three take-outs and five public houses. While this infrastructure receives much of its revenue from the many resource workers requiring temporary accommodation, it also caters to pleasure travellers drawn to the area by the assortment of tourist attractions in the region.

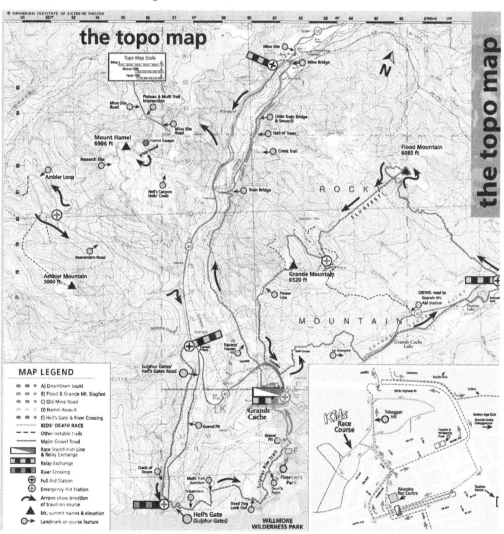

Figure 1: Canadian Death Race course topographical map. *Source:* Canadian Death Race.

A new attraction: The Canadian Death Race

The Canadian Death Race (CDR) was inaugurated in Grande Cache in 2000 and has run every year since. It is held on the August long weekend and is promoted as one of the toughest races of its kind in Canada. Individuals and teams run a course consisting of five stages totalling 125 km in distance, three mountain summits (with a 5181.6 m elevation change), and several creek crossings (sometimes with knee high water levels) (Ngiam, 2003) (see Figures 1 and 2). Runners must complete the race within 24 hours. The course winds through varied terrain including upper foothills, sub-alpine regions and lower-lying forested areas, as well as exposed alpine landscapes that serve as habitat for elk, black bear, grizzly bear and a variety of birds.

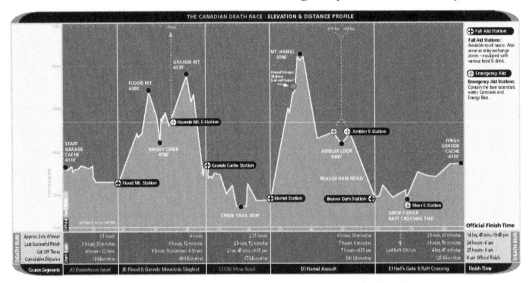

Figure 2: Canadian Death Race course elevation change. *Source:* Canadian Death Race.

The branding of the CDR (name, logo and promotional themes) builds on the challenge of the race. The original organizers of the event drew upon the Greek myth of Charon, in which a coin must be presented to a ferryman to cross the River Styx into Hades. In the CDR version, runners must provide a token to a ferryman for passage across Hell's Gate: the confluence of the Smokey and Sulphur rivers. This brand is nicely captured by the skull featured by the eye-catching if somewhat intimidating logo (see Figure 3).

Figure 3: Canadian Death Race logo. *Source:* Canadian Death Race.

While the race serves as the primary attraction, it is complemented by value-added features such as a festival and a children's race.

The frameworks presented by Hinch and Higham (2011) in their discussions of sport tourism development serve as useful tools for the examination of the opportunities and challenges associated with the CDR as a tourist attraction in Grande Cache (see Figure 4). For the purpose of this case study, three major dimensions are particularly relevant: 1) markets, 2) spatial considerations, and 3) temporal considerations.

Markets/Marketing

- Market typologies
- Active/event markets
- Marketing strategies

Spatial Dimensions

- Space
- Place
- Environment

Temporal Dimensions

- Participant experience
- Seasonality
- Long term impact

Figure 4: Analytical framework. Source: Based on Hinch and Higham (2011)

Markets

The primary market for the CDR consists of ultra-marathon runners from Alberta and British Columbia, although published race results indicate that increasing numbers are coming from other parts of Canada and the United States. Participation has risen dramatically from the 192 runners in 2000 to the over 1,600 racers in 2011 (see Figure 5). The demand for race places currently exceeds the supply.

For 2013, advanced registration has been capped at 1,400 individual and team entrants on a first-come-first-served basis, along with 250 registrations for the children's race. The 'dedicated' nature of this market is not only reflected in the challenge of the race itself and the training that is required to prepare for the race but also in the challenges presented by the limited accommodation and services that exists in the community. Once accepted into the race, registrants must quickly book their accommodations as the demand for rooms in Grande Cache during the race far exceeds the supply.

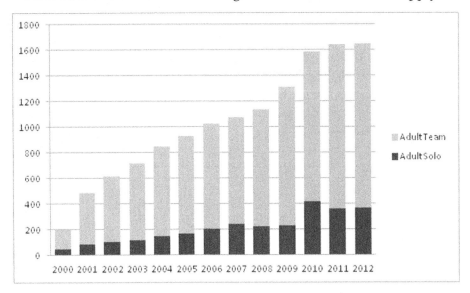

Figure 5: Canadian Death Race participation. *Source:* Drawn from race results published on CDR website, September, 2012

The second major segment for the Canadian Death Race consists of family and friends of the runners. The race organizers have consciously catered to these groups through initiatives such as the children's race, inaugurated in 2001. The town of Grande Cache also runs a festival named the 'DeathFest' that runs during the race weekend. Its 'A Killer Party' tag line picks up on the Death Race theme. Festival highlights include a carnival, beer gardens and a 'Killer Concert'.

A third significant market for the event consists of approximately 250 volunteers who are recruited to help run the Death Race. While many of these volunteers are locals, many are recruited from the broader running community in general. A similar theme is used to recruit these volunteers with a suggestion on the web page that "…the only thing harder than competing in the Death Race is volunteering for it". This is quickly followed by a list of benefits, including a pizza lunch, tee shirt and lots of smiles. Incentives, such as guaranteed registration in the following year's race, are also offered as a way to ensure that enough volunteers are signed up.

A strong brand captures the extreme challenge of the race. While 'death' may have morbid overtones for some, its use in the context of the CDR is tempered with humour and has proved popular with ultra-marathoners and with the media. The race is supported by a web site that 'lures' potential racers and backs this up with detailed information. It has also enjoyed the support of specialized media in this field including feature articles in *Trail Runner* and *Extreme Racer* magazines. The skull logo is prominently displayed on promotional items and is widely recognized. The North Face, as a supplier of outdoor clothing and equipment, is the key sponsor for the event, bringing with it recognized prestige in this particular market. A range of social media activities also promotes the event and are driven by enthusiastic supporters of the race. While such activities have definitely contributed to the growth of the CDR, they are accompanied by the risk of bad publicity if the participants' experience is not satisfying.

Spatial dimensions

Grande Cache is a relatively remote location even within the context of the Alberta market. However, this remoteness has not been a critical limitation. The relative isolation of Grande Cache actually fits nicely with the themes of challenge and endurance. For many competitors, the 'expedition' nature of the trip to Grande Cache is consistent with the challenge of the race itself. The natural assets of the region and its frontier ethic are a good fit with the underlying philosophy of the race.

The spatial dimension of the event also encompasses place meaning. Initially, the private organizers of the event received little direct support from local government. In the decade prior to its inception, the community had just experienced a series of mine closures. The initiators of the race saw the CDR as a strategy for community revitalization. Perhaps understandably, local government leaders of the day felt that after suffering the blow of losing a major employer, the optics of hosting a 'death race' were not ideal (Russell, 2009). This was not the image that they were trying to promote. In part based on of the success of the event, local government soon became supportive. Somewhat counter-intuitively, despite its name, the race's enduring message is one of survival and meeting challenges: a message that is consistent with the community's own character.

The race has certainly had an impact on the meaning that participants associate with Grande Cache. Rather than an abstract place that many of them knew only from media reports of its economic struggles, Grande Cache has become ingrained in the memories of participants as the site of a significant life experience for them. Ngiam's (2003) study of CDR runners and their racing environments found that racers had developed attachments to Grande Cache. When asked what would draw her back to Grande Cache, one of Ngiam's (2003: 156) respondents stated:

"Well, the Death Race, it is bringing me back to where I want to finish. I stayed at the Bed and Breakfast [B&B] where I met the wonderful woman that ran the B&B, so I really want to see her again. And her next [door] neighbour, she was a woman that was running and she had me over for supper so it is the people that are bringing me back, it is the race that is bringing me back. The environments, I love the mountains … So yeah, I love the mountains, I love the people and I want to finish the race. Those are the key things".

In recounting their Death Race experience, Ngaim's study respondents noted common emotional associations such as happiness, peace, sadness, pain, and frustration. Participants also highlighted the hospitality that they enjoyed while in the community. In general, their attachment was rooted in place dependence, that is, the functionality of the course, the environment, the race operations, and the host community that facilitated the experience. While their experience also shaped the way they identified with place, this was secondary to their dependence on these places, which was influenced by the generic characteristics of these types of race environments rather than the specific environment at Grande Cache. It would, however, be interesting to revisit this study now that the profile of the race has grown and the incidence of repeat competitors has increased. As the 'brand' of the CDR has developed, it is probable that participation in the race is increasingly influencing the way runners identify with Grande Cache.

The environmental impacts of the race have not been studied in detail. However, it is clear that the presence of 1,600 racers and the supporting cast that accompanies them will at least have a temporary environmental impact on the course, in the community of Grande Cache, and along the travel routes that the visitors take to the community. Probably, the most direct environmental impact is the disturbance of wildlife during the race itself and during training runs. Race organizers are cognizant of such impacts and have tried to minimize them and other negative impacts such as littering. It is interesting to note that the race rules begin with one designed to minimize environmental degradation:

"No littering - Sensitive Alpine Environment. The alpine environs of the Grande Cache area are both sensitive and diverse in animal and plant life, this combined with the frequent high winds in the area dictate that a no littering rule be imposed. Full aid stations will be equipped with a garbage bin, which Death Racers are required to use. You must either put your garbage in the bin or carry your refuse with you until you reach a garbage bin. There are no exceptions to this rule. The pristine wilderness that you are traveling through needs to be preserved and respected. Violators will be penalized, disqualified and/or fined. Crews and spectators are also bound by this no littering rule. Also, please pack out all your garbage when training on the race course. If you see someone else's careless mess please pick it up and pack it out".

Temporal dimensions

The fact that participation has grown steadily, and that demand for spaces exceeds supply, suggests that racers have been satisfied with their experience. This interpretation is complicated somewhat by competitors who may have been dissatisfied with their personal performance in a previous race and therefore register for a second race in an attempt to achieve better results. In general, however, CDR participants seem to be having good experiences.

Given the inherent challenge of running an ultra-marathon, it is not surprising that competitor emotions ranged from euphoria to heartbreak. In her study of the experience of runners in the 2002 CDR, Ngiam (2003) found evidence of the full range of emotions. For example, reflecting on reaching one of the summits on the course, one racer remarked:

> "Yeah, Flood Mountain? And you see the view of the whole town <in a gasping whisper> and I felt on top of the world. I yelled, 'YAHOO!' you know? 'I made it!' You know, I was euphoric, I went like this <two hands punching in the air> and I yelled out 'YAHOO! I MADE IT? I DID IT! I DID IT! I really did it! I got here, you know?'"

In contrast, another racer articulated her disappointment of having to pull out of the race.

> "It was a tough decision coming down Mt Hamel. That was really tough and that was disappointing … Knowing that 'oh my god, I am quitting!' You know I do not quit in things very easily and all of a sudden I am making this decision to quit and mentally it was just weird … That was not part of my mental preparation so that was very weird … I broke down, like I was really strong for my husband for about 10-15 minutes and then that was it".

Race organizers and community hosts have actively addressed the needs and wants of participants during the anticipation, actual event and recollection phases of the leisure experience (Clawson and Knetsch, 1966). Ample evidence of these efforts is provided on the Canadian Death Race web site. In terms of the anticipation and planning stage, the web site provides both teasers about the 'challenge' and concrete information about race and volunteers' registration, as well as links to accommodation and related tourism amenities. An active Facebook page is also in place to keep Canadian Death Racers in touch with each other. Strategies to address the recollection phase are just as prominent. These include the publication of competitor finishing times since the inception of the race, the distribution of awards and name plaques to recognize participation and performance, a DVD of highlights from the most recent race, and an assortment of race photos for purchase.

In terms of seasonality, scheduling the race on the August long weekend (bank holiday) means that it occurs at the peak of the summer season when many other tourist activities are in full swing. These dates make sense in terms of the relatively harsh climatic conditions that can occur in this area. Past races, have for example, included snow conditions at higher altitudes. The likelihood of this happening in the shoulder seasons – whether Spring or Fall – is much higher and while such conditions may fit in with the 'challenge' theme of the event, they would make it more difficult to run. It is interesting to note that the original concept called for and actually ran a similar snowshoeing race during the winter months. This event was, however, discontinued. While the main race is run in the very middle of summer, two formal training camps were implemented in June. Visits to these camps, along with independent visits to train, increase visitation during the spring and early summer,and help to even out the distribution of visitors.

Finally, while there are no publically available reports on the impact of the Canadian Death Race on Grande Cache, there are indications that these impacts are substantial and generally positive. In terms of the economic impact, it is clear that significant revenues are generated by hosting 1,600 racers along with their families and the large volunteer contingent. While the expenditures of these visitors are substantial, the cost of running the race has been kept relatively low by strategies such as organizing the race under the Canadian Institute of Extreme Racing (a non-profit group based in Alberta) and by drawing on a substantial volunteer base for the actual operation of the race. Based on a survey of visitors at a temporary campground set up for the 2008 race, Russell (2009) estimated that in addition to the CAN $300 registration fee, the average amount spent per campsite group for the weekend was CAN $641. Of this average, CAN $525 was spent in Grande Cache, while the balance of CAN $116 was spent in transit to and from the event. It is impossible to simply pro-rate these expenditures to all visitors who were in Grande Cache that weekend, as it is unlikely that they had similar spending patterns (e.g. those staying in motels were likely spending more). What can be concluded, though, is that the race is generating substantial revenues, much of which is remaining in the community.

Social impacts are often measured in the context of crowding, parking issues and other types of disruptions to local residents. There is no question that these types of impacts occur in Grande Cache given that the population of the town basically doubles during the race weekend. A variety of strategies have been formulated to mitigate these negative impacts. In addition, the community also enjoyed significant social benefits as a result of the DeathFest celebration. This is a community celebration that links the hosts and the guest. Grande Cache also benefited from the development of social capital through the volunteer base that has been built for the event. While many of these volunteers come from outside of the community, a significant proportion comes from inside. These individuals form a pool of social capital that can serve other events throughout the year and enjoy the added benefit of increased social bonding with their neighbours and guests. Finally, while no formal measures exist to verify this claim, it is apparent that the success of the CDR is a point of pride in a community, which prior to the initiation of this event experienced a series of economic setbacks related to volatile global resource markets. In contrast, the CDR has flourished and has fostered positive external recognition of the unique attributes of Grande Cache. More generally, the sport of ultra-marathon running has not only benefited from the significant profile of this race, but has also introduced thousands of young runners to the sport through the children's race and the interest that it generates.

Conclusion

This case study set out to illustrate the opportunities and challenges of positioning sport events as tourist attractions in isolated resource-based communities. It did this through an examination of the CDR in Grande Cache, Alberta. Students of sport have a natural interest in the dramatic growth of ultra-marathon running and can learn much from the success of this event. However, the case study was not meant to focus on the management of this event within the confines of sport performance. Rather, it was meant to highlight ways in which it contributes to tourism development in a remote resource-based community. The CDR was introduced at an opportune time and in an opportune place. Event organizers have demonstrated imagination, determination and a willingness to evolve and work with the broader sport and host community. While the case study would benefit from more detailed measures of performance in terms of tourism development, it is evident that the CDR has been a success as a tourist attraction. Organizers of other mid-sized sporting events that aspire to similar types of tourism development would be well served to study the lessons provided by the Canadian Death Race example.

References

Alberta Community Profiles. 2012. http://albertacommunityprofiles.com/Profile/ Grande_Cache/255

Clawson M, Knetsch, J. 1966. *The Economics of Outdoor Recreation*. Baltimore: John Hopkins Press.

Frontier Adventure Racing, Inc. 2001. *The Adventure Racing Industry*. Toronto: Frontier Adventure Racing Inc. Primary Market Analysis.

Higham J. 2005. *Sport Tourism Destinations: Issues, Opportunities and Analysis*. Oxford: Elsevier.

Hinch TD, Higham J. 2011. *Sport Tourism Development*, 2nd Edition. Bristol: Channel View Publications.

Hoffman MD, Ong JC, Wang G. 2010. Historical analysis of participation in 161 km ultra-marathons in North America. *The International Journal of the History of Sport* **27** (11): 1877-1891.

Jackson EL, Crawford DW, Godby G. 1993. Negotiation of leisure constraints. *Leisure Sciences* **15** (1): 1-11.

Leiper N. 1990. Tourist attraction systems. *Annals of Tourism Research* **17** (3): 367-384.

Ngiam, HS. 2003. *A Matter of Attachment: Death Runners and their Racing Environments*. Unpublished MA Thesis. University of Alberta, Edmonton, Alberta, Canada.

Okayasu I, Nogawa H, Marais D. 2010. Resource investments and loyalty to recreation sport tourism event. *Journal of Travel & Tourism Marketing* **27** (6): 565-578.

Reeves MR. 2000. *Evidencing the Sport-Tourism Relationship: A Case Study Approach*. Unpublished PhD thesis. Loughborough University, Loughborough, United Kingdom.

Russell L. 2013. *Cheating Death: The Case of the Canadian Death Race in Grande Cache*. Unpublished Major Research Essay, Cape Breton University, Nova Scotia, Canada.

Stebbins RA. 2007. *Serious Leisure*. London: Transaction Publishers.

Ancillary Student Material

Further reading

Bale J. 1989. *Sports Geography*. London: E & FN Spon.

Brymer E, Downey G, Gray T. 2009. Extreme sports as a precursor to environmental sustainability. *Journal of Sport & Tourism* **14** (2): 193-204.

Butler RW. 2001. Seasonality in tourism: Issues and problems. In Baum T, Lundtorp, S (eds) *Seasonality in Tourism: Issues and Implications*. London: Pergamon; 5-23.

Dwyer L. 2005. Relevance of triple bottom line reporting to achievement of sustainable tourism: A scoping study. *Tourism Review International* **9** (1): 79-93.

Gibson HJ. 2006. *Sport Tourism: Concepts and Theories*. New York: Routledge.

Higham J, Hinch T. 2009. *Sport and Tourism: Globalisation, Mobility and Identity*. London: Elsevier Butterworth Heinemann.

Hinch T, Higham J. 2001. Sport tourism: A framework for research. *International Journal of Tourism Research* **3** (1): 45-58.

Hinch TD, Jackson EL. 2000. Leisure constraints research: Its value as a framework for understanding tourism seasonality. *Current Issues in Tourism* **3** (2): 87-106.

Jones I. 2000. A model of serious leisure identification: The case of football fandom. *Leisure Studies* **19** (4): 283-298.

Kerstetter D, Bricker K. 2009. Exploring Fijian's sense of place after exposure to tourism development. *Journal of Sustainable Tourism* **17** (6): 691-708.

Weed ME, Bull CJ. 2009. *Sports Tourism: Participants, Polity and Providers* (2nd edition), Oxford: Butterworth-Heinemann.

Related websites

Canadian Death Race website: http://www.canadiandeathrace.com/

Grande Cache Death Fest website: http://grandecache.ca/community-living/programs-events/deathfest

Town of Grande Cache website: http://grandecache.ca/front.php

Town of Grande Cache Tourism website: http://grandecache.ca/tourism/tourism-information/tourism-information

Grande Cache Community Profile: http://albertacommunityprofiles.com/Profile/Grande_Cache/255

2010 – North Face Canadian Death Race – Video http://trailrunningsoul.com/trs/2011/01/06/video-2010-the-north-face-canadian-death-race/

Self-test questions

Try to answer the following questions to test your knowledge and understanding of the case. If you are unsure of any answers please re-read the case and refer to the references and further reading sources.

1   Why would communities that can be characterized as resource-extraction-based be interested in tourism development? What fundamental advantages and challenges do they typically have in terms of tourism development?

2   How do ultra-marathon races function as tourist attractions? In what ways are they similar to or distinct from other sport tourism attractions or activities?

3   In the case study, ultra-marathoners were categorized as 'dedicated' under Reeves's typology of sport tourism types and visitor profiles, yet family activities are an important part of the CDR weekend. How and why would you modify or apply Reeves's framework in view of these discrepancies?

4   Describe the similarities and differences between Grande Cache and other sites of extreme sport events in your region or country. What implications does your analysis have in terms of the transferability of the Grande Cache experience with the CDR to other communities?

5   What were the advantages and limitations of naming the competition the CDR? Do you think that an alternative name would have been as successful? Why or why not?

6   Do you feel that the place meaning that racers develop for Grande Cache is consistent with the meaning that locals have for it? Why or why not? How might the racers' perceptions of Grande Cache change depending on their success or failure in the race?

7   Given the relative remoteness of Grande Cache, why are so many visitors willing to drive for several hours to get to the site? What other types of mid-sized sport tourism events might match or exceed this drawing power? Why?

8   Environmental impacts associated with sport tourism can be positive as well as negative. List some of these impacts and suggest strategies for maximizing the positive impacts and minimizing the negative impacts.

9   How do the organizers of this event attempt to ensure that participants have a positive experience in terms of their anticipation/

planning for the event, the competition weekend, and their recollection of the event?

10   What were the merits of scheduling the race for the first weekend of August? How has the CDR influenced additional visits at other times of the year?

11   In addition to environmental impacts, tourism has social and economic impacts. Outline the nature of these impacts in the context of the CDR and the strategies that are being used or could be used to maximize benefits and minimize negative impacts.

Key themes and theories

The key themes raised in this case study include:

◆   Positioning extreme sport events as tourist attractions

◆   Markets for events like the CDR

◆   Spatial themes including the meaning that ultra-marathoners attach to place, the implications of location and environmental impacts

◆   Temporal themes including participant experience before, during and after the event; seasonality; and the long term impacts of the event in terms of the economic and social dimensions in addition to the environmental impacts.

A broad range of theories can be drawn on to shed light into these various themes. Samples of the most relevant include:

◆   Attractions – tourist attraction systems (Lieper, 1990)

◆   Markets – serious leisure (Stebbins, 2007), leisure constraints (Jackson et al., 1993)

◆   Spatial themes – place, space and environment (Hinch and Higham, 2011)

◆   Temporal themes – experience, seasonality and impacts (Hinch and Higham, 2011)

If you need to source any further information on any of the above themes and theories, then these headings could be used as key words to search for materials and case studies.

 Scan here to get the hyperlinks for this chapter.

4

More than a Game

Corporate Social Responsibility in Professional Football

Tim Breitbarth

Introduction

The purpose of this case study is to explore the international debate about corporate social responsibility (CSR) and to demonstrate its relevance to modern sports management. Studying the case should also provide an understanding of how the concept and methods of CSR can be applied in professional football (also known as association football or soccer). Both country-specific and club-specific approaches to CSR will be discussed, along with the links between the commercial, political, social and ethical aspects of professional football club management.

Corporate social responsibility

Situated within the broader debate about sustainable development and corporate sustainability, the corporate social responsibility (CSR) of professional sports organisations has attracted much attention from scholars, sport managers, sport sponsors, fans, policymakers and other organisational stakeholders. The European Commission (2001: 3) has defined CSR as "a concept whereby companies integrate social and environmental concerns in their business operations and in their interaction with their stakeholders on a voluntary basis".

Following the conceptual development and widespread acceptance of CSR principles, the Commission has more recently published an action agenda intended to encourage business organisations to meet their social responsibilities by integrating social, environmental, ethical, human rights and consumer concerns into their core business operations and strategies (European

Commission, 2011). The agenda encourages this integration process to be undertaken in close collaboration with the business organisation's key stakeholders, the aim being to encourage business decision-makers to attempt to maximise the creation of shared value for their owners, wider stakeholders and society at large. Integrating CSR arguably offers a variety of benefits to organisations, for example improved reputation, risk management and community relations (see Table 1).

Table 1: Business drivers linked to CSR

- Improve image, reputation, brand value

- Risk management

- Resource efficiency

- Access to financial capital, sponsorships, partnership money

- Improve employee motivation, attractiveness as an employer

- Innovation, 'new ways of thinking'

- Access to new markets

- Counter political, legislative and regulatory pressures

- Build trust and legitimisation

- Relationship-building and maintenance with stakeholders and partners

- Pass on organisational values and culture

Sources: Adapted from Herrmann (2004), Weber (2008), European Commission (2011)

Football as business

While approaches to CSR are reaching levels of maturity in some industries, it is only relatively recently that professional sports, especially football, have started to embrace the concept for its own specific purposes (Smith and Westerbeek, 2007; Breitbarth and Harris, 2008; Walters and Chadwick, 2009; Breitbarth, Hovemann and Walzel, 2011). Triggered especially by the immense commercialisation it has experienced over the last two decades, European football is now thought of as part of the wider entertainment sector and may even be considered to be an industry in its own right (Chadwick, 2009).

While some commentators have argued that sport is a distinctive socio-economic phenomenon that requires special treatment because of the way it touches people's everyday lives (European Commission, 2007; Chadwick, 2009), others consider high-profile professional sports leagues and clubs to be hardly any different from medium-sized, multinational companies: both consist of tangible, financial and intangible assets that are professionally managed and marketed (Yang and Somnez, 2005). Indeed, the title of Manchester United's then-Chairman Sir Roy Gardner's statement in the club's 2004 Annual Report was "Running a football club as a business". Meanwhile, Deloitte's (2012) Football Money League suggests that in 2010-11, the top 20 European clubs generated combined revenues of €4.4 billion: a 3% increase on the previous year and representing over a quarter of the European football market.

Undoubtedly, the political economy of professional football has changed significantly over recent decades. Breitbarth and Harris (2008) compare revenue sources of teams before and after 1990, largely confirming Andreff's (2000) assertion that the basis of football financing has changed from SSSL (speculators-subsidies-sponsors-local) to MMMMG (media-magnates-merchandising-markets-global). This shift confirms the growing need for clubs to engage in stakeholder management and dialogue in order to demonstrate sound governance and strategic orientation (Barn and Baines, 2004).

This, in turn, has made policy and ethics key values for football clubs. It has also put clubs under close scrutiny, especially from their commercial and media partners, politicians and fans. Today's football club must simultaneously uphold both the commercial and the symbolic values of its sporting products (Rouvrais-Charron and Durrand, 2009). Brand image is particularly important for European football teams because the stakeholders of the club, especially the commercially minded ones, will expect the brand to perform well (Richelieu, Lopez and Desbordes, 2008; Blumrodt, Desbordes and Bodin, 2010). If a football club failed to act responsibly, it could put the club's brand value at risk. For example, investors, sponsors and supporters with a different cultural background and operating mainly outside Europe would certainly be careful about spending money on a sporting product like a Premier League club if it had any association with racism. CSR programmes and initiatives can be used to manage such risks. As Liverpool FC states at the beginning of its Club Charter, "We do not tolerate discrimination of any sort at the club, on the pitch or in the stands. As such, we participate in a number of initiatives, some in partnership with other organisations, aimed at eliminating discrimination from football permanently".

Bradish and Cronin (2009: 692) therefore conclude that "sport is unique for being both a social and an economic institution, and as such [it is] well-suited ... to be[ing] interpreted by the business principles and practices of CSR". This means that sport clubs are in a generally good position to embrace CSR because of their traditionally deep roots into society.

Stakeholder management

It should be clear from the foregoing discussion that today's professional football clubs must be concerned with effective stakeholder management and, therefore, the integration of CSR into their operations and strategies. Figure 1 outlines the complexities that the managers of modern professional football clubs face and represents a non-hierarchical stakeholder map of a football club. It comprises both external and internal stakeholders.

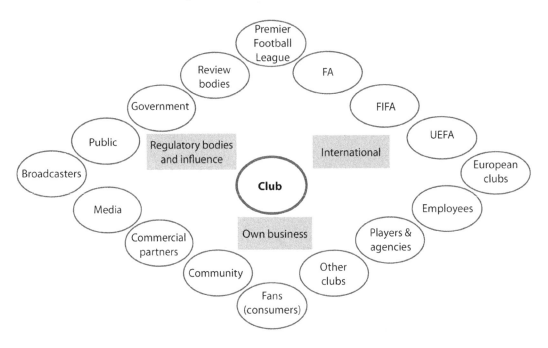

Figure 1: Non-hierarchical stakeholder map of a hypothetical (English) football club.
Source: Adapted from Bonn (2000, in Breitbarth and Harris, 2008: 183)

A particular feature of Figure 1 is the inclusion of stakeholder groups that were formerly considered to be outside the game, such as political and community actors (Bonn, 2000). This recognition has arguably become a cornerstone of the modern age of professional football management. By including these groups in their strategic management, clubs hope to gain or sustain the advantages the game holds over other sports in the global sports industry marketplace (Breitbarth and Harris, 2008). Just as with any business entity, stakeholder management can be an extremely challenging task for sports organisations, which must attempt to balance the various, often contradicting, demands and expectations of its stakeholders.

Further justification for responsible corporate behaviour comes from the fact that few football teams remain in a form that may be thought of as a 'traditional club'. In the past, sports clubs tended to draw most of their critical resources from the local and regional community (e.g. fans, players, sponsors). The traditional model of sporting clubs (or 'societies'), especially in England and Germany, was thus for the sport to be deeply 'embedded' in its societal context. Today, top clubs at the European level cannot afford to rely on such a limited resource base. The long-established grassroots links between clubs and wider society has thus become vulnerable to change. What is more, professional sport has become a commercial and, increasingly, a political domain. Professional football can be thought of as a 'platform' on which commercial (money), political (power and legitimisation), social (integration) and cultural (ethics and values) are exchanged (Breitbarth and Harris, 2008).

Because of its high public profile, professional football has come under close scrutiny from regulators (such as the European Commission), non-government organisations (such as the International Labour Organization) and community groups (such as independent club supporter groups). An example is the case of the 'Bosman Ruling'. In 1995, the European Court of Justice decided in favour of professional Belgian football player Jean-Marc Bosman's intention to freely choose a new club after his contract with his present club had ended. This was an important ruling on the free movement of labour and had a deep effect on the transfer of football players among clubs within Europe. It ended the times "of innocence when football blithely assumed that it was immune from the intervention of law" (Foster, 2000: 39). Jennings (2006), meanwhile, has prominently criticised the global football system in his book, 'Foul! The Secret World of FIFA: Bribes, Vote Rigging and Ticket Scandals', alleging widespread corruption, lack of transparency and nepotism. Accordingly, there have been symbolic and actual moves from leading football governors around the globe to mitigate the public perception of widespread unethical practice. Critics do, however, remain suspicious of such moves and demand further change.

The 'win-win-win' paradigm

There is no doubt that football has become more than a game. Today's managers and administrators have to create, direct and control resources beyond the sphere of pure sporting endeavour. Economic, political, ethical and also emotional factors have become strategic issues in football management; as indeed they have in other high-profile professional sports.

Some clubs and leagues have started to embrace CSR as a means of coping with the new circumstances, demands and pressures. Predominantly they focus on local activities, where the organisation is viewed as a citizen with a certain degree of involvement in the community (Thorne McAlister, Ferrell and Ferrell, 2005). The concept of corporate citizenship (CC) can be thought of as a local and more pragmatic expression of CSR. From a strategic perspective, improving the environment from which an organisation draws many of its human, consumer, supplier and political resources through community engagement is a winning argument for CC.

Rosca (2011: 328) further argues that:

"Football clubs … aren't only interested in how to win matches at all cost, but, as Nick Hornby writes, they also owe a sense of decency to their fans … Football clubs have a privileged position in the community, being institutions that can very good and easy represent the community to which they belong. A football club is an ambassador of its community, representing it through the results on the pitch and the activities outside the playing field, and, more important, it is an identification vehicle for the citizens".

In this way, professional football organisations also seek to counter criticisms of their legitimacy; for example, that the formation of the game in England in particular has "over the past 15 years … actually contributed to the exclusion of some groups in society, especially on economic grounds" (Brown, Crabbe and Mellor, 2006: 9). Rather than taking a reactive stance towards CSR and CC, partnership initiatives offer proactive opportunities for clubs, the public sector and businesses within the 'win-win-win paradigm' (see Figure 2).

In summary, CSR has proven its business case to companies from different industries, for example by enhancing brands and trust, building relationships with stakeholders, motivating staff, limiting business risks and helping to counter political and legislative pressures. In the context of sports, and professional football in particular, administrators and managers have started to embrace the concept for similar reasons. They also see it as a way of mitigating the downside of the commercialisation of their sport.

Clearly, the sport has to preserve both the commercial and the symbolic qualities of its sporting products in order to legitimise its powerful position and remain accepted as a partner of its commercial, media, political, supranational and other stakeholders (Rouvrais-Charron and Durrand, 2009). At a regional level, modern football clubs strategically engage with such partners as part of their CSR activities. Arguably, such projects create 'win-win-win' situations, leading to positive outcomes for the club, its stakeholder community and society at large.

This introduction has traced the international debate about CSR and its relevance to modern sports management. The following comparative cases provide an understanding of how CSR has been applied in two different football clubs. Differences are explained mainly by nation-specific CSR approaches, ownership structures and the key personalities involved. Evidently, there is no one-size-fits-all recipe for the successful integration of CSR in sport.

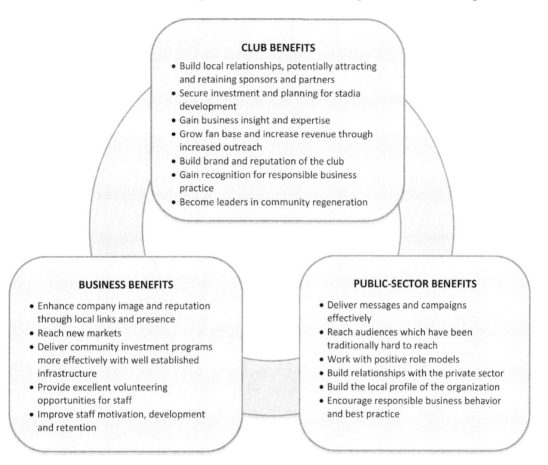

CLUB BENEFITS
- Build local relationships, potentially attracting and retaining sponsors and partners
- Secure investment and planning for stadia development
- Gain business insight and expertise
- Grow fan base and increase revenue through increased outreach
- Build brand and reputation of the club
- Gain recognition for responsible business practice
- Become leaders in community regeneration

BUSINESS BENEFITS
- Enhance company image and reputation through local links and presence
- Reach new markets
- Deliver community investment programs more effectively with well established infrastructure
- Provide excellent volunteering opportunities for staff
- Improve staff motivation, development and retention

PUBLIC-SECTOR BENEFITS
- Deliver messages and campaigns effectively
- Reach audiences which have been traditionally hard to reach
- Work with positive role models
- Build relationships with the private sector
- Build the local profile of the organization
- Encourage responsible business behavior and best practice

Figure 2: 'Win-win-win' paradigm underlying joint corporate citizenship activities in the area of sports. *Source:* Adapted from Business in the Community (2008)

The following case studies of Liverpool FC and SV Werder Bremen analyse and describe the context-specific CSR approaches of a British and a German professional football club. Learning outcomes focus on appreciating the national context of discussions and applications of CSR; learning about examples of the application of CSR and specific club projects; and recognising the value added to managing and marketing professional football, especially club brands and local, regional and international relationships.

CSR in football

There are many examples of how professional football organisations in Europe and beyond integrate CSR or aspects of the approach. In 2008, Europe's top teams (then associated under the G-14 umbrella) published a document providing insights into the contribution of European club football to community development, claiming that 'clubs are addressing more social issues than ever before ... by co-operating with governments, NGOs, sponsors, private and public sector organizations" (G-14, 2008: 5). In Sweden, 'Fotbollsalliansen' combines efforts from all Swedish elite clubs and the Swedish Football Association to help troubled teenagers and club supporters.

Teams like Chelsea FC or FC Barcelona view CSR as an integral strategic success factor, particularly when it is used a vehicle for stakeholder management. In their latest CSR report, Chelsea FC talk about how they seek to advance social inclusion, their support for the armed forces and a waste recycling scheme the club has recently developed. Due to its heritage and its role during the Spanish Civil War, FC Barcelona has become a symbol for Catalan culture and identity: hence its motto 'More than a club' ('Més que un club').

Immediately after the event had taken place, the organisers of the 2008 European Championships (EURO, 2008) published a sustainability report based on the 'triple bottom line' concept of people, planet and profit (i.e. one based on social, ecological and economic measures of sustainability). The FIFA World Cup 2010 in South Africa has seen various social development projects due to the attention and money that has come with the event. It will therefore not come as much of a surprise that the United Nations claims that "football has a great capacity as a catalyst to assist United Nations activities, such as fighting poverty, combating HIV/AIDS, promoting peace, and bringing people together" (United Nations, 2006: 11).

The following case studies describe how two clubs have framed CSR and integrated CC into their operations and strategy. Liverpool FC and SV Werder Bremen are leading clubs within their respective leagues in England and Germany. Both clubs are also proud of their long lists of national and international honours. At the same time, the position of CSR in their organisational structures and the content of their respective CSR programmes differ significantly. This can best be explained by their very different national and sporting systems, their different corporate cultures and the different policies they have had to adopt.

Liverpool FC's CSR approach

The case of Liverpool FC describes the management of CSR by a professional English football club. It considers aspects of the context, the content and the process of the club's CSR engagement.

National context in brief

CSR in the UK has deep historical roots in the massive urbanisation that took place during the rapidly unfolding Industrial Revolution. Victorian capitalism, which strongly demanded freedom from interference from the central government, further weakened community cohesion. The response was much philanthropic work, particularly on the part of prominent industrialists. Modern CSR in the UK, meanwhile, is grounded in the period of high unemployment, urban decay and social unrest that took place in the 1980s. As such, CSR in the UK requires more explicit manifestation on the part of corporations (e.g. partnership initiatives and internal staff positions) than is the case under the 'implicit CSR' of Germany's Rhenish Capitalism (Moon, 2005). This has led to a particularly community-focused approach in the UK that seeks to counter social exclusion and to support urban and regional regeneration (see, for example, Business in the Community).

Sporting context

In the UK, the process of football's transformation into a business accelerated during the 1990s, chiefly as a result of the floatation of an increasing number of clubs on the stock market and the growing significance of the game as a strategy for expansion on the part of the private-sector media (which, in turn, increased the importance of media revenues in the development of the game). At the same time, urban decay, crime and hooliganism in and around many football stadiums became a problem. Matters of football governance therefore came under increasing public scrutiny. As a result, at the beginning of the 2000s football seemed to be no longer in charge of the game or its own destiny (Hamil, Michie, Oughton and Warby, 2000). It also appeared to be suffering from increasingly intense political and media pressures.

In a coalition of interests, the Football Association (FA) and various individual clubs joined forces to tackle such problems. They began to implement stakeholder-driven CSR activities as a means of addressing football's relationship with society and reconnecting with communities (e.g. 'Football in the Community' and 'Football Foundation'). To date, such efforts have involved various campaigns, programmes, schemes and charities. The FA (2012) itself strongly believes that football has a unique place in British society and can act as a power for good off the pitch in a number of policy areas.

Tim Vine, Premier League spokesperson, describes 'Creating Chances' as the cornerstone of this ambition:

> "Social engagement has a long tradition in England. Many well-known teams participate in initiatives that use sports to change communities and society as a whole for the better. 'Creating Chances' is a fund whose goals include social integration, education, health, and equal rights for children and young adults. Since its creation in 2000, all the funding provided by top leagues is specifically transferred to social projects like 'Kickz', which has reached a large number of teenagers living in suburbs that struggle with a range of problems" (Personal communication, 30 July 2009, Bad Ragaz).

The FA and the Premier League have managed to establish, facilitate and promote a number of nationwide CSR projects that have been adapted by individual clubs. Still notable, however, is the on-going struggle to establish viable structures for the professional English football system, which was the focus of another critical report by the UK Parliament Culture, Media and Sport Committee in 2011. Other matters on English football's CSR agenda include local community involvement and making contributions to regional development, youth education and combating racism.

Profile of Liverpool FC

Liverpool FC was formed in 1892 and is one of the most successful clubs in British football with, among other titles, 18 English football championships and 11 European Cup championships. Its revenue was about US$295 million (€210 million) in 2011 and it has been consistently ranked among the Top 10 on Forbes' list of most valuable football clubs. Since 2010, the Fenway Sports Group has been the sole owner of the club. Fenway is an American sports investment company that is also the parent company of the Major League Baseball team Boston Red Sox and various other sports ventures.

It was only after fierce opposition from former owners George Gillett and Tom Hicks, and a narrow board decision in its favour, that Fenway took over Liverpool. Fenway's key people, John Henry and Tom Werner, now head the club's organisational chart as Principal Owner and Chairman respectively. Their current Managing Director is Ian Ayre, an English businessman and former CEO of several IT and sports companies in the UK and Asia.

The CSR approach

Other than FC Brentford, Liverpool is the only English sports organisation to have received the CommunityMark, a national standard of excellence in community investment, which is endorsed by the Prime Minister and HRH

The Prince of Wales. The club almost matches the 44 individual CSR programmes that make Chelsea the frontrunner in the 2010-11 Premier League season (Rosca, 2011).

Liverpool FC's CSR ambassador is Bill Bygroves, pastor at Bridge Chapel Centre in Liverpool, Club Chaplain and, since 2001, head of the club's Community Department. He also has a coaching licence and teaches at the Liverpool FC Academy. He states that:

> "Our department is responsible for the various projects. These activities range in focus, operating in the social sector on both a national and international level. They are free of charge to socially deprived and disabled children. We work in close partnership with regional schools and institutions. For example, the club engages in programmes that work to prevent drug use and fight against racism. I think one inspiring project is the 'Young Person of the Year Award', which is presented annually to children who have shown outstanding social commitment. All of our activities are financed by the club, the city, and the Premier League" (Personal communication, 30 July 2009, Bad Ragaz).

The Club Charter lists the Community Department's five focus areas: education, health, social inclusion, physical activity and charity support both home and overseas. The objectives are according to the Club Charter:

♦   To inspire people to achieve their potential

♦   To work with professional and community partners to encourage healthy lifestyles and deliver measurable improvements in them

♦   To inspire people of all ages and abilities to improve their educational achievement

♦   To contribute to safe and inclusive communities

♦   To offer a wide range of sporting activities which engage people of all ages and abilities

♦   To be a trusted partner for other charities and agencies

Table 2 and Figure 3 provide an overview of the Liverpool's CSR approach and portfolio, and show how this is featured on the official website.

Liverpool FC owner Fenway also owns the football stadium that has been the home of club since 1892. It is located in and named after the district of Anfield, which is among the most socially deprived council wards in the UK and suffers from high levels of unemployment, health problems and poor infrastructure. Consequently, the club collaborates with the City Council and other public-sector organisations to attract funding and investment to tackle a range of socio-economic problems. It is in the club's interest to operate in a sound socio-economic environment but, as with other real estate, the value of a property benefits from the value of the surrounding area being maintained in the long run.

Table 2: Overview of Liverpool FC's approach to CSR

Mission/aims	The Club recognises the role it can play in generating and supporting activity both in the local community and the wider football community
	The vision of LFC's work in communities is to use the power of the club's reputation and badge to inspire positive change, not just in its local area, but in poor communities throughout the world
	A key focus of the club is raising the aspirations and talents of young people, in particular their employability
	"People don't care how much we know until they know how much we care"
Portfolio	Truth 4 Youth (e.g. 'Young Person of the Year' award)
	Action 4 Health
	Tactics 4 Families
	Respect 4 All
	Footy 4 All
	Reduc@te
	Regeneration of Anfield
Internal organisation	Community Department, founded in 2000, with 20 full-time staff plus project-specific trainers, helpers, volunteers and seasonal workers
Main partners	Sponsors (e.g. Standard Chartered), Anfield Breckside Community Council, Liverpool City Council, local schools (about 75) and universities, Football Foundation

Source: Author

Examples of CSR activities and partnerships

The club has recently contributed €12 million to the restoration of Stanley Park, the Isla Gladstone Conservatory and other vital community institutions. Its capital investment leveraged €30 million of public-sector funding. Its involvement in the regeneration process includes the club being in regular consultation with a number of institutions: the local authority, members of the local community, residents' associations and organisations concerned with the development and regeneration of the Anfield area (such as North Liverpool Stakeholders Group, Anfield Breckfield Partnership Forum, Anfield Breckfield Community Partnership, Anfield Breckside Community Council and Breckfield North Everton Community Council).

Figure 3: Community section on Liverpool FC website. *Source:* screenshot www.liverpoolfc.tv

Another example of support for the local community is the 'Action for Health' programme, in which the club serves as the accountable body for a European-funded programme for North Liverpool (see Figures 4 and 5). North Liverpool exhibits some of the worst health statistics nationally and those health inequalities need to be addressed. The programme's activities includes a targeted healthy living programmes for young people, adults and elderly persons, including free health checks (over 4,500 had been undertaken by 2009), as well as health information points located in places such as pubs and community centres. The checks have discovered high incidences of type 2 diabetes and high blood pressure in the area.

Figure 4: Public health campaign. *Source:* G-14 (2008)

In partnership with local community agencies, further initiatives include a men's health programme, positive mental health for the over 50s, a 'Drop a Shirt Size' weight-management project and on-going support to the 2020 Decade of Health and Wellbeing in Liverpool. Independent study by the University of Liverpool shows that 67.5% of people made a healthy lifestyle change as a result of the programme (Business in the Community, 2008). The club is also a member of the European Healthy Stadia Network, where good practice is shared with other stadiums across Europe, such as the introduction of a 'Cycle2Work' scheme.

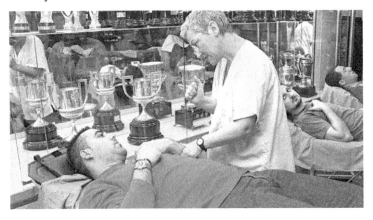

Figure 5: Free health checks for men next to Liverpool's collection of trophies. *Source:* G-14 (2008)

Star players not only contribute to the sporting success of the team, they are also viewed as key assets to represent, market and promote the club's social-responsibility projects. In particular, they help attract public participation and media attention. For example, Liverpool winger Stewart Downing joined in a tactics session with Liverpool FC's community team at a local primary school Barlow's Lane School (in Fazakerley) and helped deliver a lesson as part of the club's award-winning 'Tactics 4 Families' programme. This intends to use the language and principles of football as a mechanism to highlight the importance of strong family bonds. Using players as 'magnets' helps to engage about 22,000 young people a year in the club's CSR programmes.

There is also a positive link between the Liverpool's social responsibility activities and the strategies of the team's main sponsor, Standard Chartered Bank, which states that "We aim to lead the way in Asia, Africa and the Middle East" as the main strategic avenue to grow its global business. Being associated with one of the world's most successful football clubs, along with its extremely valuable sports brand, was an important driver behind their decision to sponsor Liverpool. As their website states "We're excited to have access to some of the most successful players in football history, past and present, as this lets us create a host of unique experiences for customers and clients around the world. Liverpool FC also has a similar heritage to ourselves – with over 100 years of history – and we share the common values of teamwork, partnership and a winning spirit. It's no real surprise then that our sponsorship of Liverpool FC is already proving popular in our markets across the world. We've been able to bring the club to events in Kenya, Hong Kong and Korea – and that's just for starters!" (Standard Chartered Bank website).

With many football brands also trying to expand into the Asian, Arabic and African markets – arguably, Manchester United has been the most successful so far – Liverpool's Commercial Director, Ian Ayre, described their partnership with Standard Chartered as a 'winning combination' when the agreement was signed in 2010. In particular, the two organisations see benefits in aligning some of their respective CSR activities:

> "Like Liverpool, Standard Chartered are well known for their charity and community work … They are currently involved in a couple of large Corporate Social Responsibility (CSR) projects, sight restoration being the biggest. Likewise, Liverpool has a lot of community projects and exciting things going on and so our objectives are to bring the two together. We're in very early talks about how we integrate with their programmes and find new initiatives. In July we're planning to run

soccer camps for them in Kenya – and that's just the start of a variety of opportunities we'll put together" (Eaton, 2010: 1).

At the international level, Liverpool FC is a partner of the Football is More Foundation. This organisation helps to develop and advance relationships around the globe that contribute to the club's agenda in respect of developing some of their strategic resources (e.g. scouting and players, publicity and brand value, doing good works and reputation, and networking and policy). In this context, the club has teamed up with the United Nations and the Aspire Foundation in Qatar to give under-privileged youths from Africa and Palestine a sporting chance. Furthermore, Gary Adlen, Liverpool FC Foundation Director, explains that developing such global relationships: "gives kids a feel for Liverpool FC [and] the chance to become ambassadors for the club and in their communities". The Executive of the Foundation, meanwhile, believes that "Liverpool gives the initiative the recognition around the globe it truly deserves".

Summary

As a member of the English business community, Liverpool FC has responded to the calls for increasing local and regional engagement with the regeneration of urban spaces and communities. The club benefits from a healthy and intact environment to operate in. The club is owned by overseas investors and is run as a business by former industry managers.

As part of a league-wide concept, Liverpool has developed a broad CSR portfolio based on various partnership and own initiatives. From a marketing perspective, this investment helps the club to foster its main assets: a global fan base and a high brand value.

SV Werder Bremen's CSR approach

The case of the SV Werder Bremen describes the management of CSR in the German context. Similar to the case of Liverpool FC, it considers aspects of the context, the content and the process of the club's CSR orientation and activities.

National context in brief

The Industrial Revolution happened later in Germany and at a much slower pace than in the UK. Strict Prussian bureaucracy demanded companies, churches and other actors to contribute to society, which enabled the state to act as an agent of modernisation (Lane, 1992). Even to the present day, the welfare state is expected to provide local public services, culture and education, and also to support research and development (Matten and Moon,

2005). Consequently, under Germany's system of Rhenish Capitalism, businesses and public institutions play a vital role in contribution to the 'common good' based on traditional and existing social agreements and regulations. This is characterised as an 'implicit' approach to CSR (Matten and Moon, 2005).

Sporting context

In Germany, sports clubs are communities of interests that are granted certain rights to govern their own affairs along with tax reductions from the public purse. The dawn of commercialisation was both later and less far-reaching than in the English football system (Skinner, 2010). Until 1998, only football teams established as 'incorporated societies' were allowed to be members of the German Football Association (DFB in German) and take part in national competitions. Consequently, the DFB is the world's largest national single-sport association, with 6.7 million society members. Today, some teams are incorporated businesses. Even so, the club or society concerned has to own 50% plus one share of the club in order to prevent outside investors dominating their business affairs (Leverkusen, owned by Bayer, and Wolfsburg, owned by Volkswagen, are exceptions to this rule for historical reasons, i.e. their corporate affiliation existed before the ownership regulation was introduced). German football clubs, as well as their governing bodies, have thus always had strong links with the local community with high-profile public administrators involved. This is exemplified by the case of SV Werder Bremen that follows.

In its statutes, the DFB proclaims that football has an immense impact on society and the environment in general. It sees as its foremost purpose the initiation and development of 'social activities', which are primarily charities, volunteer campaigns, support for disadvantaged people and humanitarian projects. However, in 2010 the DFB, together with the association of professional clubs (Bundesliga), published their first CSR strategy ('Path to Sustainability'), adding ethical, social-political and charitable goals to their core area of concern, which is, of course, the national organisation of the game.

Also only a few years ago, German football clubs started to engage explicitly with the modern CSR debate and to restructure their activities accordingly. Anna-Lisa Schwarz, the spokesperson of the Bundesliga Foundation (the foundation of the premier football league in Germany), cites the strong presence of the Bundesliga in every part of society as the main reason for the importance of its commitment to social responsibility:

> "The Bundesliga enjoys huge public popularity, with a brand awareness of 99%. Hence, our aim is to use the power and the popularity of

football to teach social values and to initiate change, for example to bring about justice, tolerance, and solidarity" (Personal communication, 31 July 2012, Bad Ragaz).

Generally, social inclusion, health and environmental aspects are on the sports CSR agenda, but so also are issues surrounding the negative impacts of advancing commercialisation and the unacceptable behaviour of some 'ultra' fan groups.

Profile of SV Werder Bremen

SV Werder Bremen e.V. is a sports club founded in 1899 and located in the northern part of Germany. Its membership is presently about 40,000 and outside of the city-state of Bremen (which has around 550,000 citizens) the club is best known for its professional football team. The club is the umbrella organisation for an incorporated society, which organises a range of amateur sports including chess, handball, gymnastics, table tennis, athletics and amateur football, and an incorporated business, a major component of which is the professional football team. The former is the sole owner of the latter. The professional football team has won ten national honours, with the latest being the German Football Association Cup (DFB-Pokal) in 2009. Among its international achievements, the club won the UEFA Cup in 1998. In 2011 its revenue was about €110 million and since 2008 it has consistently been ranked among the Top 20 on Forbes' list of most valuable football clubs.

The size of the club, along with its consistently high position in Germany's football hierarchy, has made it an integral part of the city's image, local politics, regional business and community identification. On its website, the state-city of Bremen ranks Werder Bremen top on its list of '13 Bremen icons'. The club's prominent position in the economy, along with the influence of some key personalities, has given CSR a critical role in an organisation that already had a strong community focus.

Thus, for example, the club's former Executive Director and Head of Advisory Board, Willy Lemke, subsequently became a minister of the city-state of Bremen, responsible for education, internal affairs and sports. Since 2008, he has also served as the United Nations Secretary-General's Special Adviser on Sport for Development and Peace. The current Chairman of the Management Board and Manager of Professional Football is Klaus Allofs, a former top striker, German international player and part of the German team that won the European Championships in 1980. There are hardly any business people or formally educated management experts in executive roles in German professional football, other than holders of honorary posts such as club presidents or members of advisory boards.

CSR approach

Since 2003, the club's President and Managing Director of Professional Football, Klaus-Dieter Fischer, has been a vocal ambassador for social causes and local development projects. Before leading club affairs, he worked in the civil service and as a teacher. Later he was the Director of the Bremen School Administration, which partially explains the club's innovative school partnership programme at the time. He summarises the club's approach to CSR as follows:

"We have to lead by example: in particular the team and the players because they are role models for the younger generation. Therefore, we have a social responsibility and we should positively impact on society, be it anti-discrimination, anti-violence or supporting environmental causes and amateur sports. The club has always been engaged with social and community initiatives, but in 2002 we developed the still successful project '100 schools–100 clubs' in order to frame our activities and be more explicit about it. Our motivation for this has never been financial and our CSR staff is not part of the marketing team. However, we believe that the club in general, but also our sponsors, benefit from our activities. One indication is that Werder has been voted the most friendly football club in Germany for a number of years. I think that some of the growth in club membership and fan base can also be attributed to this. However, we should be careful when we quantify and measure our social activities because it could lead to commercial pressure on our approach to CSR and competition between different of our internal departments" (personal communication).

Arguably, Werder Bremen can be considered to be the leading professional German football club in respect of the explicit integration of a CSR and CC portfolio into its management. Its social engagement includes initiatives targeting all age groups and both genders, and is prominently featured on its website (see Table 3 for an overview). The club has also consolidated its various new and long-standing projects in order to frame and communicate them more effectively in cooperation with partners to respective target groups (see Figure 6). Despite not intending to generate significant income from their community projects, Werder Bremen's use of social marketing tactics has helped it to reach out to potential participants, provide a sense of identification with respective programmes, and offered partners the opportunity to leverage their respective commitment, contributions and investments.

Table 3: Overview of SV Werder Bremen's approach to CSR

Mission/aims	General claims: Lifelong green-white; Lifelong active, Lifelong healthy, Lifelong tolerant, Lifelong helpful, Lifelong ecological
	Supporting the continuous development and growth of sports within the region, in particular among children and youth
	Raise awareness for matters like fair play, anti-discrimination, crime prevention, healthy lifestyles
	Inspire and enthuse young people about the club.
	"We cannot change the world on our own, but we are placing the first pieces of a puzzle!"
Portfolio	100% Werder Partner (e.g. '100 Schools–100 Clubs')
	100% Werder Worldwide (e.g. 'Football Clubs for Development and Peace')
	Kids-Club
	Nappy-League
	60Plus
	SV Werder Bremen Foundation
	Werder Volunteers
Internal organisation	Department of 'Social Affairs Management', six full-time staff, four interns, project-specific trainers, helpers and volunteers
Main partners	AOK Health Insurance, Kraft Foods, Scort Foundation, Bremen Police Department, ClimateHouse Bremerhaven, Home Mission, Bremen Heart Foundation, Universum Educational Science Center, Bremen Theatre

Source: Author

Figure 6: Logos used to brand Werder Bremen's CSR activities. *Source:* Screenshots www.werder.de

A key factor is the visibility of the social work done. This is because from a marketing perspective, partners wish to achieve specific publicity goals. CSR managers from Werder Bremen's partner organisations think of sports as an ideal vehicle "to reach out to young people … and to use joint programmes for image transfer and publicity" (food company; author's research interview) and "to use the sport context as a show case for a kind of healthy lifestyle" (health insurance; author's research interview). Furthermore, professional sports organisations such as Werder Bremen and their individual players symbolise 'success': an attribute that certain brands enjoy being associated with.

The club is the first professional sports organisation, certainly in Germany, to have begun implementing a CSR Performance Scorecard. The CSR Performance Scorecard is a multidimensional, criteria-based performance measurement model originally developed by a research team from the German Sport University Cologne (Breitbarth, Hovemann and Walzel, 2011). The club's progressive attitude is indicative of a more formalised and strategic attitude to CSR. Despite the president's initially sceptical view about measuring CSR activities in sports, the club became interested in further developing and integrating the concept, which provides a 'balanced' range of CSR metrics. In the specific case of Werder Bremen, key performance indicators were developed in the areas shown in Table 4.

Table 4: Key CSR performance indicators for SV Werder Bremen

Customers

- Increasing brand value

- Bonding by fans

- Bonding by strategic partners

Society

- Building up social capital

- Improving public relations

- Contributing to healthy lifestyles

- Raising awareness

Source: Walzel and Breitbarth (2012)

Examples of CSR activities and partnerships

The club's oldest CSR programme is '100 Schools–100 Clubs'. This dates back to 2002 and when it was established it was unique among its kind. Over time, other German professional clubs have tried to imitate it. The programme aims to encourage fair play, anti-discrimination and crime prevention by developing and supporting youth institutions in the wider region. The original objective was to involve 100 schools and 100 clubs but today there are actually 111 schools and 111 clubs that have been selected to be members of the programme, as well as 25 kindergartens, primary schools, vocational training schools and other community organisations. The original programme name and logo has remained because of its high level of public recognition (see Figure 6).

The SV Werder Bremen Foundation may choose to support individual activities within the broader '100 Schools–100 Clubs' programme. Participating schools, clubs and other selected institutions are encouraged to be innovative and committed to identifying projects that can link sport and social goals. In return, such institutions receive organisational support and resources to promote and operate the projects. This includes, for example, participation of the club in children's project weeks, stadium tours, free attendance at one game per season for the pupils, regular staff development sessions, donation of sports equipment and material (largely Werder-branded), educational and sports training sessions for children (see Figure 7), and participation in a special tournament for participating institutions.

Figure 7: A physiotherapist of Werder Bremen's professional football team delivering a sports training session at a partner school. *Source:* Press publication, available at www.werder.de/de/werder-bewegt/news/38460.php

Participating institutions can thus be part of a vibrant network that specifically focuses on child and youth development. Additionally, all institutions can claim to be officially associated with the club and thereby benefit from its reputation. Each institution may use an official individualised partner logo (see Figure 8). The club has accepted only about half of the institutions that have applied to be a member of the programme, mainly due to limited resources for managing the programme on a sustainable and quality level.

Figure 8: Use of '100 Schools–100 Clubs' logo on a participating school's website. *Source:* Screenshot http://realschule-diepholz.de/partner/werder-partner

Club officials are particularly proud of this programme and consider it to be the most important initiative within their CSR portfolio. The programme creates strong links not only with participating institutions but also with private partners that sponsor and support the club in other ways. In particular, food industry giant Kraft Foods and the leading German health insurer, AOK, are partners of the club. For both companies, the long-term involvement adds to their strategic marketing and their own respective portfolio of CSR activities. They invest a considerable amount of money in the programme in order to gain publicity and demonstrate their CSR. Through involvement in the programme, AOK seeks to enhance its reputation, widen its membership base and encourage children to be more active and healthier (author's research interview).

A manager concerned with the partnership describes their views as follows:

"We like to be recognised and need to be visible as a partner of this programme. In order to satisfy our executives and to demonstrate that such socially responsible activities add to our strategy, we want the partnership to be successful. In particular, high participation numbers and recognition from the public, media, politicians and others is extremely helpful. Due to German law, we are not allowed to spend money on sponsorship, so adding to Werder Bremen's widespread social activities is a suitable way to reach our goals" (author's research interview, May 2009).

Another example is that Werder Bremen's Head Coach, Thomas Schaaf, acts as an ambassador for AOK's campaign to encourage greater engagement in physical education at all school levels. The motto of the campaign translates as 'Sport in school is vital to life'.

Summary

The German social system has traditionally fostered a culture of 'implicit CSR', wherein organisations are deeply embedded in society and have become thoroughly integrated into the local community by adopting formal and informal social obligations. Werder Bremen's CSR approach has developed as part of its specific role in the socio-economic fabric of the city-state of Bremen. Top representatives and managers of the club have previously been involved in local governance and public administration. Many were formerly successful professional football players. Few have a formal 'business' background. The club is owned by the members of the SV Werder Bremen 'society': an ownership structure that meets with requirements of the German Football Association.

Werder Bremen's programmes are not the same as other clubs or the Bundesliga because of the non-centralised evolution of CSR in German professional football. Arguably, the club was the first German professional sport organisation to start measuring the performance of their CSR activities.

Conclusions

Arguments in favour of the explicit use of CSR in professional football are now able to speak for themselves. All high-profile organisations across Europe – including clubs, leagues, associations and governing bodies – have started to engage explicitly in the CSR agenda. Links between sporting matters, policy and political issues, commercial interests and social and communal development have tightened. Consequently, modern sports management requires the use of stakeholder management and a strategic CSR orientation.

A recent comparative study by Hovemann, Breitbarth and Walzel (2011) shows that the motivations and reasons for adopting CSR, the areas of CSR engagement, the extent of institutionalisation of CSR activities and the types of partnerships involved differ between selected English and German clubs. English clubs tend to demonstrate a more concerted, business-driven and well-developed approach than their German counterparts. They also tend to use a wider range of CSR activities and exhibit greater organisational integration. For example, clubs involved in the 2010-11 Premier League season hosted more than 300 CSR programmes between them.

Reasons for the differences in club structure, management and CSR approach between England and Germany can be found in their respective national governance and sporting systems. In England, football clubs became more aware of their role in society in the early 1980s. Since that time, the central government has called upon football clubs to launch social inclusion programmes and be part of regeneration projects, for example through the 'Action Sport' initiative. Such political intervention is justified by the idea that sports organisations can have strong connections to the citizens of their local communities and through these linkages have the power to improve people's quality of life. For football clubs such as Liverpool FC, it is therefore both in their interests and a political requirement that they engage systematically in CSR activities.

In comparison, the federal nature of German government has traditionally encouraged sports clubs to act as vehicles for social inclusion. Additionally, it is a requirement for any German professional football team to be owned by a collective group of individual members of a club 'society', so as to prevent commercial ownership. Pressure from investors to engage in CSR activities is less than in the UK and club leaders often have a career background in public administration, politics or the game itself. The case of Werder Bremen shows how the football club is intrinsically intertwined with the city-state itself and acts as proud ambassador on behalf of its citizens.

From a marketing and management perspective, football clubs benefit from CSR since they can build and foster regional, national and even international relationships with other influential organisations. Arguably, the most valuable asset of top football clubs is their brand value, which can be significantly enhanced by demonstrating and enacting social responsibility. This makes clubs valuable partners of industry and policy organisations such as corporate sponsors, local authorities and not-for-profit organisations. In the case of Liverpool FC, the club's efforts to expand its fan base into the Arabic and Asian regions are significantly aligned with the business strategy of its main sponsor.

In order to substantiate lasting CSR integration, however, the case of SV Werder Bremen shows a way forward to the better monitoring and communication of CSR activities. The concept of the CSR Performance Scorecard has gained acceptance within the club. At the same time, the spirit in which sports organisations are run in Germany shows that even a highly commercialised sports product such as football should not too easily be thought of simply as a business. Formal, wide-ranging evaluation and benchmarking of CSR activities in European sports is, however, still a long way off.

In summary, these comparative case studies provide contrasting pictures of how CSR is applied in professional football. Together, they provide a rationale for why football must be considered to be more than a game, and illustrate the consequences of doing so for how a professional sports product should be managed in view of national and cultural differences. Sports industry practitioners can locate their own experiences and approaches to CSR within the case studies. Researchers may be inspired to engage with the topic and may find suitable threads that they wish to develop further.

References

Andreff W. 2000. Financing modern sport in the face of sporting ethics. *European Journal of Sport Management* **7** (1): 5-30.

Barn SS, Baines PR. 2004. Fulham FC: Club-supporter relationship: 'Come all ye faithful'. In Harris, P, McDonald F. (eds) *European Business & Marketing*, London: Sage; 184-194.

Blumrodt J, Desbordes M, Bodin D. 2010. The sport entertainment industry and corporate social responsibility. *Journal of Management & Organization* **16** (4): 514-529.

Boon G, 2000. Football finances: Too much money? In Hamil S, Michie J, Oughton C, Warby S. (eds) *Football in the Digital Age*. Edinburgh: Mainstream Publishing; 28-35.

Bradish C, Cronin JJ. 2009. Corporate social responsibility in sport. *Journal of Sport Management* **23** (6): 691-697.

Brown A, Crabbe T, Mellor G, Blackshaw T, Stone C. 2006. *Football and its communities: Final report for the Football Foundation*, www.substance.coop/publications_football_and_its_communities.

Breitbarth T, Harris P, 2008. The role of corporate social responsibility in the football business: Towards the development of a conceptual model. *European Sport Management Quarterly* **8** (2): 179-206.

Breitbarth T, Hovemann G, Walzel S. 2011. Scoring strategy goals: Measuring corporate social responsibility in professional European football. *Thunderbird International Business Review* (Special Issue: Sports management - current trends and future developments) **53** (6): 721-737.

Business in the Community. 2008. *Clubs that Count: A Spotlight on Partnerships*. Report, September. London. www.bitc.org.uk.

Chadwick S. 2009. From outside lane to inside track: Sport management research in the twenty-first century. *Management Decision* **47** (1): 191-203.

Deloitte. 2012. *Fan Power: Football Money League*, Sports Business Group. Manchester: Deloitte.

Eaton P. 2010. The start of a brand new era. http://www.liverpoolfc.tv/news/latest-news/the-start-of-a-brand-new-era

EURO 2008 SA. 2008. *Sustainability Report*. November, Berne/Vienna. www.baspo.admin.ch/internet/baspo/de/home/themen/sportanlaesse/euro08_neu/english_documents.parsys.73821.downloadList.9642.DownloadFile.tmp/euro2008nachhaltigkeitsberichte.pdf.

European Commission. 2001. *Commission Green Paper, 'Promoting a European Framework for Corporate Social Responsibility'*, COM (2001) 366 Final, Brussels.

European Commission. 2007. *White paper on Sport*, COM (2007) 391 Final, Brussels.

European Commission. 2011. *A renewed EU strategy 2011-14 for Corporate Social Responsibility* COM (2011) 681 Final, Brussels.

Foster K. 2000. European law and football: Who's in charge? In Garland J, Malcom D, Rowe M. (eds) *The Future of Football*. London: Frank Cass Publishers; 39-51.

Fotbollsalliansen. 2008. Fryshuset Social Projects. Stockholm www.fryshuset.se/documents/Fryshuset/OmFryshuset/Fryshuset_english_version2.0.pdf.

G-14. 2008. Community Engagement: Insights into the Contribution of European Club Football www.bitc.org.uk/resources/publications/community_engagement.html.

Hamil S, Michie J, Oughton C, Warby S. 2000. Whose game is it anyway? In Hamil S, Michie J, Oughton C, Warby S. (eds) *Football in the Digital Age*. Edinburgh: Mainstream Publishing; 17-26.

Herrmann KK. 2004. Corporate social responsibility and sustainable development: The European Union initiative as a case study. *Indiana Journal of Global Legal Studies* **11** (2): 205-232.

Hovemann G, Breitbarth T, Walzel S. 2011. The state of development of corporate social responsibility in European professional football: A comparison of the countries of Germany, England and Switzerland. *Journal of Sponsorship* **4** (4): 338-352.

Lane, C. 1992. European business systems: Britain and Germany compared. In Whitley R. (ed.) *European Business Systems – Firms and Markets in their National Contexts*. London: Sage; 64-97.

Manchester United. 2004. Annual Report http://production.investis.com/manutd/findata/reports/annrep04/annrep04.pdf.

Matten D, Moon J. 2005. A conceptual framework for understanding CSR. In Habisch A, Jonker J, Wegner M, Schmidpeter R (eds) *Corporate Social Responsibility Across Europe*. Berlin: Springer; 335-355.

Moon J. 2005. An explicit model of business-society relations. In Habisch A, Jonker J, Wegner M, Schmidpeter R. (eds) *Corporate Social Responsibility Across Europe*. Berlin: Springer; 51-65.

Richelieu A, Lopez S, Desbordes M. 2008. The internationalization of sports team brand: The case of European soccer teams. *International Journal of Sport Marketing and Sponsorship* **10** (1): 29-44.

Rosca V. 2011. Corporate social responsibility in English football: History and present. *Management & Marketing Challenges for the Knowledge Society* **6** (2): 327-346.

Rouvrais-Charron C, Durand C. 2009. European football under close scrutiny. International. *Journal of Sports Marketing & Sponsorship* **10** (3): 230-243.

Skinner J. 2010. German model highlights Man Utd dilemma, BBC, Monday, 29 March. http://news.bbc.co.uk/sport1/hi/football/europe/8589872.stm

Smith A, Westerbeek H. 2007. Sport as a vehicle for developing corporate social responsibility. *Journal of Corporate Citizenship* **25** (7): 43-54.

The FA. 2012. Written evidence submitted by The Football Association to the UK Parliament, Culture, Media and Sport Committee, February 2012, www.publications.parliament.uk/pa/cm201213/cmselect/cmcumeds/89/89we03.htm

Thorne McAlister D, Ferrell OC, Ferrell L. 2005. *Business and Society: A Strategic Approach to Corporate Citizenship*. Boston, Mass: Houghton Mifflin.

United Nations. 2006. *Sport for Development and Peace: The Way Forward*. Report of the Secretary-General (#A/61/373). General Assembly, 22 September 2006.

Walters G, Chadwick S. 2009. Corporate citizenship in football: Delivering strategic benefits through stakeholder engagement. *Management Decision* **47** (1): 51-66.

Walzel S, Breitbarth T. 2012. Implementing the corporate social responsibility performance scorecard in professional football clubs. Abstract Book of the 20th Conference of the European Association for Sport Management (EASM), Aalborg, Denmark, 18-21 September; 188.

Weber M. 2008. The business case for corporate social responsibility: A company-level measurement approach for CSR. *European Management Journal* **26** (4): 247-261.

Yang D, Sonmez M. 2005. Intangible balls. *Business Strategy Review* **16** (2): 38-47.

Ancillary Student Material

Further reading

Babiak K, Paramio Salcines JL, Walters G. 2013. (eds). *Routledge Handbook of Sport and Corporate Social Responsibility*. New York: Routledge.

Carroll AB, Buchholtz AK. 2011. *Business & Society: Ethics, Sustainability, and Stakeholder Management*. Monson: South Western Education Publishers.

May G, Phelan J. 2005. *Shared Goals: Sport and Business in Partnership for Development*. The Prince of Wales International Business Leader Forum, www.toolkitsportdevelopment.org/html/resources/9A/9A141603-39AE-4360-8749-FB2BA9B54676/shared_goals_1.pdf

Swayne LE, Golson JG. 2011. *SAGE Encyclopaedia of Sports Management and Marketing*. Thousand Oaks: SAGE Publications.

Related websites and audio-visual materials

Websites

Liverpool FC: www.liverpoolfc.tv

SV Werder Bremen e.V.: www.werder.de

The Football Association: www.thefa.com

Deutscher Fussball-Bund e.V.: www.dfb.de

Premier League: www.premierleague.com

Deutsche Fussball Liga GmbH: www.bundesliga.de

UK Parliament: Culture, Media and Sport Committee – Seventh Report, Football Governance: www.publications.parliament.uk/pa/cm201012/cmselect/cmcumeds/792/79202.htm

Birkbeck Sport Business Centre: www.sportbusinesscentre.com/BSBCMedia

Bertelsmann-Stiftung: CSR Weltweit – 'Fussball und gesellschaftliche Verantwortung': www.csr-weltweit.de/de/im-fokus/dossiers/fussball-und-gesellschaftliche-verantwortung

Podcast

Why governance in sport matters, and what it means for football (podcast): www.ethicalcorp.com/governance-regulation/podcasts/why-governance-sport-matters-and-what-it-means-football

Videos

FIFA Football for Hope Festival 2010: www.youtube.com/watch?v=_bHhZI3043A

Fußball und gesellschaftliche Verantwortung (mostly German language): www.csr-weltweit.de/de/im-fokus/dossiers/fussball-und-gesellschaftliche-verantwortung/index.nc.html

Good energy at Manchester City FC: www.youtube.com/watch?v=8_SCqPJvGNk

'Professional Football against hunger' – 2012 campaign kick-off: www.youtube.com/watch?v=rxcKwrAle3I

More than a club: FC Barcelona and UNICEF: www.youtube.com/watch?v=KINSYKAd2Dk

Racism in association football: www.youtube.com/watch?v=-2CX5633olM

Liverpool FC United Nations partnership: www.youtube.com/watch?v=kaord6GEaz4

Liverpool FC joins forces with Football is More: www.liverpoolfc.tv/news/latest-news/lfc-join-forces-with-football-is-more

Comic

Score the goals: Teaming up to achieve the UN Millennium Development: www.un.org/wcm/webdav/site/sport/shared/sport/Score%20the%20 Goals/1001589_UNOSDP_BD_EN_Basse%20Def.pdf

Self-test questions

Try to answer the following questions to test your knowledge and understanding. If you are not sure of the answers please re-read the case and refer to the references and further reading sources:

1 How should CSR be defined?

2 Why should professional football organisations be concerned about CSR?

3 What are potential benefits of CSR and CC for football clubs?

4 What are main differences between the English and German (a) ownership systems and (b) football context that impact on their different CSR agendas?

5 Research and draw a stakeholder map of an English football club of your choice.

6 Why do clubs use star players for their CSR activities?

Key themes and theories

The key themes raised in this case study relate to the following:

Social responsibility of professional sports organisations

- ◆ Benefits of CSR for sports organisations
- ◆ Motives of sports organisations undertaking CSR
- ◆ CSR activities of professional football organisations in Germany and England
- ◆ Measuring CSR in a sports context

Commercialisation and political economy of football

- ◆ Football governance
- ◆ Economic scale and scope of professional football clubs

Strategic management of service organisations

- ◆ Sports club management
- ◆ Organisational change
- ◆ CSR integration

Sports marketing

- ◆ Celebrities and promotion
- ◆ Sports and charity
- ◆ Branding

The key theories relate to:

Resource-based view of the sports organisation

Corporate sustainability

- ◆ Corporate social responsibility
- ◆ Corporate citizenship
- ◆ Cause-related marketing

Relationship management/marketing

- ◆ Stakeholder management
- ◆ Social marketing
- ◆ Sports sponsorship

Balanced scorecard approach

If you need to source further information on any of the above themes and theories, then these headings could be used as key words to search for materials and case studies.

 Scan here to get the hyperlinks for this chapter.

SECTION TWO

IMPACTS and LEGACY

5

The Economics, Economic Impacts and Wider Legacies of Sports Mega-Events

The 2008 Beijing Olympic Games

Xi Wang and ShiNa Li

Introduction

International sporting mega-events, such as the Olympic Games, the FIFA Football World Cup and the Rugby World Cup, have become important economic phenomena. Indeed, the economic and associated benefits that such events can deliver continue to fuel the interest of national governments in bidding for, holding and financing events of this kind (Li, 2012). Many governments are eager to hold international sporting mega-events as they believe that the gross domestic product (GDP) of their country will increase, making the general population better off (Dwyer, Forsyth and Spurr, 2004). This is increasingly the case with developing countries: the 2008 Olympic Games in Beijing, the 2010 FIFA World Cup in South Africa and the 2014 FIFA World Cup and 2016 Olympic Games to be held in Brazil are all contemporary examples of developing countries being interested in hosting international sporting mega-events.

The economic effects of sporting mega-events are generated by different types of event-related investment and expenditure, such as monies spent on operations, increased tourism expenditure and investment in event venues and related infrastructure, as well as exports and foreign investment legacies after the event finishes (Li and Blake, 2009). It is only relatively recently that the organisers of sporting mega-events have started to realise the importance of legacies and actually to formulate legacy plans prior to an event taking place. The International Olympic Committee (IOC), for example, recognises the significance of legacies attributable to Olympic Games through the inclusion of an additional goal in Rule 2 of the Olympics Charter: "to promote a positive legacy from the Olympic Games to the host cities and host countries" (International Olympic Committee, 2007: 15). After organising the Olympic Games, the immediate challenge a hosting city faces is how best to utilise the sporting venues. If the venues are not profitably used, they are likely to become a financial burden for the local, regional or national government. In fact, the post-Games utilisation of venues has been a recognised problem for many years, with all Olympic cities making efforts to prolong and maximise the social and economic benefits from their Games, albeit with varying levels of success (Cashman, 2006; Preuss, 2007; Gratton and Preuss, 2008; Gold and Gold, 2010).

The above issues were of particular concern to the organisers of the 2008 Beijing Olympic Games. Much effort was invested in ensuring that the facilities would be well utilised after the Games for non-sporting purposes, such as holding large events, conferences and exhibitions. These wider uses would help contribute to the wider tourism legacy for Beijing while at the same time generating a positive economic legacy. For example, during the post-Games period of August 2008 to July 2010, the Beijing National Stadium, known as The Bird's Nest, received 13 million visitors, earning more than US$41 million. The National Swimming Centre, often dubbed as the Water Cube, received 4.5 million visitors (BODA, 2011). As such, the venues of the 2008 Beijing Olympic Games have achieved a greater level of commercial success than those of any previous Olympic Games, with people from within China forming the majority of visitors. This case examines the economics of 2008 Beijing Olympic Games with the aim of demonstrating the economic impacts and wider legacy benefits that hosting major international sporting mega-event can deliver for a host city and nation. In particular, the case considers what can be done to ensure the host leverages maximum legacy benefit long into the future.

The relationship between sports mega-events and economics

Mega-events can be defined as festivals, exhibitions, sports matches and other cultural and musical events that achieve sufficient size and scope to affect whole economies and receive sustained global media attention (Getz 1997; Roche, 2000; Horne and Manzenreiter, 2006). These include the World's Fairs (although these are now declining in influence); the World Cups in soccer, rugby union and cricket; the larger regional sports gatherings (e.g. European Championships, Asian Games, Pan-American Games and Commonwealth Games); and the Olympic Games (García, 2004; Gold and Gold, 2005).

Mega-events play significant roles in host destinations in terms of the economy, culture, society, politics and environment. In economic terms, hosting sporting mega-events, especially the Olympic Games, encourages governments to invest in sports venues, tourism facilities and other infrastructure. This may in turn lead to economic growth, urban regeneration and increased employment. The Olympic Games are not just grand sporting arenas promoting the Olympic spirit: they also represent stages upon which host cities promote themselves, enhance their image and gain long-term economic benefits. Although the economic impact of a mega-event can never capture the whole picture, it is one of the most significant indicators of its outcomes. Li and McCabe (2012), for example, summarise two main constructs used to measure the economic impact of mega-events: event-related direct expenditures and event effects. In the context of the Olympic Games, Li and Blake (2009) categorise five Olympic-related direct investments and expenditures: operating expenditures, tourism expenditures, investment in Olympic-related infrastructure, investment in Olympic venues and related facilities, and exports and foreign investment legacies. Event effects can be evaluated at both the macroeconomic (whole economy) level in terms of changes in gross domestic product (GDP), employment, economic welfare and exports (Li and McCabe, 2012), and at the microeconomic (industry) level in terms of changes in the value of labour, capital and output (Kasimati, 2003; Blake, 2005; Madden, 2006; Li, Blake and Cooper, 2011). In addition, there are other economic benefits that the Olympics may generate. These are, however, intangible and therefore difficult to quantify. Examples include increased property values and long-term promotional benefits (Dwyer, Mellor, Mistillis and Mules, 2000).

Holding a mega-event typically generates a large amount of investment and expenditure. For example, the investment in Olympic venues, related infrastructure and facilities for the 2000 Sydney, 2008 Beijing, and 2012 London Olympics was estimated to be US$3.3 billion (NSW Treasury, 1997), US$11.8 billion (BOBICO, 2001; BOCOG, 2002) and US$3.6 billion (Blake, 2005) respectively. There are other economic activities directly related to holding a mega-event (Madden, 2006). The main types of event-related expenditure include operating expenditure by the event committee, and domestic and inbound tourism expenditures (Li and Blake, 2009). These event investments and expenditures are considered to be 'new' money flowing into a host economy, which can have economic impacts on welfare, employment, prices and industries.

Holding an international sporting mega-event can bring additional positive economic impacts and other benefits (Lee, 2008):

♦   Labour and employment – hosting and preparing for the games implies a large demand for labour, which is seen as an important economic benefit by providing local and national jobs and income.

♦   Urban infrastructure – the construction of improved transport and public facilities, lighting, housing and other infrastructure can bring huge benefits for the host city.

♦   Sport facilities – the construction, refurbishment and improvement of sport facilities is regarded as having long-term value to local communities.

♦   Increased income – this is normally measured by GDP. The economic impacts of mega-events are normally criticised for being easily over-estimated. However, in many cases, mega-events do generate considerable incomes. Usually it is difficult to calculate the income accurately due to its wide dispersion throughout the economy. The impact on income from additional tax revenues also needs to be included. Indirect and induced impacts also need to be captured through the use of multipliers. This is because additional investment can also attract further investment, a feature known as the 'multiplier effect'.

♦   Improve tourism recognition – holding a mega-event can bring long-term tourism effects throughout the preparation and construction phases, during the event itself and event after the event. The mega-event can generate extensive exposure for the host city and country through media coverage. With the use of appropriate strategies, this can attract still more domestic and international tourists.

Studies on the economic impact of the Olympics

The economic impact of mega-events has been widely studied for many years. It is believed that these events can generate economic benefits and welfare for the host destination (see Table 1 for a comprehensive list of economic evaluation studies of major sports events). Furthermore, substantial social and cultural impacts on the host community are also acknowledged. This forms the 'psychic income' which, while difficult to measure, is certainly felt by the local population (Adair, 1994). Over the years, more and more researchers have taken an interest in the economic impact of the Olympics. Early studies tried to focus purely on the net financial impact: defined as the difference between event revenue (largely from ticket sales) and expenditure on building venues and running the events. Studies of the wider economic impact of the Olympics began with investigations of the 1984 Los Angeles

Olympic Games. Since the early 1990s, there has been a growing recognition of the longer-term economic benefits that hosting a major event can bring to a region through the increased profile (or brand image) of the host destination and the subsequent tourism visitation (induced tourism) that this can generate (Jago, Chalip, Brown, Mules and Ali, 2003; Macfarlane and Jago, 2009).

Table 1: A list of economic impact evaluations studies on major sports events

Authors	Publica-tion Year	Theme
Multiplier Analysis		
Gelan	2003	The tourism impacts of the British Open
I-O Models		
Economic Research Associates	1984	The impacts of the 1984 Olympics in Los Angeles
KPMG Peat Marwick	1993	The impacts of the 2000 Sydney Olympics
Humphreys and Plummer	1995	The impacts of the 1996 Olympics on the State of Georgia
Jang, Lee and Ahn	1999	The impact of the 2002 Korea-Japan World Cup
Fuller and Clinch	2000	The impact of hosting the 2012 Olympics on Washington (unsuccessful bid city)
Airola and Craig	2000	Projected economic impact of hosting the 2012 Olympics on Houston (unsuccessful bid city)
Daniels et al.	2004	Income effects of the Cooper River Bridge Run in Charleston, South Carolina, USA
Lee and Taylor	2005	The tourism impacts of the 2002 FIFA World Cup
Allan, Dunlop and Swales	2007	The impact of regular season sporting competitions
Humphreys and Prokopowicz	2007	The impacts of the Union of European Football Associations 2012 Football Championship in Poland and Ukraine
CGE Models		
NSW Treasury	1997	The impact of the 2000 Sydney Olympics
Madden	2002	The impacts of the 2000 Sydney Olympics
URS Finance and Economics	2004	The impacts of the Rugby World Cup 2003 on the Australian Economy (tourists and attendees)
Blake	2005	The impacts of the 2012 London Olympics
Bohlmann and van Heerden	2005	The impacts of the 2010 FIFA Football World Cup on the South African economy
Madden	2006	The Economic and fiscal impacts of the 2000 Sydney Olympics
URS Finance and Economics	2007	The impacts of the 2006/07 3 mobile Ashes Test and Commonwealth Bank One Day International Series on the Australian Economy (tourists and attendees)
Li, Blake and Cooper	2011	The tourism impacts of the 2008 Beijing Olympics
Giesecke and Madden	2011	The impacts of the 2000 Sydney Olympics

Authors	Publication Year	Theme
Li	2012	A simple framework for evaluating the economic welfare of a large event
Li, Blake and Thomas	2013	The economics of the Beijing Olympics under conditions of an imperfect market structure
Li	2013	Economic consequences of event infrastructure and venues
Other Methods		
Baade and Matheson	2002	The impact of the 1984 Los Angeles and the 1996 Atlanta Olympics (econometric models)
Hotchkiss, Moore and Zobay	2003	Employment and wages impacts of the 1996 Olympics in Georgia (econometric models)
Baade and Matheson	2004	The economic impact of the World Cup (econometric models)
Kasimati and Dawson	2009	The impact of the 2004 Olympics on the Greek economy (econometric models)
Kim, Gursoy and Lee	2006	South Korean's attitudes towards the impacts of the 2002 World Cup (survey and statistcs)
McHugh	2006	The impact of the Olympics (CBA)
Access Economics	2010	The Impact of the 2022 FIFA World Cup (CBA)

Source: Li and Jago (2012b)

Various methods, such as multiplier analysis, input-output (I-O) analysis, computable general equilibrium (CGE) modelling and cost-benefit analysis (CBA), have been applied to assessing the economic effects of sporting mega-events. The multiplier can be defined as "a method of assigning a numerical value to … linkage intensity" (Wanhill, 1983: 10). There are four frequently used types of tourism multiplier: sales, output, income and employment multipliers.

Multipliers can be calculated using I-O analysis, which is defined by Leontief (1986: 19) as "a method of systematically quantifying the mutual interrelationship among the various sectors of a complex economic system". An I-O model can thus capture a chain of effects in the economy initially caused by a change (decrease or increase) in demand (Blake and Sinclair, 2003).

Computable general equilibrium (CGE) modelling is an applied economic method that simulates changes in the economy when all markets clear simultaneously: that is when the quantity demanded equals the quantity supplied in each market. Such models are based on sophisticated assumed mathematical relationships between the different sectors of the economy that reflect the behaviour of the key stakeholders in the economy and provide more realistic assessments than are obtained from I-O Models (Li and Jago, 2012b). For example, CGE models put constraints on factors, allow changes in prices and more properly capture negative effects (Li and Jago, 2012b).

CBA can be used to quantify overall benefits and costs brought by holding an event. Such benefits and costs can be either economic or non-economic.

CBA and CGE thus examine two different aspects of the event effects (Dwyer and Forsyth, 2009). While CBA can evaluate the wider benefits and costs brought by an event, CGE modelling is capable of evaluating the feedback effects among industries (overall economic impacts) of an event (Li and Jago, 2012a). It is argued that since CBA can show net benefits of holding an event, it is a better tool for identifying policy implications, justifying public support and subsides (Késenne, 2005). The advantage of CGE modelling, meanwhile, is that it enables the wider economic impacts of holding an event to be captured. CBA has the strength of allowing the estimation of the value, efficiency and opportunity cost of increased expenditure involved in holding an event (Shaffer, Greer and Mauboules, 2003) and capturing non-economic effects. Therefore, the combination of both CGE and CBA is necessary to make a comprehensive evaluation of the impact and legacy effects of an event (Dwyer and Forsyth, 2009). For example, CGE can be employed to capture economic welfare: how much people are better or worse off due to event legacy effects. The CBA approach, meanwhile, can be applied to capture the further costs of economic legacies, for example stadium maintenance costs (Li and McCabe, 2012).

The 2008 Beijing Olympic Games

Beijing is the capital and political centre of the People's Republic of China and a world-renowned ancient city (see Figure 1). It has a population of just under 20 million. The metropolis, with an area of 16,801.25km², is located in northern China. Its 14 urban and suburban districts and two rural counties are governed as a directly controlled municipality of the national government (Beijing Municipal Bureau of Statistics, 2008). Beijing has long been the exemplar of China's culture, and the home of innumerable historical relics and landmarks. In recent years, China's economic growth has increased rapidly. In 2011 for example, Beijing's GDP reached RMB 47,156.4 billion (equivalent to US$7,298 billion), up 9.2% from 2010. Its GDP per capita was RMB 34,999.3 (equivalent to US$5,416.7), which was close to the developed countries (World Economic Outlook Database, International Monetary Fund, 2012). Investment, foreign trade and consumption remain the three major drivers of the capital's economy.

Figure 1: Olympic city – Beijing. Source: Wikipedia (2012)

Since the first modern Olympic Games, held in Athens in 1896, the majority of Games have been staged in developed countries in Western Europe, America and Australia. Of the 27 Olympic host cities up to and including 2012, the People's Republic of China (the 2008 Beijing Olympics) is only the third developing country to host the Olympic Games (the other two being Mexico, which hosted the 1968 Mexico City Olympics, and South Korea, which hosted the 1988 Seoul Olympics). The 2008 Beijing Olympic Games were notable for being staged by the biggest developing country in the world in terms of its population and held in the city with the longest history. Over the 16 days of competition, a total of 11,028 athletes from 204 countries and regions around the world challenged sporting and human limits, competing in 28 sports and 302 events (one event more than the schedule of the 2004 Games). An unprecedented 86 countries won at least one medal during the Games.

In 2001, the International Olympic Committee announced that having won an absolute majority of votes after two rounds of voting, Beijing had won the bid to hold the 2008 Olympic Games. The Government of China promoted the Games and invested heavily in new facilities and transport systems. China planned and built the Olympic Park, along with the 37 further stadiums and venues to host various Olympic events. Of these, 31 were in Beijing, including 12 new, 11 refurbished and eight temporary venues. The other six venues (see Figure 2) were the Qingdao Olympic Sailing Centre, the Tianjin Olympic Centre Stadium, the Shenyang Olympic Stadium, the Qinhuangdao Olympic Sports Centre Stadium, which were all newly built, and the Shanghai Stadium and the Hong Kong Olympic Equestrian Venues, which were renovated (BOCOG, Official Report of the Beijing 2008 Olympic Games-Volume III-Chapter 2 Venues, 2010). Holding the Games in other national cities can help spread the construction costs, thereby reducing the financial burden on the host city. The positive impacts brought by holding the Olympics, such as increased tourist expenditures, can also be spread out to non-host cities in this way.

Figure 2: Olympic venues in the other six host cities. Source: Adapted from Beijing Olympic Venues Tourism and Transport Map – Venues (2008)

Investment in the Olympic venues began in 2003. The 31 Beijing-based venues were divided into three categories. The first was the 'new venues', i.e. the Bird's Nest (Beijing National Stadium) and Water Cube (the National Aquatics Centre). The second was the 'existing venues refurbished', such as Yingdong Natatorium of National Olympic Sports Centre. The third was the 'temporary venues', such as the Olympic Green Hockey Stadium and Olympic Green Archery Field. After the Games, the former was turned into a body-building facility for citizens while the hockey stadium was redeveloped into seven five-a-side to nine-a-side football pitches.

One element of good practice illustrated by the Beijing Olympics was the reduction of the cost of construction. For example, a series of plans known as 'weight loss' were implemented to reduce the total costs of investment in the Olympic venues. The main saving was derived from reducing investment in the National Stadium, the total cost being cut down by nearly half to US$382 million (Jin, 2005). This was achieved by the cancelling the building of the roof and reducing the use of steel. In other Olympic venues, savings were made by cutting down the number of seats, reducing the floor areas of buildings, decreasing the number of new-built stadiums and changing some new-built stadiums into temporary stadiums. The largest structures to be built were the Beijing National Stadium, Beijing National Indoor Stadium, Beijing National Aquatics Centre, Olympic Green Convention Centre, Olympic Green, and Beijing Wukesong Culture and Sports Centre. Almost 85% of the construction budget for the six main venues (US$2.1 billion or ¥17.4 billion) was funded through corporate bids and tenders for ownership rights after the Olympics. China also constructed 59 training centres and infrastructure projects for the Paralympic Games, held in Beijing immediately after the Olympics.

Economic impact of the 2008 Beijing Games

In seeking to conduct an economic impact assessment of a mega-event, one of the fundamental inputs, irrespective of the evaluation technique used, is an estimate of the direct expenditure generated by the event. This is defined as the new spending in the host destination as a direct consequence of the event taking place. This includes not only expenditure by event attendees, but also by event organisers in operating the event and by sponsors contributing funds from outside the host region. Larger international events, such as the Olympics and the Football World Cup, also require investment in building new venues or refurbishing existing ones.

Li and Blake (2009) created a framework for measuring investment and expenditures associated with the 2008 Beijing Olympic Games at both the host-city (Beijing) and host-nation (China) levels. Using this framework, it can be seen that for Beijing the total additional investment and expenditure (that is, the economic size of the Beijing Olympics) was expected to be around US$17.61 billion (see Figure 3). More than half of the Beijing Olympic investment was in infrastructure construction (US$8,732 million). International tourism (US$2,407 million) and national tourism (US$2,541 million) due to the Olympics were predicted to bring in similar additional expenditures. These together accounted for 28% of the total. Operating expenditures by the Beijing Organising Committee of the Games (BOCOG) of US$2,369 million contributed 13% of the total, while a relatively small proportion (9%) of the total come from investment in venues and related facilities (US$1,559 million).

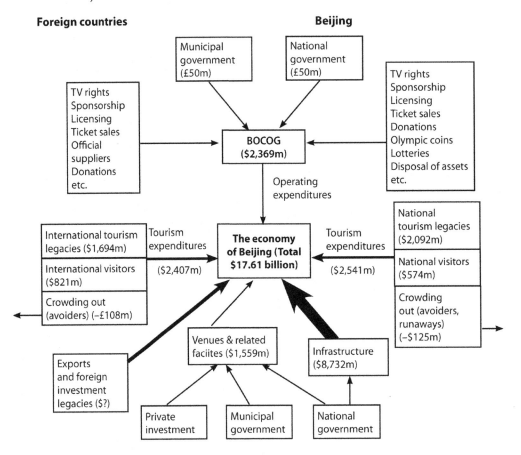

Figure 3: Framework of Olympic-related investment and expenditures in Beijing. Source: Li and Blake (2009)

This framework can also be used to trace the sources of Olympic investment and expenditure. The investment in infrastructure and venues was funded by the national and municipal governments. Tourism expenditures had three components: visitors, tourism legacies and crowding out. Visitors include spectators, athletes, officials, media visitors, volunteers, sponsor visitors and Olympics family (Airola and Craig, 2000). Tourism legacies refer to tourists who visit the host country before and after (rather than during) the Games. Crowding out refers to tourists who gave up or rearranged their travel plans to visit the host country in order to avoid the Games (Baim, 2004).

Three types of the Olympic investment and expenditures come from outside China, including sponsor operating expenditures, international tourism expenditures, and exports and foreign investment legacies. All of these were relatively small when compared with the total. Based on the assumption that half of the operating expenditures and a quarter of investment in venues were funded from abroad, it can be seen that around 80% of the total investment and expenditure was generated within China. National and municipal governments were, in fact, the most important investors of the Beijing Olympic Games, especially in terms of investment in infrastructure.

For China as a whole, Figure 4 shows that the Olympic-related investment and expenditures was expected to total US$19.68 billion. Neither the operating nor investment expenditures in Beijing and China vary in the two frameworks. In view of the lack of data, however, it is difficult to estimate exports and foreign investment legacies, which have been left as 'unknown' items in the framework.

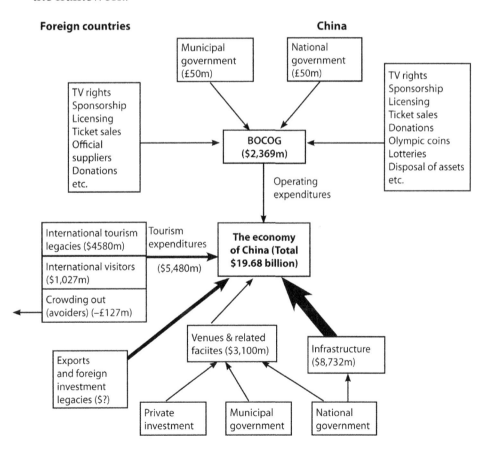

Figure 4: Framework of Olympic-related investment and expenditures in China. Source: Li and Blake (2009)

The investment and expenditures in China differ from those in Beijing in three respects. First, national tourism expenditures are not considered in the China-level framework. Second, the investment in venues and related facilities is almost doubled in the China-level framework due to additional investment in the Olympic venues in the other six cities. Third, the Beijing Olympics was predicted to bring higher international tourism expenditures in China than in Beijing, as many overseas Olympic visitors also travelled to other parts of China. Investment in Olympic-related infrastructure nevertheless accounted for the largest proportion (44%) of the total.

Economic legacies of the 2008 Beijing Olympic Games

Legacies of large mega-events are defined as "tangible and intangible elements of large-scale events left to future generations of a host country where these elements influence the economic, physical and psychological well-being at both community and individual levels in the long-term" (Li and McCabe, 2012: 3). The economic legacy is defined as "all economic effects that are left following the Games that would otherwise not have occurred without the Games" (Preuss, 2004: 266). Preuss (2004) built a framework to overview the economic legacies of Olympics consisting of three elements: financial surplus, structure and image. Since the early 1990s there has been growing recognition of the longer-term economic benefits that hosting a mega-event can bring to a region through the increased profile or brand of the host destination and the subsequent tourism visitation (induced tourism) that this can generate (Jago et al., 2003; Macfarlane and Jago, 2009).

Li and McCabe (2012) created a framework for the definition, dimensions and measurement of the legacies of mega-events. Figure 5 shows the first two parts of the framework, including the definition and dimensions of legacy and the measurement factors. Legacies are divided into three categories: economic, social and compounding legacies. Given the purpose of this case study, the focus is applied to the economic legacies which are correlated with the three elements: induced tourism, event stadiums and other economic activities. The following is the reflection on these three elements of the 2008 Beijing Olympic Games.

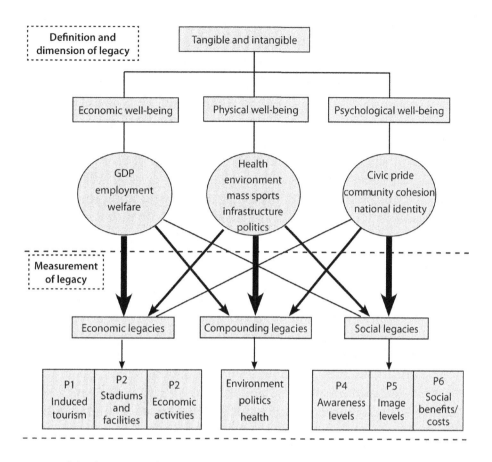

Figure 5: Part of the framework for measuring the legacies of mega-events. *Source*: Li and McCabe (2012)

Preparation for the Beijing Olympic Games was set against the background of Beijing's fast-growing economy. Investment, consumption and technological innovation stimulated in preparing for the Games brought about rapid changes in Beijing's economy. Beijing's leading edge in terms of financial services, technological innovation and tourism was strengthened by the staging the Olympic Games. Enormous resources were invested to guarantee the success of the Beijing Olympic Games, which resulted in an 'Olympic economic boom'. The preparations for the Games created approximately a million new jobs, most of which were in construction, real estate, environmental protection, information technology, sports, culture and tourism (BODA, 2011). The Games also promoted industrial restructuring, corporate brand-image and managerial innovation, thus exerting a profound influence on the economic development of the host city of Beijing in particular, and the country of China as a whole. For example, the annual GDP growth rate of Beijing during implementation of the Chinese government's 'Ninth Five-year Plan' (1996-2000) was 10%. Since 2001, after Beijing was awarded the 2008 Olympic Games, annual GDP growth reached 12.4%. By 2007, Beijing's GDP amounted to US$ 123 billion, and the per-capita GDP was US$ 7,654, reaching the level of moderately developed economies (BODA, 2011).

Furthermore, the Olympics had a significant influence on Beijing's economic development, environment, and the growth of the country's advertising, television, Internet, mobile phone, clean energy and sports sectors. Building on 30 years of economic reform and the opening up of economic relations, including the substantial economic impact of China's 2001 entry to the World Trade Organization (WTO), the excitement surrounding the Games served as the catalyst for pulling many of these sectors onto the international cutting edge. An appraisal of the impact of the Olympics presented by Sands (2008: Para.17) considered that "the huge inflows of investment to support the Olympics and recreate Beijing have had an important ripple effect on economic growth", not simply in Beijing but in areas surrounding the capital.

This development has also impacted on the protection of cultural relics, including the refurbishment of hundreds of cultural treasures and historic architectural features, including many of the city's landmarks, old streets and four-corner residences that date from the imperial period. Some 10,000 staff, 70,000 Games-time volunteers and millions of city volunteers who worked for the Beijing Olympic Games represent immeasurable human resources for the development of China. By 2008, 139 historical and cultural sites with a total area of 330,000m^2 had been repaired. In the second half of 2007, the Municipal Government also introduced an initiative aimed at bringing back the authentic ambiance of the old city, in which a first group of 44 Hutongs and 1,474 Chinese quadrangles[1] were renovated. It is estimated that spending on the Olympics has added 2.5% annually to Beijing's overall economic growth since 2002 (BODA, 2011).

Venue and infrastructure legacies of the Beijing 2008 Olympic Games

Hefner (1990) was one of the first to explain how construction of Olympic venues could benefit an economy, in that increasing investment in Olympic venues increases the demand for capital and labour in the construction

---

1   A hutong is a type of narrow street or alley that is common in Beijing, dating back to the Yuan Dynasty of the thirteenth and fourteenth centuries. A Chinese quadrangle, also known as Siheyuan, is a type of combined residence with a closed square or rectangular courtyard. These were commonly found throughout China. A Beijing quadrangle is a type of Chinese quadrangle that has a courtyard surrounded by four buildings.

industry and also the demand for building materials which, in turn, would encourage more investment, output and employment in industries that produce building materials. The venues can also bring tangible and direct legacies after the event finishes. On the one hand, Li and McCabe (2012) argue that the investment in venues and related infrastructure will be wasted unless they are used efficiently after the event. On the other hand, these venues and infrastructure can generate positive economic legacies if they can be effectively used to hold other cultural, sporting and commercial events, or converted for other uses (see Table 2 and Figure 6).

Table 2: List of major events taking place in the National Stadium (Bird's Nest) until October 2012

Time	Events
2009	
1 May	"Jackie Chan and His Friends" Concert
30 June	Summer Concert of "Charm China"
8 August	Italian Super Cup Football Match
6 October	Opera Turandot in the Bird's Nest to celebrate China's 60th founding anniversary
3 November	Race of Champions Beijing 2009
2010	
Dec.2009-Feb.2010	The First Session of "Bird's Nest Happy Snow Season"
23 April	The sixth sports meeting of Yumin Primary School
27 April	"Charm Bird's Nest" photo contest
4-13 May	Youth Football Invitational Tournament of "Bird's Nest Cup"
7 June	Schlumberger sports meeting
26 June	Sports meeting for urban construction
18 July	"Green, Environmental, Healthy New Age" concert
21 July	"Philanthropy China Tour" football match
25-30 July	International Youth Football Invitational Tournament of "Bird's Nest Cup"
27 July	"Passing on Love" charity sports meeting
2-16 August	The first Olympic cultural festival at Aocheng Square
6-10 August	Photo exhibitions on the second anniversary of the 2008 Beijing Olympic Games
6 August	"Returning to Bird's Nest" – celebrations on the second anniversary of the 2008 Beijing Olympic Games
8 August	"Barcelona in China" - match between Beijing Guo'an and FC Barcelona
20 August	Aocheng Youth Football Invitational Tournament
23 August	"Baidui Cup" football match
1 October	The drum corps of China Young Pioneers played "striving to become 'four good' teenagers"

Time	Events
3 October	The music concert held by Central Opera Theater celebrating the 61st anniversary of the People's Republic of China
23-24 October	"Bird's Nest Cup" National Interesting Track and Field Sports for Children
2011	
Dec.2010-Feb.2011	The Second Session "Happy Snow Season"
1 May	Rock 30 Bird's Nest Concert
19-21 May	Beijing International Equestrian Show 2011
28-29 May	Beijing Youth Baseball Competition
12 June	A Different Long March - 2011 Bird's Nest Feast of Patriotic Songs
16 July	Rugby Competition
20 July	"Bird's Nest Cup" Youth Mind Sports Games
6 August	Italian Super Cup-Football Match
25 September	Chinese & Japanese & Korean Music Grand Ceremony
27-30 October	Extreme Sports Final
3 December	Skiing World Match
2012	
Dec.2011-Feb.2012	The Third Session "Happy Snow Season"
29 February	Music-Man II Concert News Announcement
14 April	Music-Man II Concert
29-30 April	Mayday Nowhere Concert
10-12 May	2012 LONGINES Beijing international Equestrian Grand
14 July	BMW Joy Night
27 July	Bird's Nest Athens Games
8 August	First Children Simulation Olympic Games
11 August	2012 TIM Italian Super Cup
21 September	Attraction – Show in Bird's Nest
1-7 October	Second Children Simulation Olympic Games

Source: Adapted from the official website of National Stadium-Bird's Nest

The Beijing Olympic venues were designed for both Games-time competitions and post-Games use. In line with the concepts of 'Green Olympics', 'High-tech Olympics' and 'People's Olympics', energy-saving features and eco-friendly materials were employed in construction, while high technologies were applied. After the Games, their post-Games social benefits are considered to satisfy Beijing citizens' needs (BODA, 2012). The venues are used extensively for sports events, cultural activities, exhibitions, business, tourism and recreation. In line with the concept of achieving sustainable development and integrating art, technology and environmental protection, the venues constitute a unique Olympic legacy to Beijing.

Figure 6: Use of Beijing Olympic venues after the games. *Source*: Beijing Olympic Venues Tourism and Transport Map – Achievements (2008)

The construction of Beijing Olympic venues made full use of the existing resources and spread the positive benefits of the Olympics to other geographical and social areas. Figure 6 shows the variety of functions of the Beijing Olympic venues in the post-Games period: shopping, body-building, catering, training, exhibition, performance, competition, conferences and entertainment. Among these nine functions, body-building is the most popular and catering only applies to the National Stadium and Fencing Hall. The figure shows that the post-Games uses of the venues emphasise the sports purposes of these stadiums, such as promoting mass sports, rather than purely commercial purposes, such as entertainment and catering. The use of these venues was planned well before the Olympics, and the facilities are now operated by government offices and authorised companies. Each venue has a minimum of two functions: performance and competition. The National Stadium has the most functions, which include body-building, shopping, entertainment, catering, exhibition, performance and competition.

After more than three years of exploration, the main Olympic venues, such as The Bird's Net and Water Cube, have found a way to combine their special significance with commercial uses. For example, there were 28 events, including concerts, sports and cultural events and festivals, held at The Bird's Nest from May 2009 to July 2011 (see Table 2). These events were both international and national, both for adults and children, and both for professionals and the general public.

One of the most innovative developments was the transformation of the stadium into the 'Snow Bird's Nest'. Since the beginning of winter 2009, the Bird's Nest started to make snow on a waterproof layer covering the track and the grass (Figure 7). The average thickness of the man-made snow was 40cm with the maximum depth of 1m. Since that time it has been used in a large public event and carnival called 'Happy Snow Season'.

Figure 7: Machine creating snow in the 'Bird's Nest'. Photo credit: China.org.cn

During the event, a ski run sits at the east of the landscaped avenue of the central area of the Olympic Park. It is 10m high and 100m long with a slope of about 10 degrees: equivalent to beginner's level. The 'magic carpet' installed on the east side of the ski run transports skiers to the top of the runs with ease. Both the design and quality of the ski run are first class. The sponsors purchased 500 sets of imported snow boards, skis, snowshoes, ski boots, ski sticks and 300 sets of ski suits and gloves for rental. Compared to other artificial ski slopes, the Bird's Nest offered reasonably favourable rental fees for ski equipment: US$12.70 for two-hour rent of snow boards, skis, shoes , ski boots and sticks, with US$6.40 for each additional hour. Safety facilities were also set up at the high platform and the resting areas. Thirty qualified coaches were on the spot to teach beginners the basic skills of skiing. Numerous other activities were also provided for visitors, including ski jumping, outdoor snow games and a Frisbee snowfield. One innovative scheme was the 'Happy Snow' season ticket, which entitled visitors to enter the stadium for a whole day where they could ski (or ski jump), listen to music, participate in competitions and enjoy a large, free New Year party. Whereas most stadiums in Northern China are closed throughout the winter due to the cold weather, the large programme of activities at the Bird's Nest resulted in 220,000 visitors attending over a 66-day period. This, in turn, generated nearly US$ 4.5 million of income. In total, between October 2008 and the end of July 2012, over 60 large-scale events have been organised, with nearly 20 million visitors attending, generating just over US$124 million.

Once the Olympic Games were over, the Beijing Wukesong Culture and Sports Centre, which served as the Olympic Basketball Stadium, became an important part of Beijing's Olympic Games heritage. It was opened to the public who could enjoy various cultural, sports, leisure, recreational and commercial activities taking place there. At the beginning of 2011 it became the first Olympic venue to be rebranded commercially with Mastercard Worldwide giving its support to the stadium and associated programme of major events, branding the centre as the MasterCard Centre (see Box 1).

Box 1: Press release about 2008 Olympic Games venue rebrand

Beijing's Iconic Wukesong Arena Renamed MasterCard Center

MasterCard, Bloomage and AEG Sign Landmark Deal, Paving the Way for Beijing's Leading Sports and Entertainment Venue

Singapore, January 06, 2011. MasterCard announced today that it has obtained naming rights for Beijing's iconic Wukesong Arena, the basketball venue for the 2008 Olympic Games, in a landmark deal for China's sports and entertainment industry.

The 18,000-seat arena will be renamed the MasterCard Center or, in Chinese, Wanshida Zhongxin, in a five-year deal with the venue owners Bloomage International Investment Group and US-based AEG, one of the leading sports and entertainment presenters in the world. As the strategic partner of Bloomage, AEG, together with the US National Basketball Association (NBA), will provide consultancy support in the running of MasterCard Center.

The renaming of the stadium marks another milestone for China's rapidly growing sports and entertainment industry. It is the first 2008 Olympic Games venue to be rebranded commercially, the first arena in Beijing to be renamed in such a way, and it also marks the first time local ownership and know-how has combined with international event management expertise and sponsorship to bring the world's best performers to Beijing.

To officially launch the MasterCard Center, popular Cantonese pop singer Jacky Cheung will be performing on 21 January. Other renowned artists scheduled to perform in the arena in 2011 include American rock band, the Eagles, and Hong Kong singer, Aaron Kwok. In addition, the arena will host NBA basketball, table tennis, badminton and other sports events.

Besides being a vehicle to bring world-class performers and unforgettable, priceless moments to Chinese audiences, the MasterCard Center demonstrates MasterCard's long-term commitment to China, while helping to ensure the legacy of the Olympic Games. It leverages local resources for the benefit of consumers and stakeholders, including the local community in Beijing – especially in Haidian District where the arena is located – and the local government. It is also in line with the government's objective of maintaining economic growth through increased domestic consumption.

Jessica Guo, Deputy General Manager, Bloomage International Investment Group Inc., remarked, "As the newest, state-of-the-art multi-use arena in China, our 18,000-seat arena is already a benchmark for arenas throughout Asia. By teaming up with MasterCard, a reputable global payment solutions leader, we're really looking forward to continuing the Olympics legacy by bringing the world's finest performers to the capital to entertain Beijingers and visitors, making Beijing one of Asia's leading entertainment hot spots".

John Cappo, President and Chief Executive Officer of AEG China, said, "The Beijing Olympics was an amazing eye-opener for the world. It is great to have such a visionary partner like MasterCard who wants to continue the legacy of the Beijing 2008 Olympic arenas. This naming rights deal underscores MasterCard's long-term commitment to China and a milestone in the maturing of China's sports and entertainment industry. Together with MasterCard and our partners, we will bring world-class entertainment and Priceless experiences to the MasterCard Center".

Ling Hai, Division President, Greater China, MasterCard Worldwide, said, "We are delighted to rebrand an iconic Olympics venue as the MasterCard Center in Beijing, the capital city and an emerging market with huge growth potential. We've seen in recent years, thanks to the increasing prosperity and stability of China's economy and society, a surge in public demand1 for live entertainment and sports events, creating a prosperous and active market for such events. By providing opportunities for unique access to performers and behind-the-scenes action, we aim to bring to local consumers and businesses that we collaborate with a series of Priceless experiences in the MasterCard Center. In Chinese our name means 'everything is attainable'".

David Yang, NBA China Vice President, Business Development and Marketing Partnerships, said, "There is a growing appetite for sports and entertainment in China and the MasterCard Center will continue the legacy of the Beijing Olympics and further solidify the city as a premiere destination for world-class events. Together with our partners, we have a long-term commitment to China and we look forward to bringing NBA basketball to the state-of-the-art MasterCard Center in years to come".

Negative economic legacies can occur if the operational and capital costs of event stadiums and related facilities are high. One of the principal costs incurred is the cost of stadium conversion to ensure their effective use after the event has taken place. Conversion costs and maintenance fees can be significant, with the estimated cost of conversion of the Olympic Park in London reaching USS$370 million (Beard, 2009).

One of the key strategies adopted in Beijing was for many of the stadia built for the Games to be shared with, and eventually owned by, local universities. For example, the China Agricultural University Gymnasium is home to a wrestling arena, the Peking University Gymnasium now hosts a table-tennis facility, the Beijing Science and Technology University Gymnasium is a judo and taekwondo arena, while the Beijing University of Technology Gymnasium is home to badminton and rhythmic gymnastics. Another two universities expanded and refurbished existing venues, these being the Beijing Institute of Technology Gymnasium for volleyball and the Beijing University of Aeronautics and Astronautics Gymnasium for weightlifting. Not only will the use of these venues by students will help to make these venues sustainable in the longer term but these venues will also benefit students (see Box 2) (Li and Blake, 2009).

Box 2: Press release – 2008 Olympic Games university venues

Post-Olympic Utility of Universities Venues: Give Priority to the Demand of Students and Staff

20th April, 2009, By Li Jiangtao, XinHua Net

XinHua Net, Beijing – The 2008 Olympic Games left great legacies to Beijing and one of them are those four newly-built and two refurbished gymnasiums situated in the universities. They are well-designed and multi-functioned and have become a beautiful scene in the universities. One year has passed after the Olympics, those venues in universities have already converted their role and have started to provide services for students and staff.

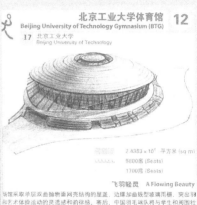

Beijing University of Technology Gymnasium

China Agricultural University Gymnasium

Beijing University of Technology Gymnasium, which successfully hold the matches of badminton and rhythmic gymnastics, is the only venue located in southeast of Beijing and also the earlier batches of venues opened to the public. At the beginning of November 2008, the freshman of the university has already started their badminton course in the warm-up venue who has become the first group utilize the venue. Both the warm-up and competition venues have already furnished more than 15 badminton fields opened for all students, staff and public. The gymnasium is now under further redevelopment and will provide more satisfactory services for public.

After a half-year refurbishment and operational test, the auxiliary venue of China Agricultural University Gymnasium has now gone into operation and it attracted lots of students and staff to exercise. After the Olympics, the university converted Wrestling warm-up area to badminton fields and went through several trail runs. There are five professional synthetic resin courts with proper temperature and light and the fitting room and rest room are also provided. Some students as being the part-time workers are responsible for court reservation, certificate approval and entrance check. Those students were selected through strictly interview and taken comprehensive training before being on duty. At eight o'clock every day, there are some coaches from the badminton club to provide professional services for students. Based on different time period, the entrance fee for students and retired staff is RMB 10-15/hour and RMB 20-30/hour for current staff.

Tourism Legacies of the Beijing 2008 Games

Olympic tourism legacies refer to tourists who travel to the host country before or after the event, with the main reason for their visit being Olympics-related (Li and Blake, 2009). However, such legacies are not automatic. For example, some previous Olympics have witnessed very limited, short-term tourism increases after the hosting of the Games. The 1988 Calgary Winter Olympic Games is an example (Chalip, 2003). The 1992 Barcelona Olympic Games, meanwhile, were considered to be the first Olympics to deliver truly long-term tourism legacies (Cashman, 2006). Only when the Olympic Games are positively supported by other factors, such as good media coverage and improvements to tourism facilities and infrastructure, will tourism legacies be possible over a longer time period (Spurr, 1999).

The Beijing Olympic Games improved the tourism infrastructure significantly and created new scenic spots which gave impetus to the local tourist industry. During the seven-day "Golden Week" National Holiday in October 2008, the number of tourists to Beijing reached 8.02 million, with a year-on-year increase of 35%. To capitalise on the post-Games period, Beijing launched a "Year of Tourism" in 2009 and converted some of the Olympic venues to tourist resorts to complement the UNESCO World Heritage Sites such as the Forbidden City, the Great Wall and the Summer Palace. This helped create new tourist itineraries combining traditional places of interest and contemporary landmarks (BOCOG, 2010b).

The changes in the South Gong and Drum Lane (Nanluogu Alley), one of the oldest hutongs in Beijing, reflect the transforming influence of the Beijing Olympics in protecting and promoting imperial Chinese architecture and building traditions, which in turn help China to impress the world with its rich history and culture (see Figure 8). An example is the South Gong and Drum alley, which is located in the vicinity of the imperial landmarks of the Drum and Bell Towers.

Figure 8: South Gong and Drum Hutong after restoration. *Sources*: Wu Hu Website (2012), Beijing Life Website (2012), Yao Lan Website (2012), Yoyoku Website (2012), Tuchong Website (20120

Business and export legacies

Holding a mega-event can also bring additional trade and business development benefits (Dwyer et al., 2000). Li and McCabe (2012) argue that a successfully held event demonstrates the capabilities of a host country in organising large events, managing venues, creating a friendly and safe environment, and formulating supportive and effective policies. Due to such demonstration effects, confidence in investment from foreign companies will help stimulate the economy, with local businesses well placed to benefit from the management skills, new technologies and innovation generated from holding such an event.

The success of the 2008 Beijing Olympic Games has often been regarded as an opportunity to build China's international prestige and demonstrate its national strength. According to A. T. Kearney Global Cities Index, Beijing ranked fifteenth among the world's best cities in 2010. 'Commercial activities' was the area where Beijing performed best, ranking sixth. This includes the value of a city's stock market, the number of headquarters of Fortune 500 companies and its attraction to talents of different groups and ethnicities. In a list of the world' s richest and most influential cities by HSBC and Knight Frank Commercial & Residential Estate Agents, Beijing ranked ninth, with New York, Paris and London being the top three. The analysis took each city's economic vitality, political influence, science and technology levels and living standards into consideration in compiling the list. The top 10 cities are New York, London, Paris, Tokyo, Los Angeles, Brussels, Singapore, Berlin, Beijing and Toronto (BODA, 2011).

Both direct and indirect economic activities concerning the Beijing Olympic Games will help improve economic efficiency, people's living standards and the degree of economic openness. Ultimately, the economic impacts brought by the Games to the host city and country will become an enduring legacy. In particular, the Games will help adjust the conventional economic models in concept, system and standards. Moreover, the cultural creative industry, generated by the combination of Olympic culture and Chinese civilisation, will be an important legacy to benefit Beijing and China (BOCOG, 2010b).

Conclusions

Holding an international sporting mega-event has become an important economic activity for host cities and their countries. The staging of such events provide good opportunities for the host, especially in developing countries, to achieve economic goals such as increasing economic growth, creating jobs or attracting foreign investment. Other goals include enhancing positive social, cultural and political impacts, which in many cases can be even more significant. Such non-economic impacts can assist in building a new image and national identity, inspiring national pride and unity, increasing public participation in sport and enhancing public health, and providing opportunities for long-term growth based on the construction of facilities and the knowledge gained during an event.

The 2008 Beijing Olympic Games promoted the Olympic ideals and promoted China's economic and social development. More importantly, it left priceless tangible and cultural heritage legacies. The extensive investment and expenditures associated with the 2008 Beijing Olympic Games, both at the host-city and host-nation levels, have been examined in this case study in attempting to explain the economic impact of the Games.

The case study has put forward a framework for the defining, characterising and measuring the impacts of mega-events that can be applied to studying the economic legacies of such events, including induced tourism, event stadia and other economic activities. To ensure the success of the Games, Beijing accelerated its urbanisation efforts, including the development of more city parks, a high-technology transportation system, new forms of clean energy, setting up a comprehensive information service and the use of advanced technologies in construction. In addition, Beijing residents have been left state-of-the-art facilities for sports and cultural events as well as better transportation services, while all Chinese nationals have been able to draw inspiration from the Olympic spirit and values.

Finally, it is important to note that despite the many positive benefits and impacts of the Olympics, there may also be opportunity costs and 'crowding out' effects that result in negative impacts to the host economy. However, such negative impacts are a relatively minor part of the larger picture which for Beijing was ultimately one of economic success.

References

Access Economics (Pty Limited). 2010. Cost Benefit Analysis of the 2022 FIFA World Cup, report for Department of Resources, Energy and Tourism. http://www.ret. gov.au/tourism/Documents/foi/cost-benefit-analysis-of-the-2022-fifa-wc.pdf

Adair D. 1994. Psychic income and the administration of English County Cricket: 1870–1914. *The Sports Historian* **14** (1): 66-71.

Airola J, Craig S. 2000. The Projected Economic Impact on Houston of Hosting the 2012 Summer Olympic Games. Houston Working Paper, University of Houston. http://action.roadshowmedia.com/houston2012/Documents/eco_impact.pdf

Allan G, Dunlop S, Swales K. 2007. *The economic impact of regular season sporting competitions: The Glasgow Old Firm football spectators as sports tourists*, Strathclyde Discussion Papers in Economics, No. 07-03.

Baade R, Matheson V. 2002. Bidding for the Olympics: Fool's gold? In Barros CP, Ibrahimo M, Szymanski S. (eds), *Transatlantic Sport: The Comparative Economics of North America and European Sports*. London: Edward Elgar; 127-151.

Baade R A, Matheson. 2004. The quest for the cup. Assessing the economic impact of the World Cup. *Regional Studies 38* (4): 343-354.

Baim D. 2004. The post-games utilization of Olympic venues and the economic impact of the Olympics after the games. In Humanistic Olympic Studies Center (ed.) *The First Olympic Economic and City Development and Cooperation Forum*. Beijing: Ren Min University of China; 71-85.

Beard M. 2009. £230 million 'is not enough' to convert venues after games. London Evening Standard. http://www.thisislondon.co.uk/standard/article-23625342-230-million-is-not-enough-to-convertvenues-after-games.do

Beijing Life (2012), http://www.beijinglife.org

Beijing Municipal Bureau of Statistics. 2008. Basic Information. http://www.bjstats.gov.cn/esite/bjsq/jbqk/

Beijing Olympic Venues Tourism and Transport Map. 2008. Beijing: SinoMaps Press.

Blake A. 2005. *The Economic Impact of the London 2012 Olympics*. TTRI Discussion Paper 2005/5, University of Nottingham, Nottingham.

Blake A, Sinclair M.T. 2003. Tourism crisis management: US response to September 11, *Annals of Tourism Research* **30** (4): 813-832.

BOBICO (Beijing 2008 Olympic Games Bid Committee). 2001. The Bidding Book of Beijing 2008 Olympic Games, prepared for the bidding of the Beijing Olympics and submitted to the International Olympic Committee.

BOCOG (Beijing Organizing Committee of the Games). 2002. The Olympic Action Plan of the 2008 Olympic Games, Beijing: Beijing Municipal Government and the BOCOG.

BOCOG (Beijing Organizing Committee of the Games). 2010a. Official Report of the Beijing 2008 Olympic Games-Volume III: Preparation for the Games: New Beijing Great Olympics. Beijing: Beijing Municipal Government and the BOCOG.

BOCOG (Beijing Organizing Committee of the Games). 2010b. Beijing Olympic Games Impact (Abstract). Beijing: Beijing Municipal Government and the BOCOG.

BODA (Beijing Olympic City Development Association). 2011. Olympic City 4.

BODA (Beijing Olympic City Development Association). 2012. Olympic City 5.

Bohlmann HR, van Heerden, J. H. (2005). The impact of hosting a major sport event on the South African economy. *Journal of Tourism 26* (4): 595-603.

Cashman R. 2006. *The Bitter-Sweet Awakening: The Legacy of the Sydney 2000 Olympic Games*. Sydney: Walla Walla Press.

Chalip L. 2003. Tourism and the Olympic games. In Moragas M, Kennett C, Puig N. (eds), *The Legacy of the Olympic Games 1984–2000*. IOC: Lausanne; 195-204.

Daniels M, Norman W, Henry M. 2004. Estimating income effects of a sport tourism event. *Annals of Tourism Research* **31** (1), 180-199.

Dwyer L, Mellor R, Mistilis N, Mules T. 2000. A framework for assessing 'tangible' and 'intangible' impacts of events and conventions. *Event Management* **6** (3): 175-89.

Dwyer L, Forsyth P. 2009. Public sector support for special events. *Eastern Economic Journal* **35**: 481-499.

Economics Research Associates. 1984 *Community Economic Impact of the 1984 Olympic Games in Los Angeles And Southern California*. Los Angeles Olympic Organizing Committee.

Fuller SS, Clinch R. 2000. *The Economic and Fiscal Impacts of Hosting the 2012 Olympic Games on the Washington–Baltimore Metropolitan Area*. George Mason University Working Paper. http://people.bath.ac.uk/ecpek/index_files/Paper1.pdf

García B. 2004. Urban regeneration, arts programming and major events: Glasgow 1990, Sydney 2000 and Barcelona 2004. *International Journal of Cultural Policy* **10** (1): 103-118.

Gelan A. 2003. Local economic impacts: The British Open. *Annals of Tourism Research* **30** (2): 406-425.

Getz D. 1997. *Event Management and Event Tourism*. New York: Cognizant Communications Corporation.

Giesecke J, Madden J. 2011. Modelling the economic impacts of the Sydney Olympics in retrospect: Game over for the Bonanza story? *Economic Papers: A Journal of Applied Economics and Policy* **30** (2): 218-232.

Gold JR, Gold MM. 2005. *Cities of Culture: Staging International Festivals and the Urban Agenda, 1851–2000*. Aldershot, UK: Ashgate Press.

Gold JR, Gold MM. 2010. *Olympic Cities: City Agendas, Planning, and the World's Games, 1896-2016*, 2nd Edition. London: Routledge.

Gratton C, Preuss H. 2008. Maximising Olympic impacts by building up legacies. *International Journal of the History of Sport* **25** (14): 1992-1938.

Hefner FL. 1990. Using economic models to measure the impact of sports on local economies. *Journal of Sports and Social Issues* **14** (1): 1-13.

Horne J, Manzenreiter W. 2006. *Sports Mega-events: Social Scientific Analyses of a Global Phenomenon*. Oxford: Blackwell.

Hotchkiss J, Moore R, Zobay S. 2003. Impact of the 1996 Summer Olympic Games on employment and wages in Georgia. *Southern Economic Journal* **69** (3): 691-704.

Humphreys JM, Plummer MK. 1995. *The Economic Impact on the State of Georgia of Hosting the 1996 Olympic Games*. Selig Center for Economic Growth: Georgia.

Humphreys B, Prokopowicz S. 2007. Assessing the Impact of Sports Mega-events in transition economies: EURO 2012 in Poland and Ukraine, *International Journal of Sport Management and Marketing* **2** (5/6): 496-509.

International Olympic Committee. 2007. *Olympic Charter*, Lausanne: the International Olympic Committee.

Jago L, Chalip L, Brown G, Mules T, Ali S. 2003. Building events into destination branding: Insights from experts. *Event Management* **8** (1): 3-14.

Jang J-K, Lee J, Ahn H-K. 1999. The Economic Impact of the 2002 Korea – Japan World Cup, Seoul. http://ref.daum.net/item/1149750

Jin S. 2005. Host the Olympic Games frugally. *Beijing Social Sciences* **2**: 29-34 (Chinese).

Kasimati E. 2003. Economic aspects of the summer Olympics: A review of related research. *International Journal of Tourism Research* **5** (6): 433-444.

Kasimati E, Dawson P. 2009. Assessing the impact of the 2004 Olympic Games on the Greek economy: A small macroeconometric model. *Economic Modeling* **26**(1) 139-46.

Késenne S. 2005. *Do We Need an Economic Impact Study or a Cost-Benefit Analysis of a Sports Event?* Working Papers 2005018, University of Antwerp, Faculty of Applied Economics.

Kim H., Gursoy D, Lee S. 2006. The impact of the 2002 World Cup on South Korea: Comparisons of pre-and post-games, *Tourism Management* **27** (1): 86-96.

KPMG Peat Marwick. 1993. *Sydney Olympics 2000: Economic Impact Study*. Sydney Olympics 2000 Bid Ltd: Sydney.

Lee C, Taylor T. 2005. Critical reflections on the economic impact assessment of a mega-event: The case of 2002 FIFA World Cup. *Tourism Management* **26** (4): 595-603.

Lee A. 2008. The impact of the Beijing Games. *The Geography Bulletin* **40** (3).

Leontief W. 1986. *Input-Output Economics*. Oxford: Oxford University Press.

Li SN. 2012. A simple framework for evaluating the economic welfare of a large event. *Tourism Analysis,* **17**(4): 395-508.

Li SN, 2013. Large sporting events and economic growth: Evidence from economic consequences of event infrastructure and venues, *Event Management* (in press).

Li SN, Blake A. 2009. Estimating Olympic-related investment and expenditure. *International Journal of Tourism Research* **11** (4): 337-356.

Li SN, Blake A, Cooper C. 2011. Modeling the economic impact of international tourism on the Chinese economy: A CGE analysis of the Beijing 2008 Olympics. *Tourism Economics* **17** (2): 279-303.

Li SN, Blake A, Thomas R. 2013. Modelling the economic impact of sports events: The case of the Beijing Olympics. *Economic Modelling* **30**: 235-244.

Li SN, Jago L. 2012a. Evaluating economic impacts of international sports events. In Shipway R, Fyall A. (eds) *International Sports Events: Impacts, Experiences and Identities*. London: Routledge; 13-26.

Li SN, Jago L. 2012b. Evaluating economic impacts of major sports events – a meta analysis of the literature. *Current Issues in Tourism* (in press).

Li SN, McCabe S. 2012. Measuring the socio-economic legacies of mega-events: Concepts, propositions and indicators. *International Journal of Tourism Research* (in press).

Macfarlane I, Jago L. 2009. *The Role of Brand Equity in Helping to Evaluate the Contribution of Major Events*, CRC for Sustainable Tourism Pty Ltd Report, Gold Coast.

Madden, J. 2002. The economic consequences of the Sydney Olympics: The CREA/Arthur Anderson study. *Current Issues in Tourism*, **5** (1), 7-21.

Madden JR. 2006. Economic and fiscal impacts of mega sporting events: A general equilibrium assessment. *Public Finance and Management* **6** (3): 346–394.

McHugh D. 2006. A Cost-Benefit Analysis of an Olympic Games, Queen's Economic Working Paper No. 1097, Queen's University, Canada. http://qed.econ.queensu.ca/working_papers/papers/qed_wp_1097.pdf

NSW (New South Wales) Treasury. 1997. Economic Impact of the Sydney Olympic Games. http://www.treasury.nsw.gov.au/ pubs/trp97_10/index.htm

Preuss H. 2004. *The Economics of Staging the Olympics-A Comparison of the Games 1972–2008*. Cheltenham: Edward Elgar.

Preuss H. 2007. The conceptualisation and measurement of mega sport event legacies. *Journal of Sport and Tourism* **12** (3-4): 207-228.

Roche M. 2000. *Mega-Events and Modernity: Olympics and Expos in the Growth of Global Culture*. London: Routledge.

Sands LM. 2008. The 2008 Olympics' Impact on China. *The China Business Review*. July-August. https://www.chinabusinessreview.com/public/0807/sands.htm

Shaffer M, Greer A, Mauboules C. 2003. *Olympic Costs and Benefits*. Canadian Centre for Policy Alternatives Publication: Vancouver; February.

Spurr R. 1999. Tourism. In Cashman R, Hughes A. (eds), *Staging the Olympics: The Event and Its Impact*. NSWUP: Sydney; 148-156.

Tuchong, Zhu Keran, 2012. http://zkrnews.tuchong.com/albums/

URS Finance and Economics. 2004. *Economic Impact of the Rugby World Cup on the Australian Economy*. New South Wales State Government, Department of Industry, Tourism, and Resources.

URS Finance and Economics (Australia Pty Ltd) 2007. *Economic Impact of the 2006/07 3 Mobile Ashes and Commonwealth Bank One Day International Series on the Australian Economy*, prepared for Cricket Australia, Australian Government.

Wanhill S. 1983. Measuring the economic impact of tourism. *Service Industries Journal* **3**(1): 9-13.

Wikipedia, Beijing, 2012. http://en.wikipedia.org/wiki/Beijing

World Economic Outlook Database, International Monetary Fund. 2012. *World Economic and Financial Surveys*, http://www.imf.org/external/pubs/ft/weo/2012/02/weodata/index.aspx

Wu Hu, Beijing Historical Sites, 2012. http://www.wuhu6.com/cn-bj/jd/%E5%8D%97%E9%94%A3%E9%BC%93%E5%B7%B7.html

Yao Lan, BBS, 2012. http://bbs.yaolan.com/thread_51369938.aspx

Yoyoku, Beijing Travel, 2012. http://www.yoyoku.com/news/beijing/lyzs/2866.html

Ancillary Student Material

Further Reading

Coaffee J. 2012. Policy transfer, regeneration legacy and the summer Olympic Games: lessons for London 2012 and beyond. *International Journal of Sport Policy and Politics*. 1-17, iFirst Article.

Fourie J, Santana-Gallego M. 2011. The impact of mega-sport events on tourist arrivals. *Tourism Management* **32** (6): 1364-1370.

Grix J. 2012. London 2012 and its legacies. *International Journal of Sport Policy and Politics*. 1-2, iFirst Article.

Jakobsen J, Solberg HA, Halvorsen T, Jakobsen TG. 2012. Fool's gold: Major sport events and foreign direct investment. *International Journal of Sport Policy and Politics*. 1-18, iFirst Article.

Maenning W, Zimbalist A. 2012. *International Handbook on the Economics of Mega Sporting Events*. Edward Elgar Publishing.

Parent MM. 2012. Mega sporting events and sports development. In Girginov V. (ed.) *Management of Sports Development*. Oxford: Butterworth-Heinemann; 147-163.

Shipway R, Fyall A. 2012. International sports events: Toward a future research agenda. *International Sports Events* **1** (55): 1-9.

Slack T. 2004. *The Commercialisation of Sport*. Abingdon: Routledge.

Walker M, Kaplanidou K, Gibson H, Thapa B, Geldenhuys S, Coetzee W. 2013. "Win in Africa, With Africa": Social responsibility, event image, and destination benefits. The 2010 FIFA World Cup in South Africa. *Tourism Management* **34**: 80-90.

Related websites

The 2012 London Olympic Games legacy: www.london2012.com/about-us/legacy/

Legacy Trust: http://www.legacytrustuk.org/

Plans for the legacy from the 2012 Olympic and Paralympic Games: http://www.culture.gov.uk/images/publications/201210_Legacy_Publication.pdf

Publications from the Department for Culture, Media and Sport, UK: http://www.culture.gov.uk/publications/default.aspx

The Official Website of the FIFA World Cup: www.fifa.com/worldcup/index.html

Youth Olympic Games: http://www.olympic.org/content/youth-olympic-games/

The Official Website of the ICC Cricket World Cup: www.iccworldtwenty20.com/

The Official Website of the Rugby World Cup: http://www.rugbyworldcup.com/

The Official Website of the European Football Championship (UEFA): http://www.uefa.com/

The Asia Games (Asiad): http://en.wikipedia.org/wiki/Asian_Games

The Pan American Games: http://en.wikipedia.org/wiki/Pan_American_Games

The Commonwealth Games: http://en.wikipedia.org/wiki/Commonwealth_Games

Commonwealth Games Foundation: http://www.thecgf.com/

The Official Website of The World's Fair: http://www.worldsfairs.com/Worlds_Fairs/Home.html

Self-test questions

Try to answer the following questions to test your knowledge and understanding of the case. If you are unsure of any answers, please re-read the case and refer to the references and further reading sources.

1 To what extent did Beijing hold a 'successful' Olympic Games and why?

2 What is the relationship between economics and large events, especially sports events?

3 Which economic methods can be used to evaluate the economic impacts or effects of large events?

4 What are the economic achievements of the Beijing Olympic Games?

Key themes and sub-themes

The key themes raised in this case study relate to the following:

Beijing 2008 Olympic Games

◆ Beijing

◆ 2008 Olympic Games

Economic impacts of the Beijing Olympics

◆ Olympic investment and expenditure

Economics of the Olympics

◆ Relationship between sports events and economics

◆ Studies on the economic impact of the Olympics

◆ Direct investment and expenditures

◆ Event effects: at both the macroeconomic level (e.g. changes in GDP, employment, economic welfare, exports) and industry level (e.g. changes in value of labour, capital and output)

◆ Opportunity costs, crowding out effects

Methods of economic modelling

◆ Multipliers

◆ Input and output modelling

◆ Computable General Equilibrium Modelling

◆ Econometric modelling

◆ Macro-economic modelling

◆ Cost and Benefit Analysis

Legacies of the Beijing 2008 Olympic Games

◆ Economic legacies of the 2008 Beijing Olympic Games

◆ Tourism

◆ Venues and infrastructure

◆ Business and exports

If you need to source any further information on any of the above themes and sub-themes, then these headings could be used as key words to search for materials and case studies.

 Scan here to get the hyperlinks for this chapter.

6

Resident Impacts of Sport Events

Leo Jago, Margaret Deery and Liz Fredline

Introduction

Sport events are increasingly being used to underpin tourism strategies in many destinations. They offer the opportunity to showcase a destination as well as the potential to provide a substantial injection of 'new' money into the host destination's economy (Jago and Dwyer, 2006). While sports events can provide a source of pride and can engender a sense of community for residents in the destination, they can also cause substantial problems for the local population, leading to frustration and possibly even anger (Balduck, Maes and Buelens, 2011). The Tour de France, for example, is just one event where the local community has examined its benefits and costs. It is critical, therefore, that sports events are well managed and the impacts on the local community are monitored to ensure that they do not cause unreasonable concerns for the host community.

Local support for a sports event is fundamental for its longer-term success given the importance that locals play in the provision of labour and services for many events. From a tourism perspective, the support of the local community is also important. It has been found that tourists generally have a strong preference to shop, dine and recreate in areas frequented by the local population. As most sports events rely very heavily on the patronage of locals, failure of locals to support an event can have serious consequences for the financial viability of the event.

Until more recent years, the impact of sports events was determined largely by the economic impact that they generate for the host community. As there was a backlash against some sports events by members of the local community, often related to motor sports, it was recognised that the social impact should also be assessed. Such assessments provide the opportunity for the organisers to take action to maximise the social benefits and minimise the social costs that are generated by the event.

Social impacts of sports events

The social impacts of sports events on communities has received increasing attention, with work by researchers such as Fredline (2005), Getz (2005), Ohmann, Jones and Wilkes (2006) and Balduck et al. (2011) examining the positive benefits and the negative effects of a range of events on the host community. In his meta-review of sport tourism, Weed (2009) argues that resident perceptions are an important part of the strategic planning process and, following Fredline's (2005) work, suggests that "local residents should be both educated about and consulted on the impacts of sport tourism" (Weed, 2009: 622).

Many of the social impact studies are based on social exchange theory which argues that people will be motivated by expected returns. As Easterling (2004: 49) states, "individuals or groups will engage in an exchange if they value that which is being exchanged, perceive that costs do not exceed benefits and that the exchange will be rewarding". With regard to tourism, residents in a tourist destination will engage with tourists as long as they perceive that the benefits outweigh the costs. Those benefits and costs, however, will vary according to a number of variables including the level of contact with tourists, whether residents are dependent on tourists for a livelihood and the level of attachment that residents have to the destination.

The number and type of social impacts have been examined by a range of researchers, and work by Ohmann, Jones and Wilkes (2006) provides an overview of the social impacts of events per se. They divide these impacts logically into positive and negative impacts with the former including:

♦   Shared experience, revitalising traditions, building community pride, improved regional identity (Hall, 1992).

♦   Sense of pride, self-actualisation, opportunities for entertainment, demonstration effect impact on fitness levels and health (Fredline, 2005).

♦   Increased community pride, strengthening of traditions and values, adaptation of new social patterns or cultural forms (Ritchie, 1984).

Additionally, Balduck et al. (2011) in their study on the Tour de France found the positive impacts to be economic and tourism development, cultural interest and consolidation, external image enhancement and interest in foreign cultures. These key issues are meta categories of positive impacts and they are, as with most social impact studies, based on the perceptions of the host residents rather than on actual impacts.

With regard to the negative impacts of events, Ohmann et al. (2006) list a range of findings from their study. These include:

♦ Disruption to community life, loss of amenity due to noise or crowds, changes in social and leisure habits, intergroup hostility, displacement of tenants due to increased housing prices (Getz, 2005).

♦ Community alienation, negative community image, bad behaviour, substance abuse, traffic congestion, theft, noise, prostitution (Hall, 1992).

♦ Rowdiness, fan delinquency, reduction in psychological wellbeing due to perceived loss of control over the local environment (Fredline, 2005).

♦ Crowding, infrastructure congestion, exclusion of local residents due to costs, disruption of local lifestyle, suppression of human rights (Higham, 1999).

Many of these impacts relate to specific types of sports events while others can be applied more generally. For example, the issue of noise would be especially relevant at motor sport events, whereas the issue of crowding and traffic congestion can apply to a range of events. Gathering data at specific events provides the opportunity to examine the specificity of these impacts and how positive or negative the impacts can be on a host community.

Assessing the social impact of sports events

Although the social impact of a sports event on the local community may be based on perceptions rather than objective dimensions, this does not make this impact any less real. As perceptions can change over time and be influenced by reports in the media and the like, it is important that the social impact is monitored on a regular basis so that action can be taken before the level of concern becomes such that it has an overall negative impact on the event.

Attempts were made by organisers to develop objective measures to assess the social impact of sports events on the local community, but it was soon realised that it was more appropriate to assess the attitudes of the community. Although there has been an increase in research in this area, the appropriate survey instruments were lacking. One of the most comprehensive attempts, however, was work by Delamere (undertaken with colleagues) in Canada (Delamere, 1997, 2001; Delamere, Wankel and Hinch, 2001) whereby research concentrated on the impacts of small community festivals rather than larger-scale events using a number of the impacts mentioned above.

In addition to the development of the measurement scale by Delemere and colleagues, the dimensions identified in Ap and Crompton's (1998) study were consistent with the event impacts proposed by Ritchie (1984). Using a principal components analysis, seven factors were identified. These were labelled social and cultural, economic, crowding and congestion, environmental, services, taxes, and community attitudes.

The research instrument used in the current study was designed using statements from previous event and tourism literature with the inclusion of additional items from the social capital literature. Many early measurement scales in this research field used Likert-type measures asking respondents to agree or disagree with an 'attitude' toward or 'perception' of tourism. However, this approach creates a level of ambiguity in interpretation (Ap and Crompton, 1998). If a respondent agrees with a positive perceptual statement, it does not necessarily imply that they are happy about impact it refers to, or that it brings benefits to them or the community. An additional difficulty with this approach is that the identification of attitudes toward tourism does not adequately identify management strategies. Rather, effective tourism management involves the development of strategies to ameliorate the negative impacts of tourism on residents' quality of life and to promote the benefits. Therefore, the critical issue in assessing the impacts of tourism is an understanding of the effect on quality of life rather than just attitudes or perceptions of tourism.

Recognising this, in the later 1990s there was a migration from the use of quite simple Likert-type measures to more complex measurement scales. Lindberg and Johnson (1997) developed a two-part scale based on the principles of Fishbein's (1963) attitude model, which proposed that the measurement of an attitude should comprise a multiplicative function of belief and affective components. The score then used as a dependent variable in the analysis was the product of the two parts of the scale. The instrument used in this research was based on one developed by Fredline (2000). The format of the instrument is shown in Table 1 and the wording of the scale in Table 2.

Following the methods of Fredline (2000), the main dependent variables, which relate to residents' perceptions of the impacts of events, were measured using the three-part scale shown in Table 2. The scale included 45 impact statements and residents were first asked to assess whether they believed the impact to have occurred because of the event and to identify the direction of the change.

Table 1: Format of instrument

Section A	Overall Impacts of the event including opportunities for open ended comment
Section B	Three-part scale measuring specific impacts of the event
Sections C-H	Measurement of independent variables: 1. Contact 2. Participation 3. Identification with theme 4. Community attachment 5. Socio-political values 6. Demographics

Table 2: Example of Section B questions

1a. Because of the event, noise levels in and around the Grand Prix have …	Decreased → Increased →	1b. How has this affected your personal quality of life?	-3 –2 –1 0 +1 +2 +3
	No change ↓ go to 2a Don't know ↓ go to 2a	1c How has this affected the community as a whole?	-3 –2 –1 0 +1 +2 +3

Case studies

The survey instrument discussed above has been used to assess the social impact of sports events on the local community in a wide range of settings. In order to provide some contrast in the findings, two studies using the same local community are discussed in this case. This has been done to illustrate how the social impacts can vary quite substantially from event to event, even in a city such as Melbourne, Australia, where there is very strong overall community support for sport events. The first sports event is the Australian Open Tennis Championship that is held in Melbourne each January. This case study examines the impact that the Australian Open Tennis Championships has had on the host resident community of Melbourne in Australia. As a major event in both world tennis and Melbourne's calendar, the Australian Open Tennis Championships has the opportunity to promote the game and the city, as well as to provide a sense of pride for residents. The second sports event is the Formula 1 Grand Prix staged in Melbourne each March. Both events have large attendances, attract many interstate and international visitors, and receive substantial international media coverage.

Case Study 1: The Australian Open Tennis Championships

Background to the event

Tennis in Australia has always been an important sport and records for tournaments date back to the 1880s (Foenander, 2010). Initially held between Australia and New Zealand, the Australian Open has undergone two major changes. The first occurred in 1927 when the competition was known as the Australian Championships, while the second occurred in 1969 when the term 'Australian Open' became the official name of the championship. In 1986, the game's governing body began trading under the name of 'Tennis Australia'. In January 1987, the Australian Open Tennis Championships became the first Grand Slam championship of the year and has continued in this position ever since. The home of the Australian Open was Flinders Park, which was later renamed Melbourne Park. Over A$25 million was spent on upgrading Melbourne Park in the 1990s and the introduction of a retractable roof on two stadia (see Figure 1) has since been emulated at other Grand Slam venues such as Wimbledon. This provides protection for players from the variable weather in Melbourne during January.

Figure 1: Melbourne Park at Night with retractable roof open. *Source:* Tennis Australia

The Australian Open location

The Australian Open is located in Melbourne, in a sporting precinct that is very close to the Central Business District (CBD). While there is easy access to Melbourne Park from the CBD, it is also easily accessed from the neighbouring suburbs and residential areas. The location of Melbourne and Melbourne Park are shown in Figures 2 and 3.

Figure 2 (left) and Figure 3 (right): Location of Melbourne within the State of Victoria, Australia. *Source:* Google Maps http://www.virtualoceania.net/australia/maps/

Crowds and the community

The Australian Open attracts large crowds, with a key aim being to provide a family atmosphere to the event. In 2011, 651,127 people attended over the course of the two-week tournament, with some days recording large audiences of over 77,000 for the day/evening matches. The 2011 Australian Open was broadcast around the world, with 11 different broadcasters officially screening the event and, for the first time in the history of the Australian Open, the qualifying competition for the main draw was streamed live on the Internet. During the first week of the tournament, 1.36 million people tuned in for the men's singles final, which was lower than the number the women's final received (Mediaspy, 2011).

For much of the history of the Australian Open, the organisers have achieved the family atmosphere they have desired. In 2007, however, charges were laid by police over an incident between Serbian and Croatian supporters, with over 20 people being ejected from Melbourne Park after a fight arose. Fights again occurred between Serbian and Bosnian supporters, and chairs were hurled in the Garden Square area of Melbourne Park. Other anti-social behaviour has occurred in the years since 2009 and the police presence has been increased. This has, of course, marred the family atmosphere image and organisers have worked hard to regain the sense of safety and community for attendees.

Measuring residents' perceptions of the Australian Open

Understanding the impact that the Australian Open has on residents is important, especially for those residents who live close to Melbourne Park and who are directly affected by it. Increasingly, researchers are turning to examine the impacts that events have on residents (see, for example, Gu and Ryan, 2008; Deery and Jago, 2010) and tourism agencies are more frequently including the social impacts of events in their strategic plans (see, for example, Tourism Victoria's Tourism and Events Strategic Plan). The research undertaken in this area provides the basis for measuring the impacts of events on the community.

Method

Population

The population of interest for this study was defined as residents of Melbourne who were interviewed via telephone with the Melbourne telephone directory (White Pages) used as a sampling frame to select telephone numbers for local residents.

Administration

The survey was administered using a telephone interview to complete a questionnaire comprising 20 questions. It took about 10-15mintues to administer, and participation was encouraged using an incentive of the opportunity to win a A$100 shopping voucher.

Sampling

A two-stage random systematic sampling procedure was used to select residents from the Melbourne telephone directory. A random-number generator was used to select pages from the directory and the first name at the top of the right column on that page was selected. This number was telephoned and interviewers were instructed to alternate between speaking with males and females whenever possible.

Gathering and analysing the data

The instrument was developed based on previous research which has been well documented in previous CRC technical reports (Fredline, Deery and Jago, 2005a, 2005b) and other academic publications (Fredline, Jago and Deery, 2003). The data collected for the study on the Australian Open comprised a sample of 299 responses to the questionnaire. The key areas for examination were the 12 items presented in Table 3.

Table 3: Key Items to examine the impact of the Australian Open on the community

Entertainment	The Australian Open gave Melbourne residents an opportunity to attend an interesting event, have fun with their family and friends, and interact with new people.
Economic benefits	The Australian Open was good for the economy because the money that visitors spend when they come for the event helps to stimulate the economy, stimulates employment opportunities, and is good for local business.
Community pride	The Australian Open made local residents feel more proud of their city and made them feel good about themselves and their community
Regional showcase	The Australian Open showcased Melbourne in a positive light. This helps to promote a better opinion of our region and encourages future tourism and/or business investment.
Public money	The Australian Open was a waste of public money, that is, too much public money was spent on the event that would be better spent on other public activities.
Disruption to local residents	The Australian Open disrupted the lives of local residents and created inconvenience. While the event was on problems like traffic congestion, parking difficulties and excessive noise were worse than usual.
Community injustice	The Australian Open was unfair to ordinary residents, and the costs and benefits were distributed unfairly across the community.
Loss of use of public facilities	The Australian Open denied local residents access to public facilities, e.g. roads, parks, sporting facilities. Public transport and/or other facilities were less available to local residents because of closure or overcrowding.
Maintenance of public facilities	The Australian Open promoted development and better maintenance of public facilities such as roads, parks, sporting facilities, and/or public transport.
Bad Behaviour	The Australian Open was associated with some people behaving inappropriately, perhaps in a rowdy and delinquent way, or engaging in excessive drinking or drug use or other criminal behaviour.
Environmental impact	The Australian Open had a negative impact on the environment through excessive litter and/or pollution and/or damage to natural areas.
Prices	The Australian Open Tennis 2003 led to increases in the price of some things such as some goods and services and property values and/or rental costs.

Case Study 2: The Australian Formula 1 Grand Prix

This case study provides a comparison of the Australian Formula One Grand Prix at two points in time, 1999 and 2002, using similar data collection instruments and research design. The 1999 study was undertaken fairly early in the history of the event to set a benchmark for community impact, while the second study was undertaken a few years later to see if the impact on the community had changed. The Australian Formula 1 Grand Prix has been staged annually in Melbourne since 1996. It is a four-day event featuring qualifying, practice and support races on the first three days and the main Formula 1 Race on the final day (a Sunday). In the early years, there was quite a lot of opposition to the staging of the event in Albert Park from local residents, who formed a vocal protest group known as 'Save Albert Park'[1]. This organisation is still in operation, 16 years after it first began protesting at the presence of the Grand Prix, although it now has a much lower profile.

The following is an example of the issues for local residents:

> "Now, sixteen years later, it is time for the wider Victorian community to understand the true price – for the community, the economy and the environment – of hosting the AGP in Albert Park. For instance, AGP currently costs Victorian taxpayers in excess of $100 million per annum, when all the government subsidies are included".

Method

Population and sampling frames

In the 1999 study, state electoral district (SED) rolls were used to provide a sampling frame, and all electoral districts for which some part fell within a 10km radius of the centre of the race circuit were included. In 2002, a proprietary list (The National Consumer File maintained by Prime Prospects List Marketing) was used to provide the sampling frame, and addresses within a 15km radius of the centre of the race circuit were purchased. The reason for the changed approach was due to the removal of the SED for use in research such as this study. Privacy laws were introduced that removed the SED as a source of resident details and so a marketing list was purchased to provide a sample of residents. As can be seen in Figure 4, however, the populations in the two studies were very similar and it is only at the margins where there were differences.

---

1   The group's blog commentary to be found at http://live.org.au/blog/?p=233.

Figure 4: Comparison of the populations used in the two studies. *Source:* Fredline, Deery and Jago (2005)

Instrument design

A similar instrument was used in the two studies. Both combined qualitative and quantitative techniques in an effort to gain as many different perspectives of the impacts as possible. The structure of the questionnaire was similar to that used in the study on the Australian Open. In the original study, 38 impact statements were included, while the 2002 instrument contained 45 statements in an effort to include more items relating to social capital impacts.

Administration

The instruments were administered in a very similar fashion across the two versions of the study. In each case, a postal survey was used and incentives were employed to enhance the response rate. In the former study 1,000 survey packs were sent out two weeks after the event had taken place. Of these, 80 were returned as non-deliverable, and 279 were completed and returned, representing an effective response rate of 30.3%. In the later study, a much poorer response rate was achieved, with only 279 usable responses from 2,400 survey packages of which 248 were non-deliverable. This represented a response rate of 13%.

Comparing the results from the Australian Open and the Australian Grand Prix

A large number of questions were asked in the questionnaires regarding the host residents' perceptions of the event in question. Both quantitative and qualitative data were collected. The studies were primarily interested in what people thought about the event in general and whether the event had an impact on residents' personal and community quality of life.

Overall perceptions of the Australian Open Tennis Tournament

Before specific impacts were presented, respondents were simply asked about the impacts of the event overall. While 55.4% of respondents rated the personal impact as positive, 43.5% of the respondents perceived no personal level impact. At the community level, 78.7% rated the impact to be positive. The results in Table 4 provide the mean score for all the responses for the personal and the community impacts (where the scale ranged from -3 to +3).

Table 4: Ratings of overall impact on personal and community quality of life

	Mean
Did the Australian Open Tennis 2003 have any effect on your personal quality of life?	1.21
Do you think the Australian Open Tennis 2003 affected the community as a whole?	1.64

It should be noted that in all of these studies that have been undertaken to date, the rating of the community impact is much higher than the rating on the individual impact. While most individual respondents do not see substantial benefit for themselves personally as a result of staging the event, they do tend to recognise the range of benefits that can be derived by the community as a whole.

Specific impacts of the Australian Open Tennis Tournament

When asked about the specific impacts of the event, as listed in the questionnaire, there were some useful findings. It is interesting to observe that the responses showed almost no perception of negative impacts. The most strongly perceived positive impacts at a personal level were entertainment, pride, the showcase effect, economic impact and maintenance of facilities (see Table 5). The same five impacts were most highly rated at the community level, although the order varied slightly.

Figure 5: Advertising at the Open. *Source:* Tennis Australia

Figure 6: Crowds at the Open watching on the big screen. *Source:* Tennis Australia

Table 5: Most strongly perceived personal and community level impacts for the Australian Open

	Personal Mean	Community Mean
The Australian Open gave Melbourne residents an opportunity to attend an interesting event, have fun with their family and friends, and interact with new people.	0.92	1.53
The Australian Open made local residents feel more proud of their city and made them feel good about themselves and their community	0.70	1.45
The Australian Open showcased Melbourne in a positive light. This helps to promote a better opinion of our region and encourages future tourism and/or business investment.	0.48	1.53
The Australian Open was good for the economy because the money that visitors spend when they come for the event helps to stimulate the economy, stimulates employment opportunities, and is good for local business.	0.38	1.52
The Australian Open promoted development and better maintenance of public facilities such as roads, parks, sporting facilities, and/or public transport.	0.38	0.97

The Australian Open is thus seen as an interesting event that encourages social interaction with a range of people at both the personal level and from the community perspective. The high scores, relative to other events examined here, also shows that it is perceived as adding to the residents' quality of life (see Figure 5 and 6).

Overall perceptions of the Grand Prix

As with the study of the Australian Open, host residents were asked about their overall perceptions of the impacts of the Grand Prix on their personal lives and on the community as a whole. The results are found in Table 6.

Table 6: Overall perceptions of personal and community impacts for the Grand Prix 2002 and 1999

	Mean	
	2002	1999
Effect on personal quality of life	0.35	0.24
Effect on the Melbourne community as a whole	1.36	0.67

In comparison to other events such as Moomba, an annual community festival held in Melbourne, Art Is, a regional Victorian arts festival for local and international artists and the Australian Open, the means for the Grand Prix were much lower, as can be seen in Table 7. What is particularly evident from the figures in Table 7 is the very low score for the perceptions of the impact of the Grand Prix on the community in 1999. The presence and sentiments of the 'Save Albert Park' lobby group were obviously very strong at this time.

Table 7: Comparison of mean overall impact ratings across a range of events

Impact		Event			
	Grand Prix 1999	Grand Prix 2002	Moomba	Art Is	Australian Open
Personal	0.24	0.35	0.41	0.72	1.21
Community	0.67	1.36	1.43	1.54	1.64

Specific impacts of the Australian Formula 1 Grand Prix

The perceptions of specific impacts changed from 1999 to 2002, with the results from the 1999 study being significantly lower than those obtained in 2002. For example, the maintenance of public facilities, noise levels, crowds and litter were all perceived to impact at the personal level to a greater extent – and negatively – in 1999 than in 2002. At the community level, respondents perceived that the noise and litter were detrimental to the community in 1999. The results of this analysis are contained in Table 8.

Table 8: The most strongly perceived personal and community impacts of the Grand Prix

Impact	Personal Impact			Community Impact		
	2002	1999	Sig.	2002	1999	Sig.
Appearance of area around track	0.60	0.75		1.20	1.44	
Maintenance of public facilities	0.71	0.97	t = -2.06, p<0.05	1.69	1.66	
Noise levels	-0.22	-0.62	t = 4.03, p<0.05	-0.80	-0.98	
Employment opportunities	0.25	0.27		1.43	1.58	
Interesting things to do	0.66	0.67		1.22	1.46	
Crowded/number of people	0.07	-0.44	t = 4.89, p<0.05	0.50	-0.16	t = 4.28, p<0.05
Property values	0.19	-0.01		0.53	0.58	
Litter	-0.03	-0.38	t = 3.13, p<0.05	-0.39	-0.79	t = 2.65, p<0.05
Relationships / interactions between locals and tourists	0.34	0.26		0.77	0.88	
Entertainment opportunities	0.57	0.61		1.28	1.47	

When compared to the results from the Australian Open, the results for the Grand Prix are in overall terms lower, showing that residents were not as favourably disposed towards the Grand Prix as they were for the Australian Open.

As shown in Table 9, the impacts rated as most important benefits and costs were fairly consistent over time, but some variation can be observed. In 2002, 'pride in Melbourne' was rated as the most important personal benefit of the

Grand Prix, whereas in 1999 it did not even make the top five. Additionally, problems with parking appeared to be an issue in 2002, while this did not really rank as being important in 1999. At the personal level, the mean score indicates some improvement in parking (though this is not significant). At the community level, however, the perception of parking as a problem had significantly worsened.

Table 9: Comparison of relative importance of impacts over time for the Australian Grand Prix (five top- and bottom-ranked impacts)

	Personal		Community	
Rank	2002	1999	2002	1999
1	Pride of residents in their city (0.77)	Maintenance of public facilities (0.97)	Visitor spending stimulates the economy (1.72)	Promotes tourism (2.12)
2	Maintenance of public facilities (0.71)	Appearance of area around track (0.75)	Maintenance of public facilities (1.69)	Showcase effect (1.95)
3	Interesting things to do (0.66)	Promotes tourism (0.74)	Promotes tourism (1.53)	Visitor spending stimulates the economy (1.84)
4	Appearance of area around track (0.6)	Showcase effect (0.69)	Employment opportunities (1.43)	Maintenance of public facilities (1.66)
5	Visitor spending stimulates the economy (0.59)	Interesting things to do (0.67)	Opportunities for local business(1.29)	Employment opportunities (1.58)
30	Prices of some good and services (-0.24)	Noise levels (-0.62)	Noise levels(-0.8)	Rights and civil liberties (-0.94)
32	A waste of public money (-0.26)	A waste of public money (-0.65)	Ordinary residents get no say in planning (-0.81)	Noise levels (-0.98)
32	Dangerous driving (-0.29)	Damage to the environment (-0.66)	Disrupts life for locals (-0.87)	Disrupts life for locals (-1.09)
33	Availability of parking (-0.37)	Ordinary residents get no say in planning (-0.71)	Availability of parking (-1.16)	Ordinary residents get no say in planning (-1.1)
34	Traffic congestion (-0.56)	Traffic congestion (-0.99)	Traffic congestion (-1.16)	Traffic congestion (-1.6)

These results imply that many of the negative impacts of the Grand Prix have been ameliorated, at least as perceived by respondents in the 2002 survey. However, there also seems to have been some sort of rationalisation with regard to the perception of the event as a panacea of benefits.

Qualitative data

The following comments provide evidence of how residents see the Australian Open Tennis Championships contributing to their personal lives and to the benefit of the community (Set 1). Following on from these positive comments is feedback on the event that is less positive, focusing mainly on the expensiveness of the event, the traffic congestion and crowding and on the bad behaviour by fans and players (Set 2).

Set 1: Some of the positive comments about the Australian Open

The most common response category related to tourism associated directly with the event and the economic benefits this brought to the community. Some examples of this type of comment appear below:

> "Good for the Australian economy - people from overseas coming here and spending money at the event and around town, news coverage overseas".

> "Trade benefits, tourism, local business increase in trade, visitors spend at open and has a flow on effect, creates jobs for locals while open on".

The next most frequently mentioned benefit related to the entertainment aspects of the event. Comments such as those below reflect the sentiments of many respondents:

> "Chance for us to go to an international event to see spectacular tennis".

> "Good tennis to watch, great way to socialise".

> "In the city a perfect setting, 1st class event, watching good people play, good entertainment".

Reference was also made to the 'showcase effect' that large-scale events such as the Australian Open are thought to have. It is interesting to note that such a large proportion (21%) of respondents had this impact at the forefront of their mind and referred to it with no prompting, especially considering that it is quite an intangible long-term potential impact rather than an immediate reward:

> "Australia on show, world aware of Australia, puts Melbourne on the map".

> "Melbourne getting a good name for hosting a great event".

Another benefit frequently mentioned was the potential of the event to promote tennis as a sport, particularly to children, to encourage healthier, more active lifestyles. Some respondents made similar comments about the promotion of appropriate values such as good sportsmanship to children:

> "A lot of interest in playing tennis after Open, wanting to join clubs, good exercise".

> "Good role models for young children to see".

> "Promotes Australian tennis, family watched it together. My children play tennis and it gave them an opportunity to watch young stars".

A few respondents mentioned the development of the tennis centre as a positive impact of the event.

> "The new Vodafone Arena is fantastic".

While many of the comments implied an increase in community pride, especially those relating to showcasing the region, only a small number of respondents specifically referred to pride:

> "Something to be proud of, beautiful to watch".

> "I'm proud it is in Melbourne, very well run, professional".

Set 2: Some of the negative comments about the Australian Open

It is interesting to note that the largest category of response was actually that there were no negative impacts associated with the event, with 44% of respondents reporting this. Where specific impacts were mentioned, only small proportions mentioned these, with the greatest being complaints about prices particularly of tickets and food and beverage at the venue:

> "Too expensive for the average person, too many tourists buying all the tickets, food and drink too expensive, costs too much money to go".

> "Difficult in obtaining good economical seats, too many celebrity types getting better seats than the public"

The second most frequently mentioned problem was the heat, which is really beyond the control of event organisers except to the extent that they may have some power to change the timing of the event or provide other mitigating strategies such as shaded seats:

> "Some days too hot, not enough seats in shade".

> "Held at the wrong time of the year: too hot for players and crowds".

There were several comments relating to disruption caused by as traffic congestion:

"Lots of congestion around tennis centre when driving to city for work"

Similarly, crowding was an issue for some. Mostly this was within the confines of the event venue, but some respondents reported feeling crowded out of public spaces such as the city and public transport:

"Too many people, the event has got too big like other sports. Don't like having to queue for tickets".

"Crowding the public transport system for commuters".

A few comments were made about bad behaviour, either by players or fans:

"Unsportsmanlike behaviour by some of the players its sets a bad example for the kids".

"Listening to the noisy group of spectators – the English, the Swedish, the Aussies are okay – some of them obviously drunk".

This Australian Open in 2003 followed a number of international incidents and there were concerns discussed in the media that large-scale events may be a target for terrorist attacks. Several respondents referred to the fear of this as a negative impact of the event:

"The fact that some people were worried about a terrorist attack on a sporting venue"

A range of other comments were made which did not really relate to the impact of the event on the community. For example some people were upset that specific players did not win the tournament, others made negative comments about commentators. Some felt it disrupted normal television viewing, or that it clashed with the cricket.

It is clear from the number of issues reported in each category that, generally speaking, there was a perception that the positives of the event outweighed the negatives, which is consistent with the quantitative data presented earlier.

Comments about the Australian Grand Prix

The approach taken to examining the comments provided by respondents on the Australian Grand Prix was slightly different from that taken for the Australian Open tennis. The comments were classified (Table 10) and the first words given to describe the Grand Prix showed that 'noise', 'inconvenient' and 'problematic' were used frequently in 1999, but in 2002, the focus had shifted to more neutral words such as 'car' and 'excitement'. The word 'inconvenient' received a much lower number of mentions (11 compared to 33 in 1999) in 2002, as did the word 'corruption' (three compared to seven in 1999). Although full comments were collected (rather than just the first words thought of with regard to the Grand Prix), Table 10 gives a flavour of the types of impressions that residents had of the event in 1999 and 2002.

Table 10: Use of first words to describe the Grand Prix

Word Category	1999 Number of mentions	2002 Number of mentions	Change over time. Use of these words has……….
Noise	64	53	Decreased slightly
Excitement	49	67	Increased substantially
Cars	35	66	Almost doubled
Inconvenient	33	11	Declined substantially
Problematic	23	8	Declined substantially
Benefit	14	15	Remained almost the same
Festival	16	5	Declined substantially
Boring	9	11	Remained almost the same
Tourist	9	9	Remained almost the same
Environmental impact	5	7	Remained almost the same
Corruption	7	3	Declined
Location	4	1	(Frequency too small to compare)
Expensive	2	3	(Frequency too small to compare)
Enthusiasts	3	1	(Frequency too small to compare)
Calendar	2	1	(Frequency too small to compare)

While there is still concern about the presence of the Grand Prix by local residents, much of the initial anger had dissipated by 2002. The organisers had addressed the concerns of deterioration to houses close to the track and had also tried to address many of the environmental concerns regarding the impact of the event due to noise and other pollution. What was still of concern to the ratepayers of Victoria (the state in which the event is run) was the enormous cost to host the event. This remained a source of discontent for many residents.

Community segmentation

In an effort to identify groups within the community with differing perceptions of the Australian Open, a cluster analysis was undertaken using the perceptions of impacts on personal quality-of-life ratings. Based on previous research, it might have been expected that either three or five clusters would emerge (with positive, unconcerned and negative perceptions being represented in distinct clusters). However, as the descriptive statistics show, very little negative sentiment was expressed toward this event. Solutions ranging from two to five clusters were inspected, and no negative group became evident. Therefore, a two-group solution was selected as the most appropriate to describe the data set in a thorough yet parsimonious manner. These groups were titled 'unconcerned' and 'positive'.

These groups were then profiled in terms of the independent variables measured in this study: identification with the theme, attendance, age and gender. As shown in Table 11, a strong relationship is observed between cluster membership and identification with tennis as a spectator sport. Over 80% of the positive group indicated an interest in watching professional tennis, while the unconcerned group were much more likely than expected to have no interest in the sport. Additionally, positive cluster members were more likely to be keen recreational tennis players.

Table 11: Profile of cluster members for the Australian Open

Variable	Response	Unconcerned	Positive
Identification with tennis as a spectator sport	I am an avid fan of professional tennis and always try to attend or watch tournaments on TV	12.2%	41.2%
	I am interested in professional tennis and see it when I can	32.5%	40.2%
	I am not particularly interested in professional tennis but I enjoy seeing it when it is in Melbourne	26.9%	14.7%
	I am not interested in professional tennis but I sometimes attend or watch it because family or friends are interested	16.2%	3.9%
	I have absolutely no interest in professional tennis or the associated festivities, even when it is held in Melbourne	12.2%	0%
Identification with tennis as a participatory Sport	I am an keen recreational tennis player who plays regularly and is involved in club competition	7.1%	14.7%
	I am an keen recreational tennis player who plays regularly but not in any formal competition	1.0%	12.7%
	I occasionally play tennis socially	15.8%	16.7%
	I used to play recreational tennis but have not played in recent years	40.8%	32.4%
	I have absolutely no interest in recreational tennis	35.2%	23.5%
Attendance	Never attended	47.2%	9.9%
	Attended previously but not in 2003	40.1%	39.6%
	Attended in 2003	12.7%	50.5%
Demographics			
Age	18-44 years	41.6%	43.1%
	45-64 years	35.0%	43.1%
	65 years and over	33.4%	13.7%
Gender	Male	35.5%	31.4%
	Female	64.5%	68.6%

In summary, the Australian Open is an event that appears to have substantial support from residents and for a wide range of reasons. It brings pride to the residents that their city is hosting the event, provides good family entertainment as well as enhancing the local economy. Although the increases in traffic congestion and crowding that the event generates can be annoying for residents, overall the Australian Open is perceived to have very positive impacts on the residents of the city of Melbourne.

When the clusters for the Australian Grand Prix were analysed, three clusters emerged that represented negative, neutral and positive perceptions of the event. The results are shown in Table 12 which compares the proportions observed in each cluster in each survey and it can be seen that the proportion in the negative group has declined over time. These proportions have been weighted to compensate for the disproportionate sampling used in 1999. Additionally, it must be noted that the cluster membership being compared here is based on two separate analyses.

Table 12: Comparison of cluster membership over time for the Australian Grand Prix

$\chi^2_{(2)} = 14.40, p<0.05$	Negative	Unconcerned	Positive
2002	9.94% ↓	50.88%	39.18%
1999	21.36% ↑	41.26%	37.38%

Summary

In summary, the Australian Open Tennis Championships and the Australian Formula 1 Grand Prix have different impacts on the host resident community. The Australian Open, on the one hand, is seen as a family-friendly and affordable event which causes little inconvenience for local residents. It also generates a great deal of pride in the city. The Grand Prix, on the other hand, is still perceived as being intrusive, not a family event and very costly for the community in terms of the limited economic returns and t he significant environmental impacts. While there is substantial local community support in Melbourne for sports events in general, the Australian Formula One Grand Prix has never fully resonated with some segments of the broader local community, even though some are staunch advocates for the event. Ultimately, for a sporting event to be well supported by the local community it needs to align with community attitudes and it is clear that the Grand Prix's alignment with community values and attitudes is much less than is the case for the Australian Open. It is important, therefore, that studies are undertaken regularly to monitor host resident perceptions so that action can be taken before issues of concern go too far.

References

Ap J, Crompton JL. 1998. Developing and testing a tourism impact scale. *Journal of Travel Research* **37** (2): 120-130.

Balduck A-L, Maes M, Buelens M. 2011. The social impact of the Tour de France: Comparisons of residents' pre- and post-event perceptions. *European Sport Management Quarterly* **11** (2): 91-113.

Delamere T. 1997. Development of scale items to measure the social impact of community festivals. *Journal of Applied Recreation Research* **22** (4): 293-315.

Delamere TA. 2001. Development of a scale to measure resident attitudes toward the social impacts of community festivals. Part 2: Verification of the scale. *Event Management* **7** (1): 25-38.

Delamere TA, Wankel LM, Hinch TD. 2001. Development of a scale to measure resident attitudes toward the social impacts of community festivals. Part 1: Item generation and purification of the measure. *Event Management* **7** (1): 11-24.

Deery M, Jago L. 2010. Social impacts of events and a model for future research: The role of anti-social behaviour. *International Journal of Event and Festival Management* **1** (1): 8-28.

Easterling, D. (2004). The residents' perspective in tourism research: A review and synthesis. *Journal of Travel & Tourism Marketing* **17** (4): 45-62.

Foenander T. 2010. History of the Australian Open: The Grand Slam of Asia/Pacific, http://www.australianopen.com/en_AU/event_guide/history/history.html

Fredline E. 2000. Host community reactions to major sporting events: The Gold Coast Indy and the Australian Formula One Grand Prix in Melbourne. Unpublished doctoral thesis, Griffith University, Gold Coast.

Fredline E. 2005. Host and guest relations and sport tourism. *Sport in Society* **8** (2): 263-279.

Fredline L, Deery M, Jago L. 2005a. Testing of a compressed generic instrument to assess host community perceptions of events: A case study of the Australian Open Tennis Tournament, Proceedings of the Third International Event Conference, *The Impacts of Events: Triple Bottom Line Evaluation and Event Legacies*, UTS, Sydney, July, 158-177.

Fredline L, Deery M, Jago L. 2005b. Host community perceptions of the impact of events: A Comparison of Different Event Themes in Urban and Regional Communities, CRC for Sustainable Tourism Pty Ltd, Gold Coast.

Fredline L, Jago L, Deery M. 2003. The development of a generic scale to measure the social impacts of events. *Event Management: An International Journal* **8** (1): 23-37.

Getz D. 2005. *Festivals, Special Events and Tourism.* New York: Van Nostrand.

Gu H, Ryan C. 2008. Constructionism and culture in research: Understandings of the fourth Buddhist Festival, Wutaishan, China. *Tourism Management* **31** (2): 167-178.

Hall M. 1992. Adventure, sport and health tourism. In Weiler B, Hall M. (eds), *Special Interest Tourism*. London: Belhaven; 141-158.

Higham J. 1999. Sport as an avenue of tourism development: An analysis of the positive and negative impacts of sport tourism. *Current Issues in Tourism* **2** (1): 82-90.

Jago L, Dwyer L. 2006. *Economic Evaluation of Special Events: A Practitioner's Guide*, Common Ground, Altona.

Lindberg K and Johnson R (1997) Modeling resident attitudes toward tourism. *Annals of Tourism Research* **24** (2): 402-424.

Mediaspy. 2011. http://www.mediaspy.org/2011/01/31/ratings-tennis-final-hit-for-six/

Ohmann S, Jones I, Wilkes K. 2006. The perceived social impacts of the 2006 Football World Cup on Munich residents. *Journal of Sport & Tourism* **11** (2): 129-152.

Ritchie J. 1984. Assessing the impact of hallmark events: Conceptual and research issues. *Journal of Travel Research* **23** (1): 2-11.

Weed M. 2009. Progress in sports tourism research? A meta-review and exploration of futures. *Tourism Management* 30 (5): 615-628.

Ancillary Student Material

Further reading

Deery M, Jago L. 2006 The management of sport tourism. In Gibson, H. (ed.) *Sport Tourism: Concepts and Theories*. Abingdon and New York; 246-263.

Deery M, Jago L. 2010. Social impacts of events and a model for future research: The role of anti-social behaviour. *International Journal of Event and Festival Management* **1** (1): 8-28.

Deery M, Jago L, Fredline L. 2004. Sport tourism or event tourism: Are they one and the same? *Journal of Sport Tourism* **9** (3): 235-246.

Deery M, Jago L, Fredline L. 2012. Rethinking social impacts of tourism research: A new research agenda. *Tourism Management* **33** (1): 64-73.

Fredline L, Jago L, Deery M. 2003. The development of a generic scale to measure the social impacts of events. *Event Management: An International Journal* **8** (1): 23-37.

Fredline L, Deery M, Jago L. 2005 *Host Community Perceptions of the Impacts of the Australian Formula One Grand Prix, Melbourne: A Comparison of Resident Reactions in 1999 with 2002*, CRC for Sustainable Tourism Pty Ltd, Gold Coast.

Fredline L, Deery M, Jago L. 2005. *Host Community Perceptions of the Impact of Events: A Comparison of Different Event Themes in Urban and Regional Communities*, CRC for Sustainable Tourism Pty Ltd, Gold Coast.

Jago L, Deery M, Lipman G. 2010. *Mega Events: Generating Tourist Spend*, VISA.

Shipway R, Jago L, Deery M. 2011. A discussion of quantitative and qualitative research tools in events. In Page S, Connell J. (ed.) *Handbook of Events Studies*. Abingdon and New York: Routledge; 450-469.

Related websites

Australian Open: http://www.australianopen.com/en_AU/index.html

Australian Formula One Grand Prix: http://www.grandprix.com.au/

Formula One Australian Grand Prix: Benefits to Victoria, Tourism Victoria, July 2011: http://www.tourism.vic.gov.au/images/stories/Documents/FactsandFigures/tourism_australian_grand_prix_report_v8_web.pdf

Moomba Festival: http://www.thatsmelbourne.com.au/Whatson/Festivals/MoombaFestival/2012/Pages/Moomba.aspx

Horsham Art Is: http://www.artis.wimmera.com.au/

Self-test questions

Try to answer the following questions to test your knowledge and understanding of the case. If you are unsure of any answers, please re-read the case and refer to the references and further reading sources.

1 Why is it important to understand host residents' perceptions of the social impacts of events?

2 What other methods could be used to determine residents' perceptions of the impact of events on the community?

3 Choose five negative impacts from the events discussed above and provide potential solutions to them.

4 If you were a member of the local council receiving the results from the studies discussed above, how would you communicate the results to the community and what would you say?

5 Prepare a press release for the community on the results from one of the events discussed in this chapter.

Key themes and theories

Social impacts of events on communities

♦   Impact evaluations of events

♦   Positive and negative impacts

♦   Individual and community impacts

♦   Heterogeneous communities

Comparative event evaluation studies over time

Changes in perceptions

Management implications

Research instrument development

♦   Underlying theory

♦   Questionnaire format

♦   Data collection issues

Key theories

Social exchange theory

If you need to source any further information on any of the above themes and theories, then these heading could be used as key words to search for materials and case studies.

 Scan here to get the hyperlinks for this chapter.

7

Cultural Programmes for Sporting Mega-Events

London 2012 – A Case Study

Nancy Stevenson

"The 2012 London Games are not just about sport – they are an opportunity to enjoy and participate in a major cultural celebration" (DCMS, 2010: 13).

Introduction: Sporting mega-events and culture

Sporting mega-events often have a cultural element. However the relationship between culture and sport is complex and there is not a standardised approach across different events. Sometimes cultural programmes are explicitly required. This is the case for candidate cities when bidding to stage the Olympic Games, where Cultural Olympiads are now a compulsory element of the bid. Whether a formal requirement or not, cities or nations that bid for sporting mega-events often choose to develop cultural programmes alongside the sporting event. Cultural programmes and activities are seen as ways of engaging more people and broadening the overall appeal of the event (see Box 1). Cultural programmes can also play a role in securing positive legacies from the event. They can do this by developing and showcasing the cultural assets of the event's location to enhance its image and attract visitors and investors after the event.

This case study focuses on three regional programmes associated with the Cultural Olympiad for the London 2012 Olympic Games (hereafter called the 2012 Games). In so doing, it sets out to explore the ideas underpinning the projects in each region. The term 'legacy' is used to explain the long-term benefits expected to be created by the programmes and which are in addition to the physical legacies of the 2012 Games such as the Olympic Stadium (see Figure 1). The website material for the case study was taken from the Legacy Trust website in January 2012. This material is included to encourage discussion about the themes and issues that arise when places develop a cultural element aligned to the staging of a sporting mega-event. Web links are provided and readers are encouraged to visit these sites in order to investigate the stories that emerge not that these projects have been delivered and their legacies begin to be formally evaluated.

Figure 1: The Olympic Stadium, London, Reproduced courtesy of Charlie Inskip

What is culture?

Cultural programmes are underpinned by a range of conceptualisations, some closely tied in with the arts, creativity and the cultural industries, and others more closely linked to ideas about culture in terms of people's lives and community identity (see Figure 2). Three dominant conceptualisations that appear to underpin the Cultural Olympiad for the 2012 Games are as follows:

♦ **Social conceptualisation.** This identifies culture in terms of community, multi-cultural expression, shared experiences, local representation and empowerment. This conceptualisation is framed within a wider social agenda and links culture to social development.

♦ **Arts conceptualisation.** Identifies culture in terms of artistic expression, accomplishments and endeavour. It includes performance, opera and theatre, music, film, visual arts and dance. This conceptualisation is often associated with notions of high and low culture.

♦ **The economic/regeneration conceptualisation.** Cultural activity is used as a mechanism to enhance or change the image of cities or places within cities. Culture is used as a catalyst for change, encouraging business to invest in the area and attracting visitors (Stevenson, 2012).

In 2008, the definition of culture associated with the Cultural Olympiad was:

"Culture covers not only pursuits such as visiting galleries, museums and theatres but also activities as diverse as carnival and street theatre, fashion, gaming, photography, heritage and the natural environment, and many more. With this in mind, our definition of 'culture' in the context of the London 2012 Games is broad and inclusive" (DCMS, 2008: 45).

Figure 2: Hackney Carnival 2008. Reproduced courtesy of permission of Charlie Inskip

Box 1: Excerpts from DCMS (2010)

"The Games also offer a once in a lifetime opportunity to showcase the best of the UK's culture, creativity, industry and innovation. As well as the estimated potential global audience of 4 billion people, we expect to welcome to London 120 Heads of State, as well as 14,700 participants, 320,000 extra visitors and 20,000 accredited journalists. If we make the most of this defining moment we will boost national self-confidence, enhance the UK's reputation abroad and fully exploit the opportunities for growth offered by hosting the Games" (DCMS, 2010: 7).

"More generally the Cultural Olympiad is already engaging millions of people in the excitement of the Games through the cultural life of the nation. More exciting projects to come will engage and inspire the next generation of performers and audiences. Plans have been announced for leading artists from around the world to come together in the

UK to deliver commissions and special projects as part of the London 2012 Festival. This will be a chance for everyone to celebrate London 2012 through dance, music, theatre, the visual arts, film and digital innovation, and leave a lasting legacy for culture and the arts in the UK. Over 1,000 events will be featured on a special website which will go live from Summer 2011. The aim is for over three million people to attend and be part of the London 2012 Festival" (DCMS, 2010: 10).

The relationship between sport and culture

The Cultural Olympiad attempts to make links between culture and sport. However linking these two elements is fraught with difficulties. Some researchers claim that the values associated with sport and culture are incompatible in modern society, with culture being the "poor relation to a globalised, mediated, profit orientated sports industry" (Inglis, 2008: 471). In this context, it is difficult to develop shared understanding across different programmes. There are huge disparities in the funding arrangements for cultural and sporting elements, with monies predominantly focused on developing infrastructure and staging the sporting events in 2012. While cultural funding is normally assigned at the outset of the project, cultural elements tend to be less physically tangible and less visible. These 'soft' elements are often seen as the easiest to cut if (and when) the Games run over budget. Sometimes budgets are cut directly, but in the case of the 2012 Games some cuts were indirect and occurred when National Lottery and Arts Council funds were redirected towards the physical infrastructure for the Games. This means the Cultural Olympiad was developed in the context of a decrease in mainstream arts funding.

The marginality of the cultural programme appears to be exacerbated by the lack of clear guidelines from the International Olympic Committee (IOC) about the nature and evaluation of cultural programmes. This has led to fragmented programmes, with minimal public and media attention. The four-year timeframe intensifies this problem, as the Cultural Olympiad evolves and objectives and priorities change over time. The evolving nature of the programme makes it difficult to identify its dimensions clearly and evaluate the outcomes of the Cultural Olympiad (Garcia, 2004).

The Cultural Olympiad for the 2012 Games

The Olympic Charter outlines the fundamental principles of 'Olympism', which are framed to include notions of social responsibility, ethics, human dignity and peace. This is a presented as a holistic philosophy, "[b]lending sport with culture and education" (IOC, 2011: 10). Countries that bid to host the Olympics must include a cultural programme known as a Cultural Olympiad, commonly a four-year programme of events which supports the delivery of legacies from the Games. In this case study, three phases of the Cultural Olympiad are identified. The first is the original programme outlined in the bid documentation in 2004. The second reflects developments prior to the launch of the Cultural Olympiad in August 2008 and in its first year of operation. The third outlines the programme that has been developed since early 2010 and is to be delivered in 2012.

The bid

When countries bid to host the Olympic Games they prepare a Candidate File defining their proposal. London's Candidate File for the 2012 Games was submitted in 2004 and described the broad approach to developing the Games and its legacies. It also outlined detailed proposals which were themed to include sport and venues, the Olympic Village, and transport. Theme 17 considered "Olympism and Culture" and identified a cultural and educational programme to link communities. London was characterised as a port city with a history of welcoming "people, ideas, information and goods from around the world". (London 2012, 2004: 173). The programme was framed around ideas of diversity, creativity, community and youth culture and was envisaged as a celebration of 'the renaissance of East London'. A central project was the Olympic Friend-ship, a boat crewed by "young people, artists, philosophers and students" travelling around the world encouraging creative dialogue and exchange (London 2012, 2004). This project also envisaged a virtual boat whose voyage would underpin a national educational programme.

When London won the bid in 2005, the major focus was on developing organisational arrangements, processes and plans to deliver the infrastructure associated with the 2012 Games. Media interest was largely focused on the development of the Olympic Park, concerns about a spiralling budget and staging the Games. Other aspects such as the Cultural Olympiad received much less attention. The House of Commons (HOC) Culture, Media and Sport Committee recognised this issue and recommended "that the Government should do more to publicise and co-ordinate it, drawing together ideas, sharing good practice, and increasing awareness of some of the more practical and imaginative suggestions which are being made" (HOC, 2000: 46).

The launch of the Cultural Olympiad and early years

The Cultural Olympiad for the 2012 Games was launched in September 2008. It claimed to be "for everyone" (LOCOG, 2008: 2), a celebration of the internationalism and cultural diversity of London and the UK, inspiring and involving young people, and generating a positive legacy. Its objectives were to:

♦   "inspire and involve the widest range of London and UK wide communities;

♦   generate sustainable long-term benefits to our cultural life;

♦   create outstanding moments of creative excellence across the full range of performing arts and creative industries;

♦   connect future generations with the UK's artistic communities and with their peers around the world;

♦   promote contemporary London as a major world cultural capital;

♦   drive tourism and inward investment and use the creative industries to boost economic regeneration;

♦   embrace the Olympic movement values of excellence, respect and friendship and the Paralympic movement vision to empower, achieve, inspire" (LOCOG, 2007: 4).

The Cultural Olympiad encompassed three main elements: the Olympic ceremonies, bid projects and a UK-wide cultural festival. It aimed to translate the IOC's cultural agenda into a range of programmes reflecting the broad objectives outlined above. Some were intended to engage and involve communities. These programmes tended to be inward facing, located within communities and focused on the needs and aspirations of those communities. Other programmes presented artistic and cultural displays. They were primarily outward-facing, aiming to appeal to and attract wider audiences.

At the outset it was envisaged that the UK-wide cultural festival would have a strong local aspect, engaging local communities and drawing from 'grassroots' community projects. The 'Inspire Programme' was set up to provide an opportunity for non-commercial organisations to bid to associate themselves with the Olympics. 'Inspire Marks' were awarded to over 2,000 projects by January 2012, allowing these non-commercial projects to link to the 2012 brand. The advantages of this were not financial but provided the potential for projects to receive wider recognition and access to broader networks (London 2012, 2012).

At the start of this phase, 10 major projects were identified. These were:

1   **Artists Taking the Lead** – encompassing 12 art commissions to celebrate local and national cultural life.

2   **Young Futures Festival** – aiming to provide creative opportunities for young people.

3   **Sounds!** music projects enabling young people to work with musicians.

4   **Stories of the World** – interpreting museum collections to inspire people to explore culture and heritage.

5   **Film and Video Nation** - involving young people in film, video and digital technology through competitions and festivals.

6   **Shakespeare Now** – widening the audience for Shakespeare's work.

7   **Extraordinary Ability** - showcasing disability arts and sport.

8   **World Cultural Festival** - celebrating international culture.

9   **Festival of Carnivals** - engaging people in street festivals and performances.

10 **Access All Areas** - widening audiences of heritage sites (DCMS, 2008).

There is consistency between the objectives set out in the bid documentation and the programme launched in 2008. However some detailed projects were not developed. For example, while many projects reflect a commitment to developing friendship, the 'Friend-ship' boat was not launched. The decision to abandon this project arose due to concerns about funding and the complexities of its enactment. The decision to scrap the 'Friend-ship' was identified as a significant broken promise (BBC, 2008).

Shaping up for the Games

The early phases of the Cultural Olympiad did not capture media and popular attention (see Box 2), and were criticised for being "ill-defined and uninspired" (Horne and Whannel, 2012: 147). In its last two years, the Cultural Olympiad evolved rapidly, spurred on by the realisation that it had to be more widely understood in order to create positive legacy outcomes. There were changes in political and operational leadership. Other changes arose in the context of economic recession and fiscal restraint in the public sector. Most major projects evolved from those envisaged in 2008 and some project titles were deleted. These included the Young Futures Festival, Shakespeare

Now, The World Cultural Festival and the Festival of Carnivals. This reflected the decision to define the programme more clearly and to increase its impact. Many projects that might have originally fallen under these headings (such as the One Hackney Festival and the World Shakespeare Festival) went ahead and formed part of the London 2012 Festival.

The London 2012 Festival ran during the 12 weeks before and during the Olympics and Paralympics. This festival was the culmination of the Cultural Olympiad and drew together the endeavours of the major projects outlined below encompassing and cultural events including dance, music, theatre, the visual arts and film.

The six major projects were:

1   **Artists Taking the Lead** – This project was led by the Arts Council and involved 12 public art commissions across the UK. One example, 'Godiva Awakes' was commissioned in the West Midlands and created of a large carnival puppet. There were a series of festival events to awaken the puppet in Coventry, to mark her journey and to celebrate her arrival in London. These formed part of the London 2012 Festival (Arts Council 2012a).

2   **Stories of the World** – This included a wide range of projects, developed and delivered at a regional and local level to showcase museum, library and archive collections and develop wider audiences. An example of this was 'CultuRISE', a regional project which ran in the North East, and projects with young people to make museums more exciting.

3   **Unlimited** – Funding was provided to support and celebrate arts, culture and sport by disabled and deaf people enabling them to create and showcase their work. Projects were developed and staged around the country and many were brought together in a festival at the Southbank Centre which coincided with the Paralympics (Arts Council, 2012b).

4   **Film Nation** – A competition for young people aged between 14 and 25, who were invited to develop three-minute films inspired by Olympic and Paralympic Values. An awards ceremony was held on the 4 July 2012 to celebrate the competitors' achievements.

5   **Discovering Places** – Launched in July 2010, this encompassed projects and events to encourage people to explore their local built and natural environment. Many were included in the London 2012 Festival.

6   Music (DCMS, 2012) – A range of music events were developed under this heading and included Music Nation in March 2012 and the River of Music in July 2012. The latter comprised a multi-venue weekend festival which brought together music from around the world.

Box 2: Excerpt from the Guardian – Interview with Ruth Mackenzie: 'There's no time to mess around'

"For the purposes of the Cultural Olympiad, Mackenzie is the cavalry, brought in after an almost two-year interregnum (her predecessor in the job, Keith Khan, resigned in March 2008). This time last year, things looked bad for the Cultural Olympiad. It was a joke within the arts world, and beyond that no one had really heard of it. "What is the Cultural Olympiad?" people kept asking. The process appeared directionless; the programme, such as it was, expressed in such indecipherable jargon as to render it meaningless. The London Organising Committee for the Olympic Games (LOCOG) looked like just the wrong outfit to be running an artistic programme, their energies, understandably, focused on producing two vast sporting events. And yet the Cultural Olympiad has the potential to be more than a glossy adjunct. Done well, it could harness the enthusiasm of millions of sports fans, here and abroad, for something that Britain is indubitably good at: art" (Higgens, 2010).

Culture and the legacies of sporting mega-events

Sporting mega-events can play a role in achieving wider objectives relating to the development and/or regeneration of places. Host countries often engage in projects and programmes in an attempt to capture legacies from events. Legacies are defined as those outcomes that arise from and outlast an event, and can be positive or negative. Positive legacies do not automatically occur after events and legacy planning is required before, during, and after the event in order to secure positive long-term effects (Smith, Stevenson and Edmundson, 2011; Miah and Garcia, 2012).

The legacy plans

Legacy planning is an essential element of an Olympic Games bid. In the pre-games phase, legacy aspirations were predominantly framed in terms of the population around the Olympic Park. Cultural legacies for the community were identified arising from cultural opportunities and training associated with the wider regeneration programme. The Candidate File for the London 2012 Games identified four legacy aspirations:

- ♦ **A legacy for sport** – After the Games, the sports infrastructure (such as the main stadium and the aquatics centre) would be converted to provide a range of national and local facilities. Wide-ranging sport programmes were also envisaged to encourage greater participation.

- ♦ **A legacy for the community** – Community legacies were framed predominantly in terms of those communities living near the Olympic Park. They included "significant improvements in health and well-being, education, skills and training, job opportunities, cultural entitlements, housing and social integration and the environment" for people "in London's poorest and most disadvantaged area".

- ♦ **A legacy for the environment** – This envisaged the "Low Carbon Games" with all spectators travelling by public transport and new standards for "sustainable production, consumption and recycling of natural resources".

- ♦ **A legacy for the economy** – This was framed in terms of those communities living near the Olympic Park and included "the creation of wider employment opportunities and improvements in the education, skills and knowledge of the local labour force in an area of very high unemployment" (London 2012, 2004: .23-25).

Figure 3: Artwork at the Viewtube 2010. Photo Credit: Nancy Stevenson

In 2008, the Department of Culture Media and Sport published Before, during and after: Making the most of the London 2012 Games. This document identified five broad legacy promises for the 2012 Games:

1   To make the UK a world-leading sporting nation

2   To transform the heart of East London

3   To inspire a generation of young people

4   To make the Olympic Park a blueprint for sustainable living

5   To demonstrate the UK is a creative, inclusive and welcoming place to live in, visit and for business (DCMS, 2008: 3).

This document identified the Cultural Olympiad as a key programme to deliver Promise 3, aiming to increase engagement in cultural activities. It was also identified as one of the programmes that would help to deliver Promise 5. It provided a platform to celebrate national identity and creativity and to use this to create an image of the UK as a welcoming place.

This document outlined specific aims for the Cultural Olympiad to "celebrate the diversity of London and welcome the world to the UK; inspire and engage young people; and leave a lasting legacy" (DCMS, 2008: 45). The following cultural legacies were identified:

♦   "UK-wide artistic and cultural events of the very highest quality, to inspire a new generation of audiences and participants;

♦   Many more opportunities for young people to engage in cultural activities;

♦   Opportunities for talented young people from all communities and backgrounds to fulfil their creative potential;

♦   A global showcase of our cultural excellence and diversity" (DCMS, 2008: 45).

After national elections in 2010, a new coalition government was formed. This did not lead to any major shifts in legacy aspirations for the Games but they were reframed around four legacy themes with an increased focus on economic aspirations for the games. Ambitions to encourage people to adopt more sustainable practices and make progress towards achieving equality for disabled people have been identified and run across the following four themes:

♦   **"Sport:** harnessing the UK's passion for sport to increase grass roots participation and competitive sport and to encourage physical activity;

♦ **Economic:** exploiting the opportunities for economic growth offered by hosting the Games;

♦ **Community engagement:** promoting community engagement and achieving participation across all groups in society through the Games;

♦ **East London regeneration:** ensuring that the Olympic Park can be developed after the Games as one of the principal drivers of regeneration in East London." (DCMS, 2011a: 1)

The projects associated with the Cultural Olympiad are diverse and span the themes identified above. Some projects offer opportunities for economic growth by developing and supporting cultural events and attracting people to visit those events, some are focused on trying to engage young people in cultural activity, and some are focused on developing cultural aspects of the regeneration of East London. The outcomes of different cultural projects vary and reflect a different mix of the themes. For example, in section 7, the Urban Games (see Box 3) encompass both sporting and community engagement elements. Theatre and music events within the London 2012 Festival and regional events like Lakes Alive (see Box 4) reflect the economic theme, attracting audiences to diverse events around the UK. The events identified in the Accentuate Project (see Box 5) are focused on a range of projects reflecting the community engagement theme and specifically aiming to provide opportunities for people with disabilities.

This study has shown that the Cultural Olympiad evolved since its inception. As it evolved, the cultural aspirations and envisaged cultural legacies also evolved. The nature and extent of any cultural legacies will be affected by a broad range of contextual factors. Since the bid was made there have been an economic downturn, a change in government, fiscal restraint and the emergence of new policy initiatives and governance arrangements. All these changes mean that the debates and definitions of the cultural legacies arising from the Games will continue to evolve as they are re-articulated and re-evaluated in a changing world.

Measuring the effects of the Cultural Olympiad

After the Games, there is to be a 'meta-evaluation' of the impacts and legacy of the London 2012 Olympic Games and Paralympic Games, coordinated through the DCMS. The overall legacy of the Games will be evaluated by pulling together the results of evaluations of individual legacy programmes, and conducting some additional research (DCMS, 2011a, b). The meta-evaluation will be structured around a range of indicators relating to the four legacy themes.

The legacy themes and indicators are outlined in Table 1:

Table 1: Summary of most important indicators by theme

Sport	Economic	Social	East London
Participation in competitive school sport Participation in sport and physical activity by adults and young people Sustainable sports infrastructure Medals won in major championships Subjective well-being	Gross Value Added (GVA) Employment Inward investment into the UK Exports from the UK Tourism visitor numbers and spend per visitor Accessible transport infrastructure Sustainable approaches to construction and event management	Cohesion Participation in volunteering Participation in culture Subjective well-being Attitudes towards disability Sustainable lifestyles	Land and property values Regional GVA Resident satisfaction Economic structure/profile Unemployment Socio-economic convergence

Source: DCMS (2011b)

The indicators in the table show that some of the Games' legacies can be clearly defined and are relatively straightforward to measure. Examples include sport participation rates, medals won in major championships, exports from the UK, tourism visitor numbers and unemployment. However, it is hard to see from this table where and how the Cultural Olympiad might be evaluated. The previous sections have identified that the Cultural Olympiad is broadly framed and comprises a multitude of national, regional and local projects around the country which run across the four themes. In this context, the evaluation of the legacies of the Cultural Olympiad will be challenging because of the range and volume of activities and the interdependencies between them. It will be difficult to measure some qualitative outcomes, such as the extent to which young people are 'inspired' and the implications of that inspiration. It will also be hard to isolate project outcomes from other contextual factors. For example, a project may provide arts training for young people but this is within a wider context of economic recession and cuts to mainstream arts funding, which means there are fewer employment opportunities. The following difficulties associated with measuring the Cultural Olympiad are recognised:

> "… the Cultural Olympiad is made up of component projects whose focus could conceivably be any one of the other legacy themes, this will mean projects may be cultural in nature but are likely to have impacts on opportunities for disabled people, tourism, the economy and volunteering" (DCMS, 2011b: 10).

There will be a number of evaluation exercises to evaluate the impact of the Cultural Olympiad. Some will occur as part of the meta-evaluation but it is also likely that individual organisations will also be evaluating specific projects.

An additional complexity arises when trying to evaluate cultural projects that have a mixture of social and economic aspirations. These aspirations are not necessarily mutually compatible and sometimes demonstrate contradictory tensions. For example, a project to stage a music festival might be simultaneously directed at attracting external visitors and media attention, while also trying to achieve local representation and empowerment of disadvantaged groups. An approach that is too focused on delivering the former might exclude local communities; while an approach focusing on the latter might create something that does not appeal to a wider audience. Evaluation of the 2012 Games needs to take account of complex and sometimes contradictory objectives. The aspect of an event that is considered the most important is not necessarily the aspect that is most easily measured. For example, it might be relatively easy to identify the number of people who attended an event but this will not always be a good indicator that the event was successful. An event which is aiming to improve community involvement and a sense of inclusion may fail in some senses if it attracts too many people from outside the local area.

Exploring three regional programmes

This section outlines regional programmes in three regions of the UK. These programmes were developed to deliver the legacy objectives outlined above and provided a way to roll out the UK Wide festival. They were supported by the Legacy Trust, which had a fund of £40 million for arts, sports and education projects to celebrate and create legacies from the 2012 Games. Across the UK there were 12 regional programmes which shared three key aims:

- ♦   "to unite culture, sport and education, in line with the values and vision of the Olympic and Paralympic Games;
- ♦   to make a lasting difference to all those involved;
- ♦   to be grassroots projects, often small in scale, and unite communities of interest at local and regional level" (Legacy Trust, 2012a).

What was envisioned, at the start of 2012, for three of the regionally-funded cultural programmes is outlined below.

Box 3: North East – NE-Generation

NE-Generation was a programme consisting of diverse projects with the following aims:

◆ To bring about a shift in the way in which children and young people and the North East's cultural sector collaborate;

◆ To develop a more relevant, children and young people focused cultural sector where young people experience, participate in and generate cultural activity on their own terms;

◆ To assist the cultural sector in becoming more responsive to and reflective of young people and their cultural needs and interests;

◆ To assist the cultural sector in playing a greater part in children and young people's lives, and increasing children and young people's self-awareness, creative opportunities for self-expression and enabling them to develop their own ideas of personal and regional identity;

◆ To incorporate the "widest possible definition of culture" (Legacy Trust UK, 2008: n.p.)

The projects were:

1. **Culturise:** This project was led by young people and aimed to create cultural resources and engage people with the existing resources in the region.

2. **Dale Force!** Aimed to improve cultural opportunities for young people in rural areas.

3. **Five Ring Circus:** Promoted youth circus across the North East

4. **Future Cinema:** Enabled young people to learn about film, animation and digital technologies.

5. **Tech Max**: Aimed to engage 'looked after' young people in cultural activities.

6. **Time Travel:** aimed to make local history interesting and accessible for young people.

7. **Urban Alchemy:** used art forms such as drama, break dancing and graffiti to celebrate young people and their cultures, imagination and aspirations.

8. **Urban Games:** comprised annual events which included breakdancing, DJing, skateboarding, BMXing and Parkour. This project is outlined in more depth below.

9. **Urban Music Training:** provided training for young DJs, producers, vocalists, rappers and instrumentalists.

There are also two overarching projects: 10th Project and Cultural Innovation Fund which provided networks and skill training for young people involved in the project and allowed them to allocate £100,000 of funding for emerging artists from the North East to work with young people.

Urban Games was a three-year project celebrating culture, creative and sporting activities. It created an annual event for young people that encompassed urban arts and sports inspired by Hip Hop culture and some extreme sports.

> "Conceived by young people on Tyneside as an alternative to the traditional sports of the Olympics, the Urban Games is for those who are more passionate about Hip Hop and urban sports and arts … The inaugural event in 2010 took place at The Sage Gateshead. For many of the young people involved in the Urban Games it was the first time they had attended an event like this, let alone run it. The Urban Games 2011 built on the experience of the previous year, developing the young people's skills and increasing the scale of the event. Taking place at the Whitley Bay links, the Urban Games attracted 8000 spectators, 400+ audience at the showcase, 100+ volunteers, 300+ competitors and performers, 20+ plus medallists, with 11 people trained as event stewards, 2 world records broken and the region's first ever Parkour Jam." (Legacy Trust, 2012b).

Websites

http://www.legacytrustuk.org/programmes/north-east/

http://www.ne-generation.org.uk/

http://www.theurbangames.org.uk/

Box4: North West – We Play

We Play was focused on digital innovation, excellence in outdoor arts and culture and sport participation. It was "… designed to elaborate on the way we think, to stimulate new experience and to provide opportunities for everyone to be a great 'player' through creative, physical, social and intellectual activity… Its series of annual programmes, collaborative projects and new commissions seek to leave a legacy of partnerships across different sectors, of a new cultural infrastructure in the North West and of artworks and events which have a life beyond 2012" (Legacy Trust, 2012c: n.p.). The annual programmes were:

◆ **Abandon Normal Devices** – A festival of new cinema, digital culture and art. It was intended to provoke "reaction, creation and experimentation between and across different disciplines and geographical locations" (Legacy Trust, 2012c: n.p.).

◆ **Blaze** – A youth-led programme which made links between culture and sport. In 2012, it produced Blaze Festival North West, a festival of culture, sport, music and art.

◆ **Lakes Alive** – A festival of outdoor performance and street arts across Cumbria. This festival was "commissioned by the London 2012 Festival to produce a new large-scale show by the French street arts company Les Commandos Percu for the first night of its opening weekend" (Legacy Trust, 2012c: n.p.).

Figure 4: Blaze Boom Bike Band. Reproduced courtesy of Brian Slater Photography

Websites

www.legacytrustuk.org/programmes/north-west/

www.blazeonline.org.uk

www.lakesalive.org

Box 5: South East – Accentuate

Accentuate was a four year programme of 15 projects which provided opportunities to develop and showcase the talents of deaf and disabled people. It aimed to change peoples' attitudes and perceptions of disabled people and to provide training and employment. The 15 projects were focused on training, developing networks and commissioning work and are outlined below:

◆ **Realise!** – Aimed to support & develop the entrepreneurial skills of young disabled people through skills-based workshops, competitions and work-placements;

◆ **Campaign!** – Created collaboration between disabled young people in the South East and competitor countries, to build campaigns to raise awareness on issues that affect them in their respective countries;

◆ **Collaborations!** – Created collaboration between disabled artists and disabled athletes;

◆ **Gaming!** – Young disabled people worked with industry gaming experts to design new, inclusive, interactive games based on the theme of the Paralympics and Stoke Mandeville;

◆ **Playground to Podium** – Provided disabled young people with opportunities to participate and excel in sport through coaching;

◆ **U Screen** – Provided opportunities collaboration between young disabled and deaf people and non-disabled young people to share stories and ideas through Screen Media;

◆ **Destination Zones** – Audits were undertaken and training developed to improve provisions for disabled people within key destinations;

◆ **Creative Landscapes** – Commissioned disabled artists to explore the historic environment for Heritage Open Days;

◆ **Sync South East** – Provided training and professional development for artists and organisations to support disabled leadership;

◆ **Fest** – Intended to raise the profile and develop networks of regional deaf and disabled artists;

Figure 5: StopGAP Dance Company, reporduced with permission of Chris Parkes (Christophotographic).

◆ **Go Public** – Developed opportunities for disabled and deaf artists in the public realm to complement 2012;

◆ **Major Events** – Aimed to attract world renowned disability sporting events to the South East;

◆ **Paralympic Region** - Improved access to Stoke Mandeville's historic archive and histories of individual Paralympic athletes;

◆ **Celebrate** – Aimed to ensure that the message of the Cultural Olympiad reached the public and influenced change in cultural provision in the future;

◆ **Commission** – Developed and commissioned work, networks and professional development opportunities which ensure equity of access. (Legacy Trust, 2012d)

Websites

http://www.legacytrustuk.org/programmes/south-east/

http://www.accentuate-se.org/homepage

Conclusion

The Cultural Olympiad has been defined broadly and its programmes draw from three conceptualisations of culture. It is perceived as a complementary element to the sporting programme, widening relevance, increasing ownership and supporting wider regeneration aspirations relating to the development and staging of the Games. The Cultural Olympiad for the 2012 Games has had a relatively low profile in comparison with its sporting aspects. Media interest has been more focused on the sporting event and the physical developments associated with the Games, and the sporting events in the summer of 2012. This uneven relationship has been identified in previous sporting mega-events, such as the 2004 Sydney Olympics (Garcia, 2004). Varied explanations have been put forward for the relatively low profile of culture in sporting events. These include the difficulties in integrating sport and culture on the basis that they lack shared values and institutional structures (Inglis, 2008); diverse interpretations of culture and tensions arising between those interpretations; lack of agreed approaches or 'success criteria' to enable evaluation of the programme; and meagre funding for cultural activities in comparison to sporting elements of the games. There is an on-going discussion about the relationship between culture and sporting mega-events and further reading on these debates can be found in the recommended reading list below.

References

Arts Council. 2012a. Artists taking the lead. http://www.artscouncil.org.uk/funding/funded-projects/case-studies/artists-taking-lead-west-midlands/

Arts Council. 2012. Unlimited. http://www.artscouncil.org.uk/what-we-do/our-priorities-2011-15/london-2012/unlimited/

BBC. 2008. London 2012 to shelve ship idea. http://news.bbc.co.uk/sport1/hi/olympics/london_2012/7290404.stm

DCMS. 2008. Before, during and after: Making the most of the London 2012 Games. http://www.thebigopportunity.org.uk/uploads/4/0/0/1/4001782/dcms2012legacyactionplan.pdf

DCMS. 2010. Plans for the Legacy from the 2012 Olympic and Paralympic Games. http://www.culture.gov.uk/images/publications/201210_Legacy_Publication.pdf

DCMS. 2011a. Meta-evaluation of the impacts and legacy of the London 2012 Olympic Games and Paralympic Games. Report 1: Scope, research questions and data strategy. http://www.culture.gov.uk/images/publications/DCMS_2012_Games_Meta_evaluation_Report_1.pdf

DCMS. 2011b. Meta-Evaluation of the Impacts and Legacy of the London 2012 Olympic Games and Paralympic Games. Report 2. http://www.culture.gov.uk/images/publications/DCMS_2012_Games_Meta_evaluation_Report_2.doc.

DCMS. 2012. Department for Culture, Media and Sport. The Cultural Olympiad. http://www.culture.gov.uk/what_we_do/2012_olympic_games_and_paralympic_games/3430.aspx

Garcia B. 2004. Urban regeneration, arts programming and major events: Glasgow 1990, Sydney 2000 and Barcelona 2004. *International Journal of Cultural Policy* **10** (1): 103-118.

Higgens C. 2010. Ruth Mackenzie: 'There's no time to mess around' Guardian 29/3/2010. http://www.guardian.co.uk/culture/2010/mar/29/ruth-mackenzie-cultural-olympiad

Horne J, Whannel G. 2012. *Understanding the Olympics*. London: Routledge.

HOC. 2007. House of Commons Culture, Media and Sport Committee. London 2012 Olympic Games and Paralympic Games: Funding and Legacy. Second Report of Session 2006-7. http://www.publications.parliament.uk/pa/cm200607/cmselect/cmcumeds/69/69i.pdf.

Inglis D. 2008. Cultural agonistes: Social differentiation, cultural policy and Cultural Olympiads. *International Journal of Cultural Policy* **14** (4): 463-477.

IOC. 2011. Olympic Charter. http://www.olympic.org/Documents/olympic_charter_en.pdf

Legacy Trust. 2012a. Leaving a lasting legacy from London 2012 in communities around the UK. http://www.legacytrustuk.org/info/About/

Legacy Trust. 2012b. NE Generation. http://www.legacytrustuk.org/programmes/north-east/

Legacy Trust. 2012c. North West We Play. http://www.legacytrustuk.org/programmes/north-west/

Legacy Trust. 2012d. Accentuate. http://www.legacytrustuk.org/programmes/south-east/

LOCOG. 2007. Cultural update. http://www.london2012.com/documents/culture/culture-update-june-2007.pdf

London 2012. 2012. Inspire Programme. http://www.london2012.com/inspire-programme

London 2012. 2004. Candidate File. Vol. 1 Theme 1. http://www.london2012.com/documents/candidate-files/theme-1-olympic-games-concept-and-legacy.pdf

London 2012. 2004. Candidate File Theme 17 Olympism and Culture. http://www.london2012.com/about-us/publications/candidate-file/

Miah A, Garcia B. 2012. *The Olympics: The Basics.* London: Routledge.

Smith A, Stevenson N, Edmundson T. 2011. The 2012 Games - The Regeneration Legacy. RICS. http://www.rics.org/site/download_feed.aspx?fileID=10510&fileExtension=PDF

Stevenson N. 2012. The cultural legacy of the 2012 Games. In Shipway R, Fyall A (eds) *International Sports Events: Impacts, Experiences and Identities.* London: Routledge; 69-83.

Ancillary Student Material

Further Reading

Khan. 2004. Just another ceremony? A sustainable cultural legacy. In Vigor A, Mean M, Tim C. (eds) *After the Gold Rush: A Sustainable Olympic Bid for London*, Institute of Public Policy Research, Demos, London; 109-129.

Kennel J, MacLeod N, 2009. A grey literature review of the Cultural Olympiad. *Cultural Trends* **18** (1): 83-88.

Poynter G, MacRury I. 2009. *Olympic Cities: 2012 and the Remaking of London.* Farnham: Ashgate.

Self-test questions

Try to answer the following questions in order to test your knowledge and understanding of the case. If you are not sure of the answers please re-read the case and refer to the references and further reading sources.

1   Explain why cultural programmes are often developed in connection with sporting mega-events.

2   Identify and account for the changes in the Cultural Olympiad for the 2012 Games since the original bid was made in 2004.

3   Identify the objectives of the Cultural Olympiad and discuss how these are met by the regional programmes.

Themes

The key themes raised in this case study relate to the following:

Culture and sporting mega-events:

◆   Cultural events – conceptualisation, context and objectives

◆   Relationship between sporting mega-events and cultural programmes

◆   The Cultural Olympiad – evolution, objectives, structures, programmes

Conceptualisations of culture:

◆   Social

◆   Arts

◆   Economy/regeneration

Legacy

◆   Defining legacy

◆   Legacy planning, monitoring and evaluation

If you need to source further information on any of the above themes and theories, then these headings could be used as key words to search for materials and case studies.

 Scan here to get the hyperlinks for this chapter.

SECTION THREE

IDENTITY and EXPERIENCES

8

Active Sports Tourism

Active Sports Tourists Competing in the 2011 MBNA Chester Marathon

Amanda Miller

Introduction

Sports tourism has received increasing attention in the academic literature of late, as well as from the industry by tourism suppliers, event organisers and destination managers. This niche market is growing in size and encompasses a wide range of tourism experiences, from taking part in sporting holidays through to spectating at sporting events. As noted by Higham and Hinch (1999), the twentieth century has seen the rapid development of both sport and tourism; both are among the largest and fastest-growing industries of our day. Moreover, the phenomena of mass participation in sport and tourism are closely related, with sport and tourism activity increasingly taking place simultaneously. From a tourism perspective, Standeven and deKnop (1999) have remarked on the sharing of resources and infrastructure that often occurs within the destination by both tourists and sports participants, while the "democratisation of sport and tourism has resulted in most sports offering the potential to generate tourist activity" (Higham and Hinch, 2002: 176).

This case study seeks to add further depth to the consideration of this vibrant sector of the tourism industry by focusing on the active sports tourist. To this end, it begins by presenting the 2011 MBNA Chester Marathon and data generated from an online survey of runners subsequent to the event. The data captured were from all runners but only the data from those participants who stayed at least one night are presented, i.e. data from the active sports tourists. The case study is then placed within the broader context of sports tourism, active sports tourism and destination marathons.

The MBNA Chester Marathon

Chester is an internationally recognised tourist destination in the North West of England, offering visitors a unique historical and cultural experience. The city is renowned in the UK for having the largest Roman amphitheatre and the most complete Roman town walls. It also has distinctive shopping arcades, known as the Rows, and a cathedral. According to Cheshire West and Chester (2009), the visitor economy is significant for West Cheshire: it is estimated that Chester alone attracts 8.4 million visitors a year, which in turn generates £500 million in income per year. With regard to employment, it is estimated that tourism-related employment accounts for 10.2% of all jobs in West Cheshire. More specifically, events are recognised by Visit Chester and Cheshire (2010) in their visitor economy framework for Cheshire as important to the branding of the destination and for the visitor experience. The '2020 Time to Meet the Challenge' document positions events in the context of the visitor economy of Chester and Cheshire.

Chester hosts a portfolio of events over the calendar year, ranging from one-off events to festivals (see Box 1). These events are run by a variety of organisations in the private, public and voluntary sectors. There are also venues such as the international race course, which hosts international sporting fixtures (horse racing and polo) and cultural events, and outdoor spaces such as the Grosvenor Park and the Roman Amphitheatre.

Box 1: Examples of events taking place in Chester, 2012

Easter 2012: Chester Food, Drink & Lifestyle Festival 2012: A three-day event of chef demonstrations, kids' workshops, CamperFest and over 120 exhibitors.

May 2012: Embrace the Games: A series of events to mark the Olympic torch visiting Chester.

2nd June to 15th July 2012: MBNA Chestival: A range of free arts events and ticketed events taking place around the city.

July to August 2012: Grosvenor Park Open Air Theatre: Outdoor theatre in the Chester Grosvenor Park.

May to September 2012: Chester Races: Horse racing throughout the summer, starting with the May Festival and culminating with the Chester Finale in September.

15th to 28th October: Essar Oil Chester Literature Festival: An annual literature event comprising author events and a children's literature festival.

2013: Chester Mystery Plays: Chester's famous medieval plays, which are held every five years. 'Chester Mystery Plays in Miniature' occur as part of Chestival 2012.

Background to the MBNA Chester Marathon

The MBNA Chester Marathon first took place in May 2010. The route for the Marathon was out of town, and all registration and facilities for runners were based at the Chester Rugby Club. Following a successful inaugural event, some changes to the route were put into place to tie it more firmly to Chester as the host city. As a result, in 2011 the Marathon moved to a city-centre start and finish from its out-of-town route in 2010. The timing of the event also moved from May to a new date in October. The event was set up by Active Leisure Events, a company founded by two friends, both dedicated runners and triathletes, who felt that Chester's failure to host a marathon needed to be rectified. The inaugural event attracted entries of 1,000 runners and this increased to 4,000 entries in 2011. The 2012 event was capped at 5,000 and used the same course as in 2011, starting and finishing at the city centre location of the Chester Racecourse. The MBNA Chester Marathon is promoted as a 'destination marathon' and an ambition of the event organisers is for the marathon to become 'the UK's favourite regional marathon'.

The 2011 MBNA Chester Marathon

On 7th October 2011, the second MBNA Chester Marathon took place. The runners gathered at the Chester Racecourse for the start of the race (see Figure 1). Spectators were able to join the runners and use the grandstand for a good view of the start of the race (see Figure 2). Runners then ran through the city centre, running through the Roman Walls four times and then passing by all the city's iconic landmarks: the Town Hall (see Figure 3), the Cathedral (see Figure 4), the Eastgate Clock (see Figure 5), the 'Rows' shopping area and the Roman Amphitheatre. The route then went into the country-side outside Chester, passing through local villages (Eccleston, Pulford, Rossett, Holt, Farndon Churton, Aldford and Huntington) and coincidentally crossing and re-crossing the border of England and Wales (see Figure 6). The route then returned to the city via the suburb of Boughton and on re-entering the city runners ran alongside the river at the Groves, for the runners to finish at the racecourse (see Figure 7). Food and water stations were provided at regular intervals and volunteer marshals were positioned along the route to ensure safe passage of the runners and to support them by name (runners' first names were printed on the race numbers). Some volunteers came forward independently but others were from community groups (the Lady Taverners), youth groups (the 610 Squadron Air Training Corps, an Explorers Scout Group and the Cheshire Army Cadets), sports groups (Chester Tri Club and Juniors, Renegades West Cheshire Athletics Club, Buckley and

Tattenhall running clubs, and Chester Nomads Football Club), sponsoring organisations (MBNA, Grosvenor Garden Centre, BAM Nuttall, Alan Morris Transport and HSBC) and local charities (Hospice of the Good Shepherd and Claire House).

Figure 1: Chester Racecourse: the start and finish of the MBNA Chester Marathon. Photo credit: J. Beavan

Figure 2: The start of the 2011 MBNA Chester Marathon. Photo credit: R. Groome

Figure 3: Chester Town Hall. Photo credit: S. Gregory

Figure 4: Runners alongside the Chester Cathedral. Photo credit: S. Gregory

Figure 5: Runners passing under the iconic Eastgate Clock, Chester. Photo credit: J. Beavan

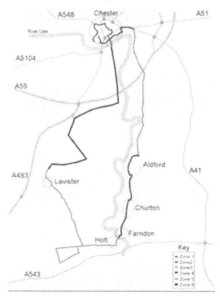

Figure 6: The Chester Marathon route. Map credit: Active Leisure Events

Figure 7: The winner crossing the finish line at the Chester Racecourse. Photo credit: R. Groome

On the day there were also other activities and support services, for both spectators and runners, including:

1   **A mini-marathon** – this raised funds for and was organised by the Hospice of the Good Shepherd. The one-mile run started at 10.00am, after the Marathon had started, and was conducted wholly within the racecourse, finishing in front of the County Stand. Registration was available online prior to the event and on the day at the Mini-Marathon Registration Point and in the Children's Zone. Places were limited but the event was open to all.

2   **Children's activities** – a children's activity centre was located at the Hospice of the Good Shepherd Children's Zone.

3   **Massage** – post-race massage, physiotherapy and podiatry advice was provided for a £5 donation. The money so raised was split between the main race charities.

4   **Meeting up with friends and family** – a special area to meet up with friends and family was designated.

5   **Race charity stall** – a number of the official race charities had awareness stands situated in the Athlete's Village.

Special provision was also made for the elite athletes, as the organisers wished to encourage and cater for the needs of elite athletes in order to make the MBNA Chester Marathon a competitive event and one that continued to attract runners of the highest possible calibre. To this end the organisers consulted widely and offered the following additional facilities to elite athletes: preferential start, elite athletes' drinks, massage facilities, and a hospitality box.

Sports events tourists at the 2011 MBNA Chester Marathon

Following the 2011 MBNA Chester Marathon, a survey was mailed out to the runners seeking to gain information on their demographic profile, their spending and their opinions on the event. Of the 2,414 runners, 1,054 completed and returned questionnaires; of these, 49.3% made an overnight stay. Overall, a high proportion of runners (91%) did not live in Chester and, significantly, participating in the MBNA Chester Marathon was the only reason why 79% of runners were visiting Chester on that day. The importance of Chester as the event destination was confirmed by the majority of runners, in that 57.1% of runners stated that their reason for participating in the marathon was that Chester was the host city: an increase of 4.4% from the previous year. Of respondents, 99.1% (n=1003) reported they would visit Chester again. A high proportion of respondents intend to run in the next MBNA Chester Marathon (67.2%) and almost all said that they would recommend the MBNA Chester Marathon to others (98.9%).

For 49.3% of runners, their visit involved an overnight stay and the dominant category of accommodation (60.8%) was hotels. With regard to the type of accommodation, serviced accommodation (hotels and B&Bs/guesthouses) was most popular, with non-serviced accommodation (i.e. caravan/camping and self-catering) accounting for a small proportion (see Table 1). Interestingly, a comparatively small proportion of runners did not pay for accommodation and stayed with friends and family (18.9%, n=92).

Table 1: Type of accommodation favoured by runners (n=487)

Accommodation type	Percent	Serviced/non-serviced	Response count
Hotel	60.8%	Serviced	296
With friends/family	18.9%	Non-serviced	92
B&B/guesthouse	15.4%	Serviced	75
Caravan/camping	2.3%	Non-serviced	11
Self-catering	2.7%	Non-serviced	13

Of those who stayed overnight (n=487), the majority stayed either for one night (58.6%) or two nights (28.6%). Only exceptionally did people stay longer, with 11.1% of those questioned staying for three nights and 1.2% staying for seven. For those staying overnight, the majority stayed in the City of Chester (77.5%), with Cheshire in second place at 10% (see Figure 8). Anecdotal evidence suggests that the organisers noticed that the city-centre accommodation was fully booked at the time of the 2011 event and are currently 'promoting' this on their 2012 MBNA Chester Marathon website.

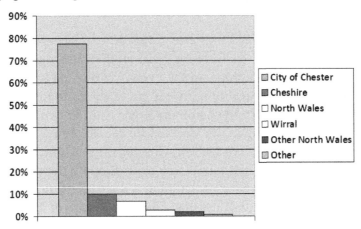

Figure 8: Places where runners stayed overnight

In the main, the active sports tourists travelled with other people: only 55 travelled on their own and 391 travelled with one or more adults. Participants typically travelled with one adult (n=206), while interestingly there were some larger groups travelling together of six adults and over (see Table 2). Of these 391 active sports tourists, 119 (30%) were travelling in family groups and had at least one child with them.

Table 2: People in the 'party'

Adults in party	Count	Children in party	Count
On own	55	1 child	44
With 1 adult	206	2 children	58
With 2 adults	84	3 children	11
With 3 adults	51	4 children	4
With 4 adults	26	5 children	0
With 5 adults	5	6 children	2
With 6 adults	19		

Table 3 indicates the various categories of expenditure by the runners. The greatest spending was on accommodation and on food and drink, with travel to Chester and shopping each also accounting for an important share of total spending. The total spending for the runners included in the survey was £129,891, which accounted for 84% of the total expenditure of all runners recorded in the overall questionnaire survey.

Table 3: Expenditure by category of the 2011 MBNA Chester Marathon runners

Expenditure item:	Spend (£)
Accommodation	46,281
Food and Drink	32,334
Travel to Chester	22,314
Shopping	16,841
Running gear	3,849
Entertainment	2,008
Car parking	1,480
Souvenirs	1,364
Visitor attractions	1,220
Transport around Chester	1,128
Other purchases	1,072
TOTAL	129,891

Charity fundraising was also determined from the questionnaire survey. A total of 109 respondents were raising money for charity. Of these, 106 declared sponsorship totalling £86,842, and of these, 105 named 68 charities of which the following were named more than twice: Cancer Research (n=10), Macmillan Cancer Support (n=6), Alzheimer's Society (n=6), Breast Cancer Campaign (n=4), Parkinson's (n=4), Click Sargent (n=3) and Guide Dogs for the Blind (n=3). This reflected the intent of the organisers, Active Leisure Events, to raise money for charities, both local and national, and to ensure that charities benefited from the event.

While the case study focuses upon the active sport tourists, the survey from which the contribution of the active sports tourists was extrapolated also captured information from tourists and locals. From this broader survey data, it is interesting to note the channels of communication for the event. The importance of a range of marketing activity is emphasised by the runners' identification of how they knew about the MBNA Chester Marathon (see Table 4). Of these channels of communication, the most important were: race listing in Runner's World (24.4%), recommendations (including race forums, 21.6%), the race website (19.9%) and advertisements in Runner's World (11.7%). The importance of the Runner's World is significant and the magazine was cited by over one third of respondents as the source from which the Chester Marathon was discovered. Other minor categories identified were: race flyers (3.6%), men's and women's Running Magazine advertisements (2.6%), exhibition stands (2.5%), know the organisers (1.8%), local press feature (1.6%), other event listings (1.4%), bill-board advertising (0.7%) and other press feature (0.6%).

Table 4: Ranking of how runners found about MBNA Chester Marathon (n=1036)

	Response Percent	Response Count
Runner's World race listing	24.4	253
Recommendation (including race forums)	21.6	224
Race web site	19.9	206
Other	14.2	147
Runner's World advertisements	11.7	121
Through my running club	9.7	100
Other race listings	8.3	86
Ran last year	5.5	57

From this broader survey data, it was also noted that the MBNA Chester Marathon continues to contribute significantly to the City of Chester economy. The year-on-year increase in spending that has been noted in successive surveys could be attributable to the increasing number of runners, its ability to attract a strong regional field of runners, the increased number of runners staying overnight, and its route having moved to a city-centre start and finish. As a best estimate, the economic spend of all the runners was £512,081, with accommodation and food and drink being dominant categories, but this does not necessarily include the expenditure of their supporters who accompanied them. Of the runners, 75.9% identified supporters who watched the event and this spend was not captured by the survey instrument. The economic value of the event can also take into account the money generated for charity, which totalled an estimated £453,518. The questionnaire captured the runners' contribution to the Chester economy, but it needs to be noted that it is not a full and comprehensive indication of economic benefit of the event as it excludes other interested stakeholders such as local businesses and Active Leisure Events themselves.

Who are sports tourists?

In understanding this case study, it is necessary to appreciate the definitional debates, particularly with regard to the broader concept of sports tourism.

Robinson and Gammon (2004) have commented upon the awkward marrying together of these two separate disciplines. Nevertheless, one of the first categorisations was provided by Gibson (1998: 45), who divides the phenomenon into three domains: "active sport tourism, which refers to people who travel to take part in sport; event sport tourism, which refers to travel to watch a sports event; and nostalgia sport tourism, which includes visits to sports museums, famous sports venues, and sports themed cruises". The separation of activity and non-activity is reinforced by Ritchie and Adair (2002), who summarise sports tourism as being travel to participate in passive or active sports holidays. Passive sports tourism refers to spectating and visiting sports museums, while active sports tourism refers to engaging in sports. Ritchie and Adair (2002) further qualify that either sport or tourism maybe the main motivator. To further corroborate this distinction, Sugden's (2007) study on the Cuban Marathon presents three categories of sports tourism: 'incidental sport tourism', where the sport experience is a casual, unplanned part of the holiday; 'residual sport tourism', where tourism is a by-product of the sport experience itself; and 'integral sport tourism', where central to the tourism experience is sports participation.

Further attention and clarification has been suggested by the development of sports tourism frameworks. Jackson and Weed's (2003) sports tourism demand continuum considers the type of participation, ranging from incidental to driven, and summarises the behavioural characteristics of these six types of participation. To understand the MBNA Chester Marathon runners in this context, it could be naively assumed that they are erring towards one end of the spectrum due to the high level of commitment required in order to participate. It could be assumed that the nature of the activity requires them to be categorised as regular or committed. Corresponding to Jackson and Weed (2003) assumptions, the Chester Marathon sport tourists were predominantly taking short holidays or weekend breaks, while the demographic profile was dominated by those age groups among whom bringing along children was uncommon practice. The survey results also confirm the importance of spectator tourism, in the form of people travelling to watch a family member or a friend compete in an event: only 12% of respondents travelled on their own to participate in the event.

Another framework for consideration is by Gammon and Robinson (2004), which focuses on whether sport or tourism is the primary motivation for the sports tourism experience. 'Sports tourism' is identified as involving those for whom sport is the prime motivation for travel, while 'tourism-sport' involves those for whom sport is a secondary activity. In this framework, the initial divide is by motivation rather than by level and type of engagement in sport, with both active and passive participation embedded in the respective categories. The MBNA Chester Marathon offers the opportunity for sports tourism and according to Gammon and Robinson's (2004) framework it would be of the 'hard' rather than 'soft' category. This is because the runners are actively participating in a competitive sporting event. The role of motivation is further identified by Kotze (2006), who contends that both extrinsic and intrinsic motivations influence the decision to engage in sports tourism. Intrinsic reasons relate to one's emotions, a need to escape and a desire for involvement. Extrinsic motivations, meanwhile, relate to rewards, recognition and prestige. Specifically, the motivations aligned to sports tourism are said to be physical motivators, cultural motivators, interpersonal motivators, and status and prestige motivations (Kotze, 2006).

Definitions have also evolved from the type of product being engaged in, as well as the motivation for participating in sports tourism. There is a growing market and interest in sports and tourism, and this is reflected in the industry offering. Specialist sports tourism operators offer various packages to facilitate competitive sports participation (such as marathon and triathlon packages), sports participation (such as training camps, skiing and cycling tours) and event spectating. With regard to the product and demand for event participation and active sports tourism, Kurtzman (1995) identifies the reasons for the increasing interest by the industry and growth in the market as being:

♦ The increasing popularity of international and national sporting events.

♦ The wider understanding and acceptance of the health benefits of sports participation.

♦ The role and value of sport to the economy and international relations being acknowledged and appreciated by governments.

♦ A wide and sophisticated programme of sporting events having evolved internationally, across the year, thereby offering year-round opportunities for sports spectators and participants to engage.

♦ The increasing mobility of sport-minded people, aided by improvements in communications technology.

Kurtzman (2000) later refers to six main sports tourism product categories: sports tourism attractions, sports tourism resorts, sports tourism cruises, sports tourism tours, sports events tourism and sport adventure tourism. A product focus is further emphasised in Pitts' (1999) two categories of sports tourism: sports participation travel and sports 'spectatorial' travel. In the context of the MBNA Chester Marathon case study, the focus is on the sports tourist and the sports tourist that participates in a particular sporting event. For this reason, the case study conforms to Pitts' (1999) category of sports participation travel, Kurtzman's (2000) sports events tourism, and Gibson's (1998) and Ritchie and Adair's (2002) active sports tourism/tourist.

Active sports events tourists

To consider the case study further, it is necessary also to place it in the context of the academic literature on active sports event tourists. According to Getz (2003), there is no conformity or agreement in defining sports event tourism. This variability is attributable to whether sports events tourism is considered from the differing perspectives of the destination, the organisers or the consumer. To illustrate this, Getz (2003: 50) contends that for consumers "it is travel for the purpose of participating in, or viewing, a sport event", while for the event organisers "tourists might be one of several target markets to attract". With regard to sports events and active sports tourists as event participants, Kurtzmann and Zauhar (2005: 44) state two requirements of sports events for them to be considered touristic in nature, those being either/or:

"A. Tourists travelling distances to see present and past star athletes or winner teams;

B. Tourists attending or participating in sports activities formally planned or informally organised".

The MBNA Chester Marathon runners, who are the focus of this case study, can be regarded as conforming to Getz's (2003) view, as they travel to participate in an event, and the second of Kurtzman and Zauhar's (2005) categories.

Getz and McConnell (2011) remark on the increasing popularity of sports tourism and events. Studies further examining this context of sports event tourism have focused on the spectator (e.g. Gibson, Willming and Holdnak, 2003; Gibson, 2005) and more recently on participants (e.g. Shipway and Jones, 2007; Miller 2012). While there has been a greater attention given to spectators in academic studies, this imbalance is being addressed. Weed (2006) acknowledges the need to understand experiences rather than just describing them. Kaplanidou and Gibson (2010: 164) also accept the increasing popularity of events for active sports tourists and suggest that "the use of the term active event sport tourists to describe participatory sports-related travel associated with event participation". This definition would indeed seem to suit the runners in the MBNA Chester Marathon, who were staying overnight in order to take part in the event.

Active sports event tourists and destinations

While considering the sports tourism and sports events tourism product, the destination itself is of importance. Indeed, "sport tourism is about an experience of physical activity tied to an experience of place" (Standeven and De Knop, 1999: 58). Hinch and Higham (2001) contend that sports tourism has three dimensions – activity, space and time – of which Weed and Bull (2004) further suggest that the interaction of people, activity and place is related to motives of sports tourists. The consensus appears to be that the integral components of the active sports tourism experience indicate the importance of place, i.e. the destination. In relation to the destination, the value of smaller-scale events is particularly noted. According to Higham (1999), not only can these small events use existing infrastructure but they also require smaller investment of funds, can potentially minimise tourism seasonality and can be more manageable than larger events. In the context of Chester and the destination marketing organisation framework for the visitor economy, events per se are seen as having this importance and potential.

In understanding the value of sports events to destinations and the tourism economy, it is accepted that sports events can be important contributors to the economic development of cities and regions. According to Hall (1992), there is a range of techniques for calculating the expenditure effects of events. These include surveying participants, sponsors and visitors; gaining information from recipients of expenditure such as shops, accommodation providers and petrol stations; and collecting statistics on attendance and participation. The present case study focuses solely on the expenditure of participants. Gratton, Shibli and Coleman (2006) note the need to look beyond economic benefits and present a 'balanced scoreboard' approach to evaluating events, acknowledging the need to consider the event's aims, economic impacts, sports development, place marketing effects, media and sponsor evaluation. Further attention is given to place marketing by Chalip and McGuirty (2004), who emphasise the need to maximise opportunities for bundling together destination attractions and to use the sports event as leverage for marketing. While academic literature has tended to focus upon large spectator events, such as 'hallmark' or 'mega-events', and event sports tourism, Kotze (2006) shows how this has been at the expense of small-scale sports events. The accrued economic benefits from the active sports tourists at MBNA Chester Marathon further confirms the value of such small-scale sports events both to the visitor economy and to destination marketers, and emphasises the importance of not overlooking them.

Studies have shown the effect of event participation on return visits to the event and/or the destination (Kaplanidou and Vogt, 2007; Miller, 2012).

Kaplanidoiu and Vogt (2010) identify how a good event experience can lead to a greater likelihood of future return visits to the event destination. Miller (2012), meanwhile, identified how the return to the destination could be connected to competing again in the event or using the area as a training destination. For the purpose of MBNA Chester Marathon, as 2011 was only in its second year of running, it is too early to see evidence of this loyalty and destination relationship developing. The active sports tourists in the survey did nevertheless express a strong intent to revisit the destination (99.1%) and to run in the next MBNA Chester Marathon (67.2%). Kaplanidou and Gibson (2010) further identify the importance of event satisfaction and the linkages to return participation in the event or similar events organised by that community. The need for the basic requirements of a successful event is magnified by the effort and expectation of these travelling participants as they look for exceptional facilities and outstanding event management. "Signage, competent officiating, punctuality in starting events on time, and an overall sense of efficiency are what participants expect, particularly those who are active event sport tourists" (Kaplanidou and Gibson, 2010: 175). Kaplanidou and Gibson's (2010) study further reinforces the importance of destination image to both event organisers and tourism agencies, and so the need for working together to fulfil the sport tourists' needs and for the host community to maximise the benefits. Images and iconic landmarks of a city and engagement with the destination are indicative of how an event can be used to create and enhance destination image.

Destination marathons

Running is considered to be one of the top ten participation sports and is one of the fastest-growing activities alongside cycling, canoeing and tennis (Mintel, 2009). Parallel to the popularity of taking part in running is the increasing number of people participating in marathons and even combining this interest with tourism. Sugden (2007: 235) notes the preponderance of marathon running, "with more than 130 officially sanctioned events [marathon running] has developed to become a key feature of the international sport tourism calendar". Attention has been given to marathons within the active sports tourism academic literature and from perspectives focusing on the destination marketing potential of marathons (Chalip and McGuirty, 2004; Getz and McConnell, 2011), marathon runners' behaviour and motivations (Funk and Brunn, 2007; Shipway and Jones, 2007; Sugden, 2007; Hallmann and Wicker, 2012), and the economic value of marathons (Agrusa, Tanner and Lema, 2006; Agrusa, Lema, Kim and Botto, 2009; Lapeyronie, 2009).

The co-branding potential of marathons and bundling of activities is examined by Chalip and McGuirty (2004), wherein events are considered as opportunities to combine running with a holiday at the host destination. In the context of MBNA Chester Marathon, this is starting to develop, as evidenced by the range of activities taking place at the main site of the Chester Racecourse for both runners and spectators. The potential items for bundling can be linked to event elements and destination elements (Chalip and McGuirty, 2004). An example of an event that has extended activities over its lifetime is Baltimore Running Festival (see Box 2), where extra events have been developed on the back of a successful running event. Studies such as McGehee, Yoon and Cardenas (2003) focus on recreational runners' involvement in travel to road races and travel behaviour characteristics, and a focus on travel behaviour in their study led Hallman and Wicker (2012) to propose three different profiles of marathon runners: holidayers, socialisers and marathoners. The profiles proposed by Hallmann and Wicker (2012) evolved from an extensive survey of marathon runners at three German marathons, and focused upon their behaviour and consumption patterns (travel means, length of stay and spending behaviour).

A particular focus within academic literature, as well as popular publications such as magazines and newspapers, is that of economic benefits. Academic studies have highlighted the substantial potential of international marathons in this respect. Kotze (2006) highlights the value of the Comrades Marathon in South Africa, which was estimated as generating R20 million from tourists. Agrusa et al.'s (2009) detailed study of the 2007 Honolulu Marathon, the third largest marathon in the USA and sixth largest in the world, identified how over 72% of participants were from outside the state of Hawaii. The study concludes that the marathon generated an economic impact of US$108,890,000 and, in turn, US$3.7 million in state taxes. The direct linking of a marathon event to tourism activity is encapsulated by Damien O'Looney, the Edinburgh Marathon Marketing Director who said how "the marathon draws thousands of people to Edinburgh who would not otherwise come to the capital. Many of these runners come with friends and family and stay in the city for several days. This year there are over 1,500 runners coming from outside the UK from over 40 different countries across the world including the US and Germany and from as far afield as South Africa, Mexico, Ukraine to China and New Zealand. Last year's event benefited the economy by over £5 million and over 200 Scotland and UK charities benefited by an overwhelming £3 million (taking the total amount of money raised since the start in 2003 to over £10 million)" (Anon, 2010: n.p.).

Box 2: Smaller scale marathons in the USA: Facts and figures

Baltimore Running Festival (Dance, 2009):

Started: 2001

Runners (2009): 20,364

Visitors (2009): 57,000

National and international participants: 40% of the runners came from outside Maryland, from all 49 other states and 44 countries

Estimated US$25 million in economic impact for the city of which:

- US$5.4 million was spent on both restaurants and hotels
- US$3.8 million was spent on retail
- US$4.4 million was spent on transportation
- US$6.3 million was spent on entertainment
- US$830,000 charity donations

Rock 'n' Roll Seattle Marathon and Half Marathon (Lamppa, 2009):

Started: 2001

Runners (2009): 25,000 registered

Visitors: 16,353

National and international participants: 12,076 participants from out of town, representing 50 states and 27 countries

Estimated economic impact of US$30.8 million for the city of which:

- 12,223 hotel room nights
- More than US$1.8 million in new tax revenue and other tourism-related fees collected
- Visiting runners brought over US$18.9 million in direct spending from outside the region, including expenditures on food, travel, lodging and entertainment
- Average length of stay was 3.4 hotel room nights
- The Port of Seattle collected US$47,068 in Passenger Facility Charge fees

Of note is the significant impact of the top five major marathons: London, New York City, Boston, Berlin and Chicago. The ING New York City Marathon was first established in 1970, when it saw 127 runners paying the $1 entry fee to participate in a 26.2-mile race that looped several times within Central Park. The race now brings in an estimated US$220 million in economic impact to the city and is regarded as the highest-grossing single-day sporting event in New York. In 2008, the marathon's estimated impact was US$205 million and it had more than 37,000 runners, 2.5 million spectators and a worldwide television audience of more than 300 million in 2006 (Anon, 2007). Significantly in terms of sports tourism, 88% of the runners were from outside New York City and nearly 50% came from outside the United States. Of the runners who come from overseas, their stay in the city is for an average of six days. Overall in 2008, the marathon participants and spectators spent US$71 million on hotels, US$45 million on food and beverages, US$42 million on retail merchandise, over US$16 million on entertainment, US$14 million on transportation, and US$11 million on running and fitness gear at the ING New York City Marathon Health and Fitness Expo (Anon, 2007). A recent study undertaken by Sheffield Hallam University highlights the tremendous economic impact of the London Marathon. The London Marathon was estimated to generate over £100 million of UK economic activity each year. London accommodation and catering sectors were among the main beneficiaries, having received £13.2 million in 2011. The runners and spectators were responsible for 83% of economic impact on London and other beneficiaries were noted as charities (£50 million was raised in 2010). Other benefits attributable to the marathon related to the spending of overseas visitors and television rights-holders (£3.85 million). The economic benefits of such events are not generated solely by major marathons and are also experienced by smaller-scale events (see Box 2). The benefits of a small-scale event can equally be highlighted with the MBNA Chester Marathon as presented in Table 3.

Conclusion

In keeping with academic studies, the significance of the MBNA Chester Marathon must be considered broader than simply the economic expenditure generated. While acknowledging the economic benefits of the active sports tourists participating in the event (detailed in Table 3), there are also wider issues that need to be considered. The importance of Chester as the event destination was clearly supported by the survey respondents. The strength of intention to compete in the following year's marathon and to return to Chester shows both event and destination loyalty beginning to form. As Getz and McConnell (2011: 335) contend that active sports tourists can be seen as "primary targets for destinations seeking competitive advantages through event tourism". The MBNA Chester Marathon clearly provides such an opportunity.

In some cases, the lucrative nature of events for tourism is evident through the setting up of destination organisations, as is the case of Durban Events Corporation, which was specifically set up sport events opportunities in Durban (Turco, Swart, Bob and Moodley, 2003), and this might be an opportunity for Chester and the area. Equally, the opportunity to bundle events with the marathon to extend the offering is possible as part of a consideration of the overall annual event portfolio for the city of Chester. The role of the marathon in generating a fitting and appropriate image for the city is also worthy of further consideration.

References

Agrusa J, Lema JD, Kim SS, Botto T. 2009. The impact of consumer behaviour and service perceptions of a major sport tourism event. *Asia Pacific Journal of Tourism Research* **14** (3): 267-277.

Agrusa J, Tanner J, Lema D. 2006. Japanese runners in the Honolulu Marathon and their economic benefits to Hawaii. *Tourism Review International* **9** (3): 261-270.

Anon. 2007. ING New York City Marathon economic impact grows to $220 million. http://www.coolrunning.com/engine/3/3_2/ing-new-york-city-maratho-5.shtml

Anon. 2010. The impact of Edinburgh Marathon. http://www.edinburgh-marathon.com/?news12

Chalip L, McGuirty J. 2004. Bundling sport events with the host destination. *Journal of Sport Tourism* **9** (3): 267-282.

Cheshire West and Chester. 2009. *Topic Paper - Image, Identity and Tourism*. http://consult.cheshirewestandchester.gov.uk/portal/cwc_ldf/cwc_cs/cs_io/tp_iit_io?pointId=801032

Dance S. 2009. Baltimore Running Festival generated $25million in economic impact. Baltimore Business Journal. http://baltimore.bizjournals.com/baltimore/stories/2009/11/23/daily22.html?t=printable

Funk DC, Brunn TJ. 2007. The role of socio-psychological and culture-education motives in marketing international sport tourism: A cross-cultural perspective. *Tourism Management* **28** (3): 806-819.

Gammon S, Robinson T. 2003. Sport and tourism: A conceptual framework. *Journal of Sport Tourism* **8** (1): 21-26.

Getz D. 2003. Sport event tourism: Planning, development, and marketing. In Hudson S. (ed.) *Sport and Adventure Tourism*. Birmingham: Haworth Press; 49-88.

Getz D, McConnell A. 2011. Serious sport tourism and event travel careers. *Journal of Sport Management* **25** (4): 326-338.

Gibson, HJ. 1998. Sport tourism: A critical analysis of research. *Sport Management Review* **1** (1): 45-76.

Gibson, HJ. 2005. Towards an understanding of 'why sport tourists do what they do'. *Sport in Society* **8** (2): 198-217.

Gibson HJ, Willming C, Holdnak A. 2003. Small-scale event sport tourism: Fans as tourists. *Tourism Management* **24** (2): 181-190.

Gratton C, Shibli S, Coleman R. 2006. The economic impact of major sports events: A review of ten events in the UK. *The Sociological Review* **54** (2): 41-58.

Hall CM. 1992. *Hallmark Tourism Events: Impacts, Management and Planning*. London: Belhaven Press.

Hallmann K, Wicker P. 2012. Consumer profiles of runners at marathon races. *International Journal of Event and Festival Management* **3** (2): 4-27.

Higham J. 1999. Commentary: Sport as an avenue of tourism development: an analysis of the positive and negative impacts of sport tourism. *Current Issues in Tourism* **2** (1): 82-90.

Higham J, Hinch T. 1999. The development of Super 12 and its implications for tourism. Industry report. http://otago.ourarchive.ac.nz/bitstream/handle/10523/1466/RugbySuper12.pdf?sequence=3

Higham J, Hinch T. 2002. Tourism, sport and season: The challenges and potential of overcoming seasonality in the sport and tourism sectors. *Tourism Management* **23** (2): 175-185.

Hinch TD, Higham JES. 2001 Sport tourism: A framework for research. *International Journal of Tourism Research* **3** (1): 45-58.

Jackson G, Weed M. 2003. The sport-tourism interrelationship. In Houlihan B. (ed.) *Sport in Society*. London: Sage; 235-251.

Kaplanidou K, Gibson H. 2010. Predicting behavioural intentions of active sport event tourists: The case of a small-scale recurring sports event. *Journal of Sport and Tourism* **15** (2): 163-179.

Kaplanidou K, Vogt C. 2007. The interrelationship between sport event and destination image and sport tourists' behaviours. *Journal of Sport and Tourism* **12** (3-4): 183-206.

Kaplanidou K, Vogt C. 2010. The meaning and measurement of a sport event experience among active sport tourists. *Journal of Sport Management* **24** (5): 544-566.

Kotze N. 2006. Cape Town and the Two Oceans Marathon: The impact of sport tourism. *Urban Forum* **17** (3): 282-293.

Kurtzman J. 1995. Sport tourism categories revisited. *Journal of Sport Tourism* **2** (3): 6-11.

Kurtzman J. 2000. Economic impact: sport tourism and the city. *Journal of Sport Tourism* **10** (1): 47-71.

Kurtzman J, Zauhar J. 2005. Sports tourism consumer motivation. *Journal of Sport Tourism* **10** (1): 21-31.

Lamppa R. 2009. Inaugural Rock n' Roll Seattle exceeds economic impact projections. www.coolrunning.com/engine/3/3_7/inaugural-rock-n-roll-sea.shtml.

Lapeyronie B. 2009. Socio-economic consequences of sporting tourism: Examples of marathons in France. *Teores, Revue de Recherche en Tourisme* **28** (2): 37-44.

McGehee NG, Yoon Y, Cardenas D. 2003. Involvement and travel for recreational runners in North Carolina. *Journal of Sport Management* **17** (3): 305-324.

Miller A. 2012. Understanding the 'event' experience' of active sports tourists: Long distance endurance triathletes. In Shipway R, Fyall A. (eds) *International Sports Events*. London: Routledge; 99-112.

Mintel. 2009. Top ten participation sports in the UK. Mintel International Group.

Pitts B. 1999. Sports tourism and niche markets: Identification and analysis of the growing lesbian and gay sports tourism industry. *Journal of Vacation Marketing* **5** (1): 31-50.

Ritchie B, Adair D. 2002. The growing recognition of sport tourism. *Current Issues in Tourism* **5** (1): 1-6.

Robinson T, Gammon S. 2004. A question of primary and secondary motives: Revisiting and applying the sport tourism framework. *Journal of Sport Tourism* **9** (3): 221-233.

Shipway R, Jones I. 2007. Running away from home: Understanding visitor experiences and behaviour at sport tourism events. *International Journal of Tourism Research* **9** (5): 373-383.

Standeven J, de Knop P. 1999. *Sport Tourism*. Leeds: Human Kinetics.

Sugden J. 2007. Running Havana: Observations on the political economy of sport tourism in Cuba. *Leisure Studies* **26** (2): 235-251.

Turco DM, Swart K, Bob U, Moodley V. 2003. Socio-economic impacts of sport tourism in the Durban Unicity, South Africa. *Journal of Sport and Tourism* **8** (4): 223-239.

Visit Chester and Cheshire. 2010. 2020 Time to Meet the Challenge. http://www.whycheshire.com/dbimgs/VEF_001.pdf

Ancillary Student Material

Further reading

Agrusa J, Kim SS, Lema JD. 2011. Comparison of Japanese and North American runners of the Ideal Marathon competition destination. *Asia Pacific Journal of Tourism Research* **16** (2): 183-207.

Bull CJ. 2006. Racing cyclists as sports tourists: The experiences and behaviours of a case study group of cyclists in East Kent, England. *Journal of Sport and Tourism* **11** (3): 259-274.

Getz D. 2008. Event tourism: Definition evolution and research. *Tourism Management* **29** (3): 403-428.

Gibson HJ. 1998. Active sport tourism: Who participates? *Leisure Studies* **17** (2): 155-170.

Morgan M. 2007. 'We're not the Barmy Army!' Reflections on the sports tourist experiences. *International Journal of Tourism Research* **9** (5): 361-372.

Shipway R, Jones I. 2008. The great surburban Everest: An insiders' perspective on experiences at the 2007 Flora London Marathon. *Journal of Sport and Tourism* **13** (1): 61-77.

Weed M. and Bull C. 2004. *Sport Tourism: Participants, Policy and Providers*. Oxford: Butterworth Heinemann.

Related websites and audio-visual materials

MBNA Chester Marathon: http://www.activeleisureevents.co.uk/

Welcome to Chester and Cheshire: http://www.visitchester.com/

MBNA Chester Marathon 2011 short clip: http://www.youtube.com/watch?v=_PFafDQZIgc

Tony Audenshaw completes the MBNA Chester Marathon 2011: http://www.youtube.com/watch?v=iz9Hs3vItXw

Visit Chester: http://www.youtube.com/watch?v=jX50GBj6UtA&feature=related

Self-test questions

Try to answer the following questions in order to test your knowledge and understanding of the case. If you are not sure of the answers please re-read the case and refer to the references and further reading sources.

1   What is sports tourism?

2   What are active sports tourists?

3   Identify the importance and value of the sports tourism market to destinations.

4   How did MBNA Chester Marathon benefit the city of Chester?

Key themes

The key themes raised in this case study relate to the following:

Sports tourism

♦   Understanding the definitions of sports tourism

♦   The market for sports tourism

♦   The demand for sports tourism holidays

♦   Case studies of specialist sports tourism operators

Sports tourism and destinations

♦   The usefulness of sports tourism to destinations.

♦   The benefits of sports tourism to destinations

♦   Case studies of destinations which are branded as sports tourism destinations

Sports events and destinations

♦   The use of sports events to attract tourists to destinations

♦   The range of sports events available at destinations

♦   The benefits of small scale sports events to a destination's visitor economy

♦   Case studies of small scale sporting events as tourism attractions

If you need to source further information on any of the above themes and theories, then these headings could be used as key words to search for materials and case studies.

 Scan here to get the hyperlinks for this chapter.

9

Sporting Identities in Youth

Examining Mountain Biking Lifestyles

Katherine King

Introduction

Young people participate in sport and leisure as an expression of their lifestyle, and the meanings they attach to such participation inform their personal identities. This case study will show how youth lifestyle and identity are shaped by participation in mountain biking. Consumer research suggests mountain biking is one of the most popular lifestyle sports among young people in the UK (Mintel, 2005). Moreover, previous research has recognised the presence of a mountain-biking 'community' based on shared lifestyles and identities, and that participants demonstrate a strong sense of identity with the activity (e.g. Ruff and Mellors, 1993; King, 2009). Despite this, mountain biking has received less attention in the literature than other lifestyle sports such as skateboarding or surfing. Moreover, research has tended to focus on adult participation, rather than on the identities and lifestyles of young people.

This case study explores the personal meanings attached to mountain biking by participants aged between 13 and 25 years old. It examines the ways in which young people express their own identities in relation to their participation in mountain biking, and consequently the role sport and leisure can play in processes of lifestyle identification and differentiation. To this end, the findings of the evaluation of a government health initiative in England are presented. The initiative aimed to increase young people's participation in sport and physical activity by promoting mountain biking at a forest location in the South East of England.

Mountain biking and the activity agenda

The government health agenda in the UK seeks to encourage active lifestyles and has identified young people as a target group whose participation in active forms of leisure is low but for whom regular exercise can help to prevent obesity, heart disease and other health problems associated with sedentary lifestyles. Government policy in England is therefore emphasising the importance of creating a wider 'culture' of sport and physical activity participation through schemes such as 'Sportivate', 'Active England' and other mass-participation projects inspired by the 2012 London Olympic and Paralympics Games. Of particular significance for young people are those activities collectively referred to as 'lifestyle sports'. Consumer research suggests that these sporting activities have the highest rates of participation among people under 25 years old (Mintel, 2005). The term 'lifestyle sports' refer to a range of land-, air- and water-based activities – such as snowboarding, mountain biking, bicycle motocross (BMX), skateboarding and surfing – which encompasses a wide variety of activities often termed 'adventurous', 'extreme' or 'alternative'. It is claimed that participation in these forms of sports provides an important mechanism through which young people can explore their identities. This is because participants seek sporting experiences that are distinctive and provide them with exclusive social identities (Wheaton, 2004).

Tomlinson, Ravenscroft, Wheaton and Gilchrist (2005: 34) have argued that the promotion of leisure activities that appeal to young people's identities and lifestyles may have a particularly important role to play in the new activity agenda, suggesting that:

> "... given the continuing decline in curriculum physical activity at school and the often limited availability of non-school sports activities, regular participation in lifestyle sports between the ages of 15 and 24 could be highly significant in terms of government targets".

In addition to their limited participation in sport and physical activity, recent government policy in England has also identified that young people's participation in countryside recreation activities is in significant decline. According to Natural England (2011), between 2010 and 2011 the number of visits to the countryside by people aged between 16 and 24 years fell by 17%. This is despite a long-running discourse which maintains that experiencing the natural environment in childhood and youth can be beneficial to people's cognitive and social development, as well as to their overall health and well-being (Bell, Ward Thompson and Travlou, 2003; Bingley and Milligan, 2007).

Policy initiatives have therefore focussed on promoting active forms of sport and leisure, as well as attempting to increase young people's engagement with the countryside. Research has shown that where young people do engage in countryside recreation, it is often in the form of high-adrenaline or adventurous outdoor activities that translate to wider lifestyle patterns, rather than traditional countryside activities (Henley Centre, 2005). Lifestyle sports such as mountain biking can make an important contribution to policy agendas that seek to re-engage young people with countryside spaces and emphasise the role of physical activity in promoting health. Mountain biking is a sport which is often performed in countryside spaces, usually woodlands and forests or upland areas, and is considered to achieve many positive benefits for those who participate, including socialisation and confidence-building, as well as further benefits for mental health, physical health and wellbeing (EKOS Ltd and Tourism Resource Company, 2007). This case study focuses on the Bedgebury Forest Active England Project, which embodies these principles by promoting the participation of young people in mountain biking.

Mountain biking at Bedgebury Forest

Partly in response to the growing health-related evidence and national government policies discussed above, the Active England programme was established in 2003 with Big Lottery and Sport England funding of £94.8 million (Sport England, 2009). The aim of the programme was to increase community participation in sport and physical activity in England. Funding was awarded to the Forestry Commission to develop several woodland sites, one of which was Bedgebury Forest in Kent.

Figure 1: Map of Bedgebury's location. Reproduced by kind permission of the Forestry Commission

Bedgebury Forest is located in a rural location, on the border between Kent and East Sussex, approximately 16 miles northwest of the town of Hastings and 12 miles southeast of Tunbridge Wells (see Figure 1). Alongside the forest is Bedgebury National Pinetum, which at over 300 hectares and containing 12,000 trees from 1,800 different species is considered a conservation site of national importance (Forestry Commission, 2012)

Bedgebury received £2.1 million in funding and was redeveloped from a working timber forest to a leisure destination, orientated towards encouraging active lifestyles. The 850 hectares of timber-producing forest was converted into a centre for developing active lifestyles for people of all ages and all abilities under the tagline 'adventure in a world of trees'. The project set out to achieve the following objectives (Forestry Commission, 2009):

◆   To enable greater access to Bedgebury for visitors of all ages and abilities, especially children and the disabled.

◆   To develop potential for lifelong learning through schools and educational outreach.

◆   To stimulate new interest in outdoor activities throughout the year by delivering high-quality facilities and services, delivered in partnership with businesses and community groups.

◆   To strengthen the local economy by attracting visitors, and offering related business opportunities such as a café and bike-hire centre.

◆   To make Bedgebury financially self-sustaining, safeguarding its long-term future.

The project was hailed as an important opportunity to create ways of encouraging new engagement with sport and physical activity in key under-represented groups, identified as women and girls, the 45 years and over age group, people on low incomes, black and minority ethnic groups, people with disabilities, and young people (O'Brien and Morris, 2009). For young people, the programme focussed on providing infrastructure for equestrian, orienteering and adventure play, as well as making a significant investment in mountain biking facilities. The site was officially opened in April 2006, with new facilities for mountain biking including the following (Figure 2):

◆   An all-ability, 10km family cycle track

◆   Cycle hire and cycle-washing facilities

◆   A challenging, 13km single-track route for cross-country mountain biking

◆   A professionally designed freeride area for downhill, dirt-jump and freeride mountain biking, featuring dirt-jumps and raised wooden

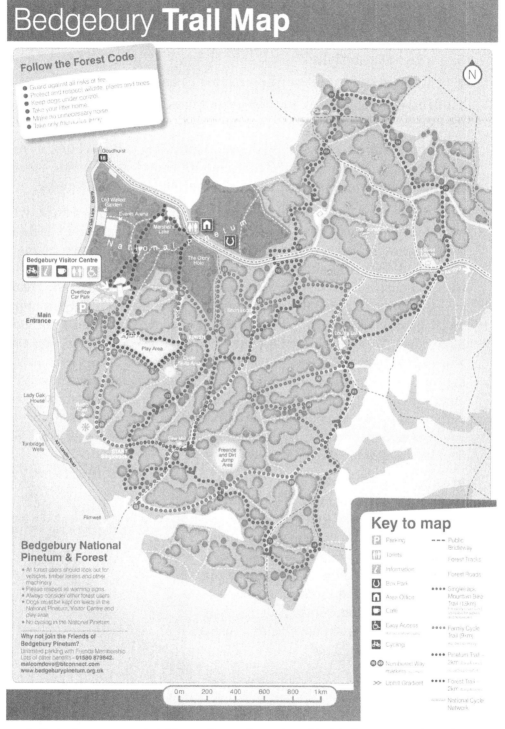

Figure 2: Bedgebury mountain biking trail map. Reproduced by kind permission from the Forestry Commission

North shore apparatus such as seesaws and narrow platforms for more experienced mountain bikers, with 'baby' North Shore equipment including lower balance beams for beginner riders to practice their skills[1].

♦   Cycle maintenance courses provided by an on-site cycle shop.

Youth coaching initiatives and mountain biking events in partnership with the local cycle club and British Cycling.

According to those participating in mountain biking at Bedgebury, there are two types of mountain biking: dirt-jump, downhill and freeride forms of mountain biking (collectively referred to as DDF); and cross-country.

DDF takes place largely in the freeride area of Bedgebury Forest, which provided some of the most challenging mountain-biking terrain, including steep narrow routes and dirt jumps. These forms of mountain biking are considered high risk, and all disciplines require specialist mountain bikes with full suspension. During weekends and school holidays, the freeride area is frequently populated by several different groups of DDF mountain bikers of varying ages and abilities, and is also used by a small number of BMX riders. The freeride area provides a social space for young people and, when not riding, young people participate in other activities such as sharing tips and techniques with other riders, discussing equipment, watching others or hanging around with friends. The freeride area is therefore largely dominated by young people and provides an informal leisure setting where young people are able to practice cycling skills away from other more heavily used areas of the forest.

In contrast, cross-country mountain biking involves cycling long distances following a designated cycle trail known as the 'single track' (see Figure 3). Participants are therefore less likely to congregate in one place. Cross-country mountain bikers adopt slightly different equipment to followers of the other disciplines, such as 'hardtail' mountain bikes which have front suspension but none at the rear.

Figure3: The single track. Photo credit: Forestry Commission, Bedgebury.

---

1   The wooden structures in the freeride area have since been ̶̶̶̶̶̶̶̶̶̶̶̶̶̶̶̶, ̶̶̶̶̶̶̶̶̶̶̶̶̶̶̶̶ their natural life.

Alternative sporting identities

Commentators have argued that lifestyle sports embody an alternative ethos to traditional sports (e.g. Beal and Weidman, 2003), and for mountain bikers these distinctions are especially clear. For participants at Bedgebury, mountain biking was considered more meaningful for personal identity than other mainstream forms of sport, which were sometimes described as exclusionary and over-competitive. Unlike many other sports that young people take part in, mountain biking is not generally organised or run by adults, and Bedgebury participants valued its casual approach to leisure, its onus on participant-made rules and the absence of 'adult' authority. In the same way, mountain biking lifestyles were considered by participants in the study to be self-regulated, free from external controls, and celebrated the freedom of 'just messing around'. As one participant noted:

> "I don't like mainstream sports, I don't like it. I find it ... God, this is one of those subjects I could talk for ages. Like, my brothers are in a hockey team, roller hockey, and they like try it all the time, they're always doing it, but there are people in the team that are better than them and they never get to play and it's just not my idea of fun,. Like, I can go out on my bike and ride when I want and, whatever, how I want" (Minty, 17 years old).

Attitudes towards competition are particularly significant in the expression of alternative sporting identities for mountain bikers. Observations at Bedgebury revealed that some forms of competition were integral to the performance of mountain biking. For example, young people would often race each other, set time records, engage in trick competitions or compete through their knowledge of equipment. Importantly, these competitions were informal, consensual and self-organised. Youth mountain bikers were often critical of those who became too competitive, or displayed 'jock-ism', and took part in what they termed 'friendly competition' without pressure from outsiders. According to one participant:

> "I've never been very good at team sports at school or anything. I'm not really into competitive stuff but it's (mountain biking) actually quite a really nice kind of competitive atmosphere" (Russell, 16 years old).

In addition to these perceived differences from mainstream sports in terms of attitudes towards competition, participants separated mountain biking from mainstream sports by framing mountain biking as an alternative cultural construct. For example, one participant stated:

"I like doing something that not everyone else does 'cause you're not mainstream then, are you?" (Boris, 16).

Some explored this identity in more subtle and implicit ways by playing down the importance of this alternative status:

"I don't do it just 'cos it's different, I do it 'cos I got hooked" (Damien, 18).

For youth mountain bikers, self-perceptions of being alternative or nonconformist change as riders increase in age or as participants become more involved in the lifestyle, taking a more subtle stance. Even so, participants' identities generally retain an oppositional element: for example toward mainstream youth sport or leisure practice, or toward adult forms of mountain biking practice.

Risky identities

Risk is considered to be an integral feature of many contemporary leisure experiences. It is sought particularly by those who seek adventure as part of their engagement with sport and leisure, who appropriate it into their lifestyle patterns. This is especially the case among young people (Mitchell, Bunton and Green, 2004). Young people chose to perform several different types of mountain biking at Bedgebury and risk played a role in shaping mountain bikers' individual identities in each of these practices.

For DDF forms of mountain biking, lifestyles were performed around thrill-seeking and risk-taking, and identities were construed as those of "adrenaline addicts". Dirt-jump mountain bikers travel at high speeds up to jumps to perform tricks in the air (see Figure 4); freeride mountain biking involves the negotiation of narrow wooden paths, seesaws and jumps high above the ground; while downhill participants follow tight paths on uneven terrain at intense speeds. Although participants indicated that they were aware of the dangers involved in these types of activities, most claimed that it "was worth the risk" and integral to their performance of the sport.

"I love that for the adrenalin rush, for going far too fast, and cutting that fine edge between you and falling off and hitting a tree very hard" (Pete, 22 years old).

"It's scary, it's brave it's A.R.D[2]" (Mike, 14 years old).

Youth mountain bikers present their experiences of risk-taking as playful and embodied. The following extract echoes the sentiments of Le Breton

---

2   A.R.D is a variation on the term "hard".

(2000), who has previously described the sudden rush of sensation that can overwhelm participants who participate in extreme sports:

> "… and the best feeling ever is when you're sitting at a huge jump you've never done before and your sitting at the run-in which goes down before you do the jump, and your heart's pounding and you suddenly just drop down and the minute you land it and you haven't crashed it is the best feeling in the world, like your hands are shaking" (Jumper Boy, 15 years old).

Figure 4: Dirt-jump mountain biking. Photo reproduced by kind permission of jab-ride.co.uk

It is claimed that younger mountain bikers show a higher preference for more risky cycling landscapes than adults (Symmonds, Hammitt and Quisenberry, 2000) and research at Bedgebury showed that attitudes towards risk were often employed to emphasise a 'non-adult' approach to mountain biking. Adults were considered to be more tentative in taking risks. However, for young people, as one participant remarked:

> "If you're not crashing, you're not pushing yourself" (Arnie, 16).

> "It's for teenagers. Teenagers who are looking for a bit of a thrill, who are young and fit, do freeride … you need very good reaction skills to be able to freeride, so you need a youthful body really" (Paul, 16).

Risk-taking behaviours were employed to demarcate participants from others and recollections of risk-related experiences were often drawn upon in exchanges between mountain bikers as part of the expression of individual identity. The appropriation of risk influenced the way in which youth mountain bikers chose their leisure spaces. Consequently, many young people chose to spend time in the freeride area, which offered the most risky terrain.

Space and identity: 'being outdoorsy'

Different views exist in the literature on the significance of nature for lifestyles oriented around adventurous activities. Some have argued that the relationship between nature as part of the place or context of a sport or leisure experience is of minor importance (e.g. Cater, 2007), while for others the presence of nature is often intrinsic to the authenticity of the experience: as in 'confronting the wild' (Becker, 2003; Waitt, 2008). The significance of being in the outdoors, particularly spaces in the countryside, emerged as integral to the construction of identity for young people participating in mountain biking at Bedgebury.

Ease of access to countryside spaces, particularly woodlands, was one of the most common ways in which young people became involved in mountain biking. For participants living in rural areas surrounding Bedgebury, mountain biking was an integral part of their 'rural' identity and represented a response to the lack of other leisure opportunities available to young people living in rural areas. Mountain biking offered a way of overcoming isolation and gave them what they termed a 'freedom', both as a form of transport and as a sport and leisure activity in its own right. Yet regardless of whether the young person lived in an urban or rural area, the countryside often featured in the construction of their identity as a mountain biker. As one participant argued:

> "I s'pose I'm a country bumpkin like that, just hang around out here with my mates ... it's just what we do" (Cheech, 16).

> "You won't find anyone more woodlandy than me" (Jimmy, 18 years old).

Woodlands, in particular, appealed to youth mountain bikers as landscapes which offered significant visual attraction while riding, with participants commenting on the importance of the presence of trees in that:

> "… it's better than being surrounded by bricks" (Hank, 25).

Some participants expressed a general distaste towards using urban spaces for sport and leisure, preferring the calm of the countryside:

> "I don't really find it that much fun just like hanging around in towns, I hate towns ... I like to be out there digging trails" (Nichols, 18).

Youth mountain bikers associated symbolic meaning with the countryside and being active in outdoor space. Participants described how mountain bikers embodied a particular identity that was linked with living an active and healthy lifestyle, and placed this with a particular outdoor ethic:

> "Being outdoors, I hate being indoors, it makes me ill-ish. Like, you know when you're inside in the winter, and sort of all day for a week you just sort of feel rubbish and tired and I sort of get that in the summer so I'm always outside" (Arnie, 16).

For mountain bikers, the body was instrumental in distinguishing those who were 'outdoorsy' from those who were not. For some there was something recognisable and embodied in mountain biking identities that displayed the connection with active or extreme forms of sport and leisure:

> "You can tell some people just watch TV and some people come out and do stuff like this" (Kenny, 15).

> "You can just tell who rides ... you can see someone walking down the street and they look like they ride or they do something extreme, even if it's rollerblading. You can more tell people were into sports, as opposed to not, like if they do something half extreme or if they just sit around playing Play Station" (Damien, 18).

While the countryside provided an important space for the performance of mountain biking, attitudes towards the nature of these environments were more complex. Whereas respect for the environment was considered important by young people who visited woodlands for mountain biking, nature appreciation in itself was considered a more adult ideal; one that did not resonate with their own identities and lifestyles. Nevertheless, participants were positive about the distinctive opportunities offered by the countryside as a space for sport and leisure, particularly compared to those provided for urban lifestyle sports such as skate parks.

Differentiated identities and lifestyles

Being a mountain biker was a significant marker of identity for young people, providing a connection to a collective culture that could be individually interpreted and expressed. Within youth mountain biking communities, subtle differences emerged between DDF mountain bikers and those who chose to pursue cross-country styles of mountain biking. DDF riders separated themselves from cross-country riders through adopting what they considered to be a more hedonistic approach to mountain biking. In contrast, young people who took part in cross-country were constructed as 'more civilized' and 'less crazy':

> "Cross-country riders seem to be a lot more careful in the way they ride. They're good at riding and they can go fast but they are more

careful of what they're doing, whereas the downhillers I know are just crazy" (Arnie, 16).

Many of the young people who took part in mountain biking at Bedgebury described cross-country riding as more competitive than the DDF styles, but agreed that cross-country riders were less likely to be confrontational in demonstrating their skill:

> "Yeah, cross country is more laid back in a way. There isn't bragging and stuff about it. Whereas downhill, everyone's like 'oh, I learnt this amazing new jump', bigs it all up" (Bill, 13).

While young people described differences between the 'scenes' experienced by those who took part in the different mountain-biking disciplines, some participants were hesitant about 'putting themselves in one box' by rejecting either the DDF or the cross-country identity. Instead, some young people preferred to emphasise the importance of individual style and personal interpretation, positioning themselves as part of a wider youth mountain-biking culture, within which they negotiated their own identities and asserted their own style of riding:

> "I think people get too serious about separating all the types of mountain biking because you have to do a bit of cross-country to do dirt-jumps and you have to do a bit of jumping in cross-country. So I'd say I do a bit of everything" (Sharpshooter, 21).

> "'I think there's a whole range of different lifestyles people lead through mountain biking, and I just think mine ... I don't know, I just make it my own" (Jimmy, 18).

In addition to the differences between mountain-biking disciplines, the 'youth' element of mountain-biking identities was dependent on disassociation with adult styles of participation in the sport. Young people often wore very different styles of clothing than adult participants, and this was considered representative of the differences between their approaches and philosophies to participation more generally. Young people described how they valued a more casual approach to the sport, expressing this in their choice of clothing as a style 'in between skater and grunge clothes'. Cross-country mountain bikers were more likely to wear what one participant termed "a sort of higher-end of mountain bike clothing" (Joel, 16 years old). However, it was the clothing worn by a group of adults known as 'the lycras' clothing that they associated with "slippery, streamlined account men" (Chrome Rider, 25), that youth mountain bikers strongly rejected:

"… they look and they ride really bad, their style is really bad, and they shave their legs and things like that for streamlining or whatever" (Damien, 18).

Youth mountain bikers, and DDF mountain bikers in particular, criticised the 'serious' attitude to leisure adopted by 'the lycras'. Adults were considered to be preoccupied with expensive equipment and clothing, too avoiding of risk and adventure, and too focussed on competition.

Lifestyle, identity and sport policy

Youth cultures constructed through sport and leisure are key to the formation of youth tastes, preferences, lifestyles and identities. As Roberts (2006) has argued, individuals incorporate their leisure choices into their wider lifestyles, which in turn inform their social identities. Lifestyles are a medium for the expression of identities, and, as such, are informed and moulded through the collection of experiences, attitudes and objects that participation in sport and leisure provides. Participation in lifestyle sports involves the adoption of shared values and attitudes to create a variety of identity positions. However, each sport has its own ethos, philosophy, codes and rules that participants may utilise or manifest in different ways to differentiate themselves from others and to express their distinctive identities.

Youth mountain bikers considered their identities to be 'alternative' when compared to other youth leisure cultures, particularly those associated with mainstream sports, and also when compared to adult mountain biking identities. Young people preferred mountain biking over team or formally organised sports because it gave them the freedom to express themselves in alternative ways. In privileging a more casual approach to leisure, oriented around the individual experience, lifestyle sports have the potential to appeal to 'hard-to-reach' young people whose participation in mainstream forms of sport may be limited. Lifestyle sports may be a significant alternative to traditional sport provision in relation to government targets to improve participation in physical activity (see also Wheaton and Gilchrist, 2011).

While some have claimed that the countryside may not be to the taste of young people (Henley Centre, 2005), the participants in this study, who included many urban dwellers, were demonstrably positive about the opportunities offered by the countryside as a leisure space. The marginal position of the countryside, in contrast to what were considered more popular youth spaces such as skate parks, did in fact contribute to its appeal because participants could share their lifestyles with others who were 'outdoorsy'. Crucially, countryside spaces offered vastly different opportunities for leisure in comparison to spaces such as skate parks or urban streets, and youth mountain bikers created a lifestyle that was orientated around particular a set of attitudes towards the countryside.

This case study demonstrates that mountain biking represents an important tool for engaging young people in outdoor recreation in countryside spaces. Providing opportunities to participate in sport and leisure experiences that appeal to young people's identities and lifestyles can be hugely effective in increasing youth engagement with the countryside and promoting positive associations with countryside space. As policy makers have previously claimed, the countryside offers a distinctive opportunity for the negotiation of identity "as young people discover new worlds and develop new skills, they also discover themselves" (Countryside Agency, 2005: 79). The countryside provides young people with a space they can "carve out for themselves", perform various forms of 'risky' behaviour and challenge the adult hegemony of public space (Bell, Ward Thompson and Travlou, 2003: 97).

Conclusions

This case has demonstrated just some of the complex ways in which identities and lifestyles are built on participation in sport. Constructing legitimate identities as part of youth mountain-biking lifestyles often depend on an intense immersion within the lifestyle and the community, and participants in this study talked passionately about their own experiences of mountain-biking culture and the ways in which these were imprinted on their own identities. Just as the construction of identity implies involvement in a collective culture with others who share philosophies, ideals and attitudes, forming identity through sport participation is dependent on differentiation from others.

Visual signs of identity such as clothing and equipment are important in lifestyle sporting groups and it is these aesthetic signs which enable young people to present a meaningful identity which is recognisable within global youth culture. Yet in addition to these outward expressions of identity, less-visible indicators are often of greater importance to the process of identity construction. In the case of mountain biking, participants differentiated themselves through choice of clothing, yet it was the sporting performance that often bore the most significance. At Bedgebury, the opportunity to pursue a range of mountain-biking disciplines saw different lifestyle groupings emerge, in part according to the style of mountain-biking participation. Mountain-biking identities were therefore diverse and myriad, and while differences between disciplines such as DDF and cross-country mattered to participants, distinguishing themselves collectively from adults or indeed from other less-active, 'outdoorsy' or mainstream forms of sport and leisure participation was perhaps most significant for identity development.

This case has shown the different values young people place on the countryside as a space for sport and leisure in comparison to other public leisure spaces. For example, urban leisure space was constructed as congested and hostile, while the countryside was depicted as free and hidden away. Youth mountain bikers sought risk-taking experiences in countryside spaces that offered them a sense of adventure and a feeling of wellbeing associated with being outdoors. Mountain biking at Bedgebury also offered young people a liberating context for identity formation removed from institutional, social or traditional sporting contexts. Importantly, it was considered an activity that was free of adult control.

References

Beal B, Weidman L. 2003. Authenticity in the skateboarding world. In Rinehart RE, Sydnor S. (eds) *To the Extreme: Alternative Sports, Inside and Out*. Albany: State University of New York Press; 337-352.

Becker P. 2003. The intense longing for authenticity or why people seek out adventure. In Humberstone B, Brown H, Richards K. (eds). *Whose Journeys? The Outdoors and Adventure as Social and Cultural Phenomena. Critical Explorations of Relations between Individuals, Others' and the Environment.* Penrith: The Institute for Outdoor Learning; 91-104.

Bell S, Ward Thompson C, Travlou P. 2003. Contested views of freedom and control: Children, teenagers and urban fringe woodlands in central Scotland. *Urban Forestry and Urban Greening* **2** (2): 87-100.

Bingley AF, Milligan C. 2007. Restorative places or scary spaces? The impact of woodland on the mental well-being of young adults. *Health and Place* **13** (3): 799-811.

Cater CI. 2007. Adventure tourism: Will to power? In Church A, Coles T. (eds) *Tourism, Power and Space*, Abingdon: Routledge; 63-82.

Countryside Agency. 2005. What about us? Diversity review evidence - part one. *Challenging Perceptions: Underrepresented Groups Visitor Needs*. ETHNOS Research/ Countryside Agency.

EKOS Ltd and Tourism Resources. 2007. 7 Stanes phase 2 evaluation. *A Report for Forestry Commission Scotland*. EKOS Ltd and Tourism Resources Company.

Forestry Commission. 2009. Bedgebury National Forest and Pinetum. Forestry Commission, Edinburgh. http://www.forestry.gov.uk/pdf/se-casestudies-bedgebury.pdf/$FILE/se-casestudies-bedgebury.pdf

Forestry Commission. 2012 Active England Bedgebury National Pinetum and Forest. http://www.forestry.gov.uk/forestry/INFD-6LJHZA.

Henley Centre. 2005. Paper 2: Demand for outdoor recreation. *A Report for Natural England's Outdoor Recreation Strategy*. Henley Centre / Headlight Vision, London.

King, K. 2009. Youth, leisure, lifestyles and identities: Mountain biking in the English countryside. Unpublished PhD thesis. University of Brighton.

Le Breton D. 2000. Playing symbolically with death in extreme sports. *Body and Society* **6** (1): 1-11.

Mintel. 2005 Extreme sports. *Leisure Intelligence*. Mintel International Group Ltd, London.

Mitchell W, Bunton R, Green E (eds). 2004. *Young People, Risk and Leisure: Constructing Identities in Everyday Life*. Basingstoke: Palgrave Macmillan.

Natural England. 2011. *Monitor of Engagement with the Natural Environment: The National Survey on People and the Natural Environment*, Natural England, Sheffield.

Roberts K. 2006. *Leisure in Contemporary Society*. 2nd Edition. Wallingford: CABI.

Ruff AR, Mellors O. 1993. The mountain bike. The dream machine? *Landscape Research*, **18** (3): 104-109.

Sport England. 2009. *Active England: Final Report*. Report by Hall Aitken and Bearhunt for Sport England, London.

Symmonds MC, Hammitt WE, Quisenberry VL. 2000. Managing recreational trail environments for mountain bike user preferences. *Environmental Management*, **25** (5): 549-564.

Tomlinson A, Ravenscroft N, Wheaton B, Gilchrist P. 2005. *Lifestyle Sports and National Sport Policy: An Agenda for Research*. Report to Sport England. Sport England, London.

Waitt G. 2008. 'Killer waves': Surfing, space and gender. *Social and Cultural Geographies* **9** (1): 75-94.

Wheaton B. 2004. Introduction: Mapping the lifestyle sport-scape. In Wheaton B. (ed.) *Understanding Lifestyle Sports: Consumption, Identity and Difference*. London: Routledge; 1-28.

Wheaton B, Gilchrist P. 2011. Lifestyle sport, public policy and youth engagement. *International Journal of Sport Policy and Politics* **3** (1): 109-131.

Ancillary student material

Further reading

Cater CI. 2007. Adventure tourism: will to power? In Church, A, Coles, T. (eds) *Tourism, Power and Space*. Routledge, Abingdon; 63-82.

Hudson S. 2003. *Sport and Adventure Tourism*. New York: Haworthy Press Inc.

King K. 2010. Lifestyle, identity and young people's experiences of mountain biking. Research Note. Forestry Commission. http://www.forestry.gov.uk/pdf/FCRN007.pdf/$FILE/FCRN007.pdf

Louv R. 2005. *Last Child in the Woods: Saving our Children from Nature Deficit Disorder.* Chapel Hill, North Carolina.

Miles S. 2000. *Youth Lifestyles in a Changing World*. Open University Press, Buckingham.

O'Brien E, Morris J. 2009. Active England: Bedgebury National Pinetum and Forest. Edinburgh: Forestry Commission. www.forestry.gov.uk/pdf/active_england_bedgebury_site_report.pdf/$FILE/active_england_bedgebury_site_report.pdf

Rinehart RE, Sydnor S. 2003. *To the Extreme: Alternative Sports, Inside and Out*, Albany: State University of New York Press.

Wheaton B. 2004. *Understanding Lifestyle Sports: Consumption, Identity and Difference*. London: Routledge.

Related websites

Sport England: http://www.sportengland.org/

Natural England: http://www.naturalengland.org.uk/

Forestry Commission: http://www.forestry.gov.uk/

International Mountain Biking Association: http://imba.org.uk/

Bedgebury Forest: http://www.forestry.gov.uk/bedgebury

Self test questions

Try to answer the following questions to test your knowledge and understanding. If you are not sure of the answers please re-read the case and refer to the references and further reading sources.

1   What are the defining features of youth mountain-biking identities?

2   How is sport used as a tool of differentiation among young people who participate in mountain biking?

3 What is the link between identity and leisure space?

4 How do risky sporting experiences shape self-identity?

Key themes and subthemes

The key themes raised in this case study relate to the following:

Lifestyle sports

♦ Characteristics of lifestyle sports

♦ Mountain-biking communities

Outdoor recreation

♦ Sport and leisure in rural environments

♦ Outdoor lifestyles and identities

Leisure experience

♦ Human-nature relations

♦ Social relations

Sporting identities

♦ Youth identity formation

♦ Alternative sporting identities

Sport policy

♦ Sport, physical activity and health

♦ Youth sport participation

Countryside access

♦ Countryside policy and lifestyle sports

♦ Barriers to access in youth

If you need to source further information on any of the above themes and theories, then these headings could be used as key words to search for materials and case studies.

 Scan here to get the hyperlinks for this chapter.

10

Nostalgia and Sport

Sean Gammon and Gregory Ramshaw

Introduction

The relationship between sport and nostalgia is both a strong and an abiding one. The longevity of their close association is founded on the fact that each one nourishes and feeds off the other, equating to a perfect symbiosis. At first glance, sport and nostalgia would appear to be rather strange bedfellows – the former tending to be more strongly associated with the young; the latter with the older generation – but bearing in mind that people's positive memories of the past often relate to sporting achievements, perhaps it is not so surprising that sport can be an important subject of nostalgia. Moreover, the association between sport and nostalgia has become stronger in recent times as the global population profile has grown older. For example, the number of people over the age of 65 in the UK increased by 20% between 1985 and 2010, due mainly to the large baby boomer generation reaching this age. Many businesses have responded by harnessing nostalgia, building it into their products and services so that they can be used to target the senior market. Nostalgia is not, however, solely for the aged: today we are also seeing the younger generations looking back fondly at the more recent past. This case sets out to investigate what has fuelled this trend. In doing so, it will outline the development and use of the term nostalgia, and how it manifests itself in the sporting world. Furthermore, it will highlight emerging markets in sport-related nostalgia and discuss the reasons for their success.

Background to nostalgia

The old joke that 'nostalgia is not what it used to be' is, of course, a long way from the truth: nostalgia has probably always been part of the human condition. As Holbrook and Schindler (1991: 330) succinctly put it, "the phenomenon of nostalgia is almost as old as life itself". What then is nostalgia and what function does it hold for those that practice it? In very simple terms, it involves an affection and/or preference for objects – such as people, places and events – as they were when we were younger or even before we were born. So nostalgia involves looking back fondly to the past, to times that we miss: times that we know have gone forever. Consequently the nostalgic experience is bittersweet, involving positive and often uplifting memories that are tainted with the realisation that we can never return to that yearned-for time.

Before analysing the nature of the term further, it is worth mentioning that while nostalgia has been alluded to in ancient texts, such as the Bible and Homer's The Odyssey, the term itself is actually a relatively new one. The term was first coined by a Swiss physician in 1688 as a neurological disease that occurred in soldiers who were away fighting in countries far from where they lived. It was, in essence, an extreme type of homesickness that brought on bouts of weeping, anorexia and suicide attempts (Sedikides, Wildschut and Basen, 2004). The only effective treatment was for the sufferer to return home, or at least to be offered the promise of return. The etymological root of the term is the compound of the Greek words Nostos (to return home) and Algos (pain, longing), which still holds resonance in contemporary usages of the word. So nostalgia is about remembering, but remembering in an affectionate and often inaccurate fashion to times past. It is not just a memory but "… memory with the pain taken away" (Goulding, 1999: 2).

There are also other characteristics which help distinguish nostalgia from other forms of remembrance, least of which is that it is restricted to pleasant and positive memories. One cannot form nostalgia from memories of horror, anguish, pain or humiliation, although we can look back at such times positively by rooting out affirmative memories connected to, for example, special friendships, the closeness of family and the optimism experienced in the face of great adversity (see Davis, 1979). It is this careful editing of the past that characterises the process of nostalgia. Therefore, nostalgia-driven memories can be thought of as a 'patchwork quilt', comprising only the best memories (which may be real or concocted), which are then stitched carefully together in order to form an idealised version of the past. This new account of the past will often carry more currency as time progresses: the stitching will fade and repetition will strengthen the conviction that the new interpretation is in fact the authentic one. The practice of nostalgia is therefore not just about fondly recalling times past: it is a specific way of remembering that has been carefully edited or in some cases partly constructed. The catalyst for why the past should be treated in this way has been identified as a reaction to the here and now (Davis, 1979; Batcho, 1995; Chase and Shaw, 1989). Increasingly people perceive the present day with dissatisfaction or unfamiliarity, while the future offers no solution or respite. This drives them back to look back to a time which they deem to be superior in some way, as well as being more familiar to them. To return, through nostalgic recollections, provides comfort and solace, and feeds the basic human need to belong.

Unsurprisingly, older generations are those most frequently identified as being most susceptible to nostalgia. This is the result of social, cultural and technological changes overtaking them, rendering them strangers in an unfamiliar world. There is, however, evidence that even younger generations are becoming more prone to nostalgia as they too struggle to keep up with the many changes and developments that the 21st century demands (Gammon, 2002; Goulding, 2002). Younger people (aged under 40) yearn for more recent pasts, although undoubtedly no less enthusiastically than their older counterparts. The present global economic downturn may serve as a potent catalyst for nostalgia, urging us to look back to times of optimism and plenty before the recession hit.

Nostalgia takes many forms, each of which raises specific issues for both those who experience it and those businesses which hope to benefit from it. For example, 'personal nostalgia' relates to memories particular to our personal biographies: nostalgic reflections about our own lives and times. 'Collective nostalgia', in contract, relates to memories that we are able to share with others, involving events deemed important to groups of various sizes (from friends to an entire nation). Understandably, it is quite common for the objects of someone's 'personal' and 'collective' nostalgia to overlap.

What, then, of times or eras that were not experienced or lived through, yet are still looked upon with nostalgia? Simply put, is it possible to be nostalgic about a period which pre-dates your birth? In the academic literature there is some contention concerning this question. Davis (1979), for example, believes that for someone to be truly nostalgic they must have lived through a particular time; that we feel differently about periods that we have actually lived through and those that have been interpreted to us by others through the media of film, books, advertising, and so on. Other authors, however, contend that it is possible to have positive feelings towards times and episodes that took place before one's birth. This they refer to as 'vicarious nostalgia' (Belk, 1988; Holbrook and Schindler, 1994; Goulding, 2002). To what extent 'vicarious nostalgia' generates the same types of feeling as other forms of nostalgia is a matter of debate, though this seems to matter little to the many businesses that utilise it in their product development. In fact, according to Hutcheon (1998: 7) it is this 'commercial nostalgia' that "…teaches us to miss the things we have never lost…". Commercial nostalgia has arguably grown into an industry all of its own. The 'retrofication' and resurrection of bygone products and brands is now commonplace across a number of industries, as businesses compete to profit from customers who are nostalgically drawn to the comforting and familiar shapes, sounds, smells and textures of these products. Whether it's the retro VW Beetle, a re-packaged aftershave from the 1970s or the reintroduction of familiar packaging such as the old-style Coca Cola bottle, the message is clear: the future success of many businesses are largely dependent on the nostalgic reactions of an ever-growing market.

Nostalgia thus has many uses, not only to the individuals and groups who seek comfort and familiarity in a world of increasing change and uncertainty but also to the many businesses who believe that nostalgia-themed products and services tap into a rich vein of almost endless possibilities. There is little doubt that baby boomers represent the biggest market in this respect, although there is a growing awareness that nostalgia is not just the preserve of older members of society and is now increasingly being practiced by younger generations.

Nostalgia and sport: A perfect match?

For many people, sport generates powerful and extremely resilient forms of nostalgia. Moments of personal achievement, coupled with memories connected to the deeds of the teams and individuals we supported when young, all represent potential sources of nostalgic recollections (Snyder, 1991; Fairley and Gammon, 2005; Ramshaw, 2005). These affectionate personal and collective memories hold great meaning and value to those who experience them. They are an opportunity both to re-concoct past events and to recalibrate past achievements with the sporting feats of today. In other words, the sporting past is warmly recalled in order to put the accomplishments of today's players and teams into perspective. As Fairley and Gammon (2005: 185) note:

> "To gaze back, albeit selectively, to a time and age when an individual was young, active, fit and healthy may act as a partial remedy to the fearful future, whilst also acting as a means of devaluing the present by comparing it with a superior past".

Sport can act as a trigger for nostalgia, as well as being a source in its own right. Playing the sports we played when younger or watching a match in familiar surroundings can often take us back to earlier days spent with family and friends who are perhaps no longer with us. Sporting events therefore have the ability to generate non-sporting reflections related to how we were back then, as well as triggering bittersweet memories of the people who shared our lives at the time. Furthermore, due to its wide appeal, sport can act as a rich source of collective nostalgia: creating important and memorable life moments that can be experienced both by fans and an entire nation.

Producers of films and documentaries are all too aware of the appeal of nostalgically delivered stories that hark back to the 'golden age' of a sport, player, event or team. Indeed, films such as Field of Dreams hark back to the more innocent days of baseball, which not only prompts baseball fans to reflect on the way the game has changed but also provides an entire nation with the opportunity to gaze back to the way things were, or perhaps to the way they should have been. These images and narratives not only play upon the emotions of older generations but also influence younger audiences' interpretation of eras and times: times that often pre-date their births and perhaps even those of their parents.

It is little wonder that so many industries view the sporting past as an effective angle through which to sell their products and services: the combination of sporting memories viewed through a nostalgic lens undeniably adds up to more than the sum of its parts. Indeed the term 'sportstalgia' has sometimes been used (mostly in blogs) to denote this blatant form of commercialisation of nostalgia.

Sport halls of fame

Arguably the most obvious manifestation of sport-based nostalgia can be found in halls of fame. The raison d'etre of the sport hall of fame is to celebrate and venerate the greats of whatever sport or country it chooses to represent. They can be virtual or housed collections, outlining the exceptional achievements and records of individuals who contributed in some way to any given sport. Usually they honour ex-players (both living and dead), though coaches, managers and journalists are often inducted. Voting usually takes place on an annual basis. This is either undertaken through a fan-based voting system or, more commonly, through a panel of experts. Halls of fame are often referred to as 'shrines' where fans pay their respects to the players they followed when they were younger (Redmond, 1973; Snyder, 1991; Gammon, 2004). Each hall of famer is allocated a distinct place within the attraction which will normally include a plaque (see Figure 1), career statistics and often various equipment and/or jerseys that were used or worn by them. Halls of fame are frequently linked with sport museums and are generally situated within or near to places that have some association with the sport. An example is the National Baseball Hall of Fame in Cooperstown, which is considered to be the spiritual home of baseball. More often than not they are virtual repositories, organised and managed by governing bodies in order to pay homage to past heroes while at the same time satisfying the collective need to protect and glorify the past. Examples of virtual halls of fame are the England Athletics Hall of Fame and the International Rugby Board Hall of Fame.

Figure 1: Babe Ruth: Hall of Fame plaque. *Source:* http://baseballhall.org/

Nostalgic sports events

Nostalgia is also a significant part of many contemporary sporting events although, at times, nostalgia is only a by-product of the event, rather than the central feature. Certain events, such as the spate of outdoor ice hockey games that have occurred throughout North America and Europe over the past decade (see Box 1) are created specifically to sell nostalgia: be it former ways of life, ex-players or nostalgia-based products.

This type of event harks back to an uncomplicated time (either real or, more often the case, imagined) when sport was accessible, equitable and fun, especially in comparison to the hypercompetitive and complex sporting environment of today. As such, the act of 'nostalgising' and celebrating the past becomes far more important than the result of the event itself. This is not to suggest that the result does not matter at all to the participants as their passion to win, unlike their abilities, has not dimmed with time. Masters tournaments, such as the Aegon Tennis Masters held in the Albert Hall in London and the many senior golf tours taking place around the world, illustrate well the popularity of such events. Not only do these events give the public the opportunity to see their heroes perform once more but they also offer a chance for the players to have one last bite of the cherry and benefit from their success. For example, the winner of the PGA Senior Championship can expect to receive winnings of around $360,000, while the total prize money for the European Senior Tour is over €9,000,000.

In other cases, nostalgia becomes part of the sporting event, although this is not necessarily the reason for the event to exist. For example, baseball games in the United States are traditionally described as a bonding time between parents and children, and tickets to these are often positioned as an opportunity to revisit (or, indeed, create) nostalgic memories of long summer days at the ballpark. Other types of sporting events are so steeped in tradition that they either consciously or unconsciously evoke nostalgia about earlier times. Attending a county cricket match in England, for example, can provide a 'quintessential' nostalgic view of rural English culture. However, in both the baseball and cricket examples, these types of sporting event do not exist for nostalgic purposes alone. In fact, the result of the match is paramount, and nostalgia is just one way of understanding and experiencing the event.

Box 1: Heritage Classic Outdoor Ice Hockey, Edmonton, Canada

The Heritage Classic Outdoor Ice Hockey event created an entirely new sports landscape from a pastiche of images, traditions, history, nostalgia and fiction. The event, held in November 2003 as a one-off celebration of the heritage of outdoor ice hockey in Canada, featured "two of Canada's premier 'heritage' teams, the Edmonton Oilers with five Stanley Cup Championships, and the Montreal Canadiens with 24 Stanley Cup Championships" (Heritage Hockey Classic, 2003: n.p.). Two games were played during the event, the first being a match between former star players from past Edmonton and Montreal teams, and the second being a regular season game between the current squads of the Oilers and Canadiens. Played in the outdoor venue of the Commonwealth Stadium in Edmonton (See Figure 2), rather than the normal indoor setting, the game was billed as a revisiting of ice hockey's greatest teams in a 'natural environment', evoking memories of the game's outdoor past, which are particularly resonant in Canada. Increasing tourism in Edmonton, particularly during a time of the year when tourism numbers tend to be quite low, was one of the event's main selling features. The games reportedly attracted 14,000 visitors, some coming from as far away as Finland and Norway (Cormier, 2003a; Cormier, 2003b; Stock, 2003), although the scarcity of tickets limited significant tourist visits. There was considerable media interest, with many national and international media companies sending sports columnists to cover the event. Meanwhile the domestic television audience reached nearly 2.5 million viewers, a record for a regular season ice-hockey broadcast in Canada (Anon, 2003).

Figure 2: The Heritage Classic: Edmonton 2003. *Source:* www.onfrozenblog.com/2007/07/10/
cooling-thoughts-amid-mercury-madness-the-heritage-classic-a-reminiscence.html

The centrepiece of the event, however, came in its construction of an antiquated sports
landscape. The outdoor rink, whether it is a rural frozen pond, an urban backyard or a
community league recreation facility, has become a "facet of northern recreational heritage" (Falla, 2000: 54). The stadium was dressed as a prairie farmyard, with a pond, bales
of hay, old Ford trucks and covered wagons for the Heritage Classic, while the teams
and officials wore jerseys from the 1940s through to the 1980s. As one participant put it:

> "… we're trying to make sure that people's experiences (at the Heritage Classic)
> are magical – that they come in here and the first thing they do is drop their jaw
> and go, 'Wow!' It's going to look like a farmyard with a pond in the middle …
> a magical wonderland. It's kind of what brings us back to where is all belongs"
> (Howell, 2003: B1).

In many ways, the constructed landscape of the Heritage Classic was seeking to redeem
the game of ice hockey, particularly in Canada:

> "[The Heritage Classic] returns hockey, our game, to its primal, Canadian roots.
> It doesn't just put the stars of our youth back on the ice. It takes us back to the
> days when hockey wasn't an elite caviar entertainment for overpaid adults, but
> a rough-and-tumble winter sport, something any kid with a pair of skates could
> play. Is there anything more absurdly, quintessentially Canadian than the idea of
> sitting outside in the cold and snow of November to watch a hockey game? But,
> today isn't just a couple of games. It's the repatriation, the redemption, of our
> national sport." (Simons, 2003: B1-B2).

In the years leading up to the Heritage Classic, the National Hockey League (NHL) had
seen labour strife, the relocation of franchises from Canada to the United States, and
few approachable superstars to represent the game. The cost of playing the game
at the amateur level had increased dramatically and the price of attending profes-

sional games was – and remains – unthinkable for many families. The Heritage Classic attempted to repatriate the game, placing it back in its essential landscape, bringing back its most memorable players – particularly Wayne Gretzky of the Edmonton Oilers and Guy LaFleur of the Montreal Canadiens – and attempting to remake the game as non-codified and inclusive. There was certainly a novelty element: despite the 'heritage' moniker, the event represented the first time the NHL had played a regular season game outdoors in the 87 year history of the league, and few professional or semi-professional teams had played outdoors since the very early twentieth century. However, placing ice hockey in its perceived 'natural environment' created both a popular and evocative display of heritage. In the years since the Heritage Classic, no fewer than 50 outdoor games – many of which have incorporated heritage and nostalgia motifs – have been played at various venues and at different levels of elite ice hockey throughout the world. Most notably, beginning in 2008 the NHL used the Heritage Classic model in the creation of an annual 'Winter Classic' game, played each 1 January. Interestingly, some incarnations of the Winter Classic have attempted to blend various sport heritage/nostalgia landscapes together by placing the game in historic baseball stadia, such as at Wrigley Field in Chicago in 2009 and Fenway Park in Boston in 2010. At these events in particular, the nostalgic markers for outdoor hockey – such as the retro jerseys and a snow-covered landscape – were blended seamlessly with the familiar and recognisable baseball landscapes of each particular city, such as the famous 'Green Monster' wall in left field of Fenway Park. As such, the outdoor ice-hockey game became more than a placeless event (Ramshaw and Hinch, 2006) and became a place-based nostalgic spectacle.

Did you know…

◆ That the attendance for the Heritage Classic was 57,167 which, at the time, was the largest crowd in NHL history?

◆ That the Heritage Classic had an economic impact of nearly $25 million Canadian dollars?

◆ That only 7,000 Heritage Classic tickets were available to the general public (after season ticket holders, sponsors, league officials, and dignitaries received their tickets), and that the event organisers received over three million requests to purchase these remaining tickets?

◆ That the venue for the Heritage Classic, Commonwealth Stadium, is best known as the home of the Canadian Football League's Edmonton Eskimos, and was also the host venue for the 1978 Commonwealth Games, 1983 World University Games, and 2001 World Athletics Championships?

Sport fantasy camps

For those individuals not satisfied with viewing the paraphernalia of their sport through the glass of a display case or their heroes from the stadium stands, fantasy camps offer the serious fan the opportunity to be coached and play alongside the players from their past. The first camps emerged during the early 1980s in the USA and were set up by former Chicago Cub player, Randy Hundley (Schlossberg, 1996). Baseball camps continue to be extremely popular (see Figure 3) and the concept has spread to many other sports such as ice hockey, football, basketball, cycling and many more. These camps blatantly feed off both 'personal' and 'collective' nostalgia, and provide memorable experiences that encourage individuals to fulfil their early sporting fantasies and become the child they once were.

Figure 3: New York Yankees Fantasy Camp. *Source:* mlb.mlb.com/nyy/fan_forum/fantasycamp.jsp

The appeal of such camps is multi-faceted and can be identified through the promotion of one or more of the following:

♦ **The event** – where the interest lies in the desire to be connected with a famous event, such as the World Series, the Olympic Games or the Tour de France.

♦ **The stadia/venues** – where the aspiration is to experience a famous and/or meaningful location (for example, Fenway Park), or to train at the same facility as the professionals.

♦ **The team/club** – usually connected with a supporter or fan of a club or of a particular famous team (for example, Chicago Cubs, Cincinnati Reds, and Detroit Tigers).

♦ **The players and coaches** – where the fantasy revolves around the opportunity to play alongside and/or to be coached by famous individuals. These can be players from the past or famous coaches.

♦ **The sport:** here the motivation is generated through a general interest in the chosen sport as a whole. These camps tend to focus primarily on educating the attendees, so they usually (though not exclusively) attract younger individuals who wish to improve their game. The fantasy revolves around the opportunity to play and to be coached in their favourite sport along with other like-minded enthusiasts. These are not fantasy camps in the traditional sense, that is, they rarely deal with the history of the game or involve famous players from the past. (Adapted from Gammon, 2002).

A further nostalgic feature of the fantasy camp is that they present the opportunity for ex-professionals to reflect upon the past: they too have a chance to shine one more time and be the sports star they once were. Another salient feature of such camps is the social interaction that occurs between and among players and attendees. Indeed, many camps have an alumni feature, which encourages campers to meet up with the friends they made at the camps and to talk about their experiences and memories: equating to a double type of nostalgia.

Fantasy camps are primarily a North American phenomenon, although similar experiences are offered in Europe, just not under the fantasy camp banner. As a result, the market in Europe remains somewhat fragmented and less organised than its North American counterpart. Time will tell whether an aging market, for example in the UK, will demand these sporting fantasies, growing it into a more global phenomenon.

Sport and merchandising nostalgia

It will come as no surprise that an aging market will not only demand experiences related to their pasts but also tangible products that more obviously represent the sporting eras that they identify with. As a result the 'retrofication' of sport products continues to be a key facet of many sport manufacturers' designs. These retro products are more commonly associated with relatively small goods such as training shoes, jerseys/shirts and various sporting equipment. However, in some cases retro theming can be implemented on a much larger scale, influencing the design and style of new stadia, as outlined in Box 2. Such initiatives illustrate well the marketability of creating sporting environments that attempt to recreate an event ambiance that is reminiscent of times past (Ramshaw and Gammon, 2007; Seifried and Meyer, 2010). To what extent such venues represent an accurate portrayal of old ball parks is a moot point, but their interpretation of the past will undoubtedly influence younger spectators' perceptions of the way a sport was consumed in earlier days.

Case 2: Oriole Park at Camden Yards, Baltimore, USA

Oriole Park at Camden Yards (OPCY), built for the Baltimore Orioles baseball club, was the first of many 'retro' baseball park constructions in the United States. Completed in 1992, the stadium served as the anchor of Baltimore's Inner Harbour redevelopment, transforming the area from a derelict industrial wasteland to a spectacular urban space. The defining feature of the redevelopment was the incorporation of the industrial architecture into the ballpark, as an early twentieth century warehouse serves as the backdrop for the right field wall. The design also features a pastiche of styles from ballparks of the early twentieth century:

> "Oriole Park is state-of-the-art yet unique, traditional and intimate in design. It blends with the urban context of downtown Baltimore while taking its image from baseball parks built in the early 20th century. Steel, rather than concrete trusses, an arched brick facade, a sun roof over the gentle slope of the upper deck, an asymmetrical playing field, and natural grass turf are just some of the features that tie it to those magnificent big league ballparks built in the early 1900's. Ebbets Field (Brooklyn), Shibe Park (Philadelphia), Fenway Park (Boston), Crosley Field (Cincinnati), Forbes Fields (Pittsburgh), Wrigley Field (Chicago), and The Polo Grounds (New York) were among the ballparks that served as powerful influences in the design of Oriole Park" (Baltimore Orioles, 2012: n.p.).

OPCY encompasses, and perhaps even started, the trend of the 'retro' sport landscape. The stadium is at the heart of the Inner Harbour 'tourist bubble' and, along with the Baltimore Raven's (National Football League) stadium, "have made the list of must-see attractions for many visitors to the city, even on non-event days" (Chapin, 2004: 201). The stadium offers not only a venue to see a sporting event but also a nostalgic sporting experience (Mapes, 2001), encompassing both the style and atmosphere of traditional baseball settings. With its pastiche of designs and novel eccentricities taken from other ballparks, OPCY also attempts to connect Baltimore's past with other American cities, while also connecting its civic identity to baseball:

> "It is perhaps in this sense that OPCY most vividly, and indeed, randomly cannibalizes the past, as storied baseball signifiers are torn from the spatial and temporal moorings and unselfconsciously juxtaposed in a pastiche of postmodern baseball historicism" (Friedman, Andrews and Silk, 2004: 128).

Finally, OPCY offers nostalgia as a remedy to the codified nature of the sport spectator experience. While OPCY is designed to generate significantly more revenue than any of the ballparks it mimics (Friedman, Andrews and Silk, 2004), the experience of going to a ballgame in an environment that evokes a 'golden age' for both the sport and the nation is akin to Bale's (2003) image of village cricket in 'Merrie England'. The landscape makes the visitor comfortable and "insist(s) that life was once liveable and, yes, yes, if we looked long and hard enough at some right thing in our past, it would be right again" (Lowenthal, 1985: 13). Many US cities with major league teams, such as Detroit and San Francisco, also incorporated the retro style for their new ballparks, while many smaller US cities – with baseball teams in various levels of the minor leagues – have also built smaller retro stadia as part of urban redevelopment initiatives. While some recent stadium constructions, such as in Washington and Minneapolis, have opted for a more 'retro-modern' feel that uses more glass and steel than brick, the influence of OPCY and its nostalgic tones are still a part of many US cities.

Did you know…

◆ That Oriole Park at Camden Yards has actually decreased capacity over the years? When the park opened in 1992, the capacity was 48,041; after recent renovations, the park now seats 45,971.

◆ That there is a statue of Babe Ruth outside of the Oriole Park at Camden Yards? Ruth never played for the Orioles but he was born in Baltimore. In fact, his birthplace is only two blocks from the stadium and is now a museum!

◆ That Oriole Park at Camden Yards was once a rail yard for the B&O (Baltimore and Ohio) Railway? The infamous brick building in right field was the B&O Warehouse, and is now used for team office space, reception rooms, and restaurants.

Other retro sporting goods, together with original memorabilia items, continue to generate significant interest across all sports, whether it be cycle racing jerseys, football and rugby shirts, ice-hockey jerseys or training shoes, the retro market remains buoyant (Farrar, 2011). The demand for such products is complicated and context driven. For example, some football fans will purchase retro shirts as a means to connect to previous teams and past successes which will be recalled vicariously or first hand, while others may be drawn to them simply for aesthetic reasons. Other products, such as the old-style football sold in the Manchester United team shop (see Figure 4), symbolically communicates how the game has changed, as well as acting as a personal reminder, to older patrons, of the way they played the game in their younger days. The myriad of retro sports accessories found on innumerable websites is testament to the increasing demand and supply of such products, and as populations age and grow, markets will undoubtedly adapt in order to offer a conduit to whichever past is longed for at the time.

Figure 4: Retro Football. Manchester United Store. Photo credit: Sean Gammon

Conclusions

Nostalgia is a powerful emotion that predominantly occurs as a negative assessment by individuals and groups of present-day events and situations. The future is perceived with uncertainly and mistrust, which drives us to consider the journey of our own lives, along with the events we experienced and the people with whom we were share those experiences. The past then becomes a comforting place to re-visit, though such visitations are viewed through a forgiving lens that is imbued with sentiment and selectivity. Consequently, it is those from older generations who are more prone to such nostalgic recollections, although recently there is evidence that younger people are looking back romantically, predominantly as a consequence of faster societal changes. Sport can act as an effective anchor to help us stop and look back to simpler, more innocent times. Viewed through the lens of nostalgia, the deeds achieved by the players and teams of the past take on a more noble quality, especially when compared to the accomplishments of their present-day counterparts. An example of the juxtaposition between old and new can be seen in the Heritage Classic event discussed in Box 1. On this occasion, essentially two events took place: the regular NHL game and, of course, the legends game, which undoubtedly generated the primary demand for tickets. But the connection between sport and nostalgia is not just about recalling the feats of yesterday's legends, for participation in sport today, whether actively or as a spectator, can also act as a powerful reminder of those people who shared in the numerous memories that sport evokes. Such memories could involve a fan recalling when they first attended a game, and with whom, or a player reflecting on games played many years ago with old friends.

It should come as no surprise that businesses are keen to offer products and services that both meet and create nostalgic demand. In terms of sport retro products, the offerings are many and varied. They are popular in all countries that have an interest in sport, although some products such as fantasy camps and halls of fame are more developed in North America. The Oriole Park development at Camden Yards (discussed in Box 2) illustrates well how some sports venues have been designed in order to appeal to a market which hankers back to a more traditional environment in which to watch their favourite sport. As populations age, the demand for such products will surely grow, even if the manner in which they are delivered will no doubt change and progress. Today's sport will become tomorrow's nostalgia, but the fashions and events that will fuel this future demand are as yet unknown.

References

Anon. 2003. Very hot ratings for very cold game. *The Edmonton Journal*, November 25 http://www.canada.com/edmonton/edmontonjournal.

Baker S, Kennedy F. 1994. Death by nostalgia: A diagnosis of context specific cases. *Advances in Consumer Research*, 21: Provo UT: Association for Consumer Research.

Bale J. 2003. *Sports Geographies* (2nd Edition) London: Routledge.

Baltimore Orioles. 2012. http://baltimore.orioles.mlb.com/bal/camdenyards20/history.jsp#history.

Belk RW. 1988. Possessions and the extended self. *Journal of Consumer Research* **15** (2): 139-153.

Batcho K. 1995. Nostalgia: A psychological perspective. *Perceptual and Motor Skills* **80** (1): 131-143.

Chapin TS. 2004. Sports facilities as urban redevelopment catalysts. *Journal of the American Planning Association* **70** (2): 191-209.

Chase M, Shaw C. 1989. The dimensions of nostalgia. In Chase M, Shaw C. (eds) *The Imagined Past: History and Nostalgia*. Manchester: Manchester University Press; 1-17.

Cormier R. 2003a. Cool experience lures thousands of visitors. *The Edmonton Journal*: B3, November 22.

Cormier R. 2003b. A little frost couldn't chill the most devout fan. *The Edmonton Journal*: A9, November 23.

Davis F. 1979. *A Yearning for Yesterday: A Sociology of Nostalgia*, London: Collyer MacMillan.

Fairley S, Gammon S. 2005. Something lived, something learned: Nostalgia's expanding role in sport tourism. *Sport in Society: Cultures, Commerce, Media, Politics* **8** (2): 182-197.

Falla J. 2000. *Home Ice: Reflections on Backyard Rinks and Frozen Ponds*. Toronto: McClelland & Stewart.

Farrar ME. 2011. Amnesia, nostalgia, and the politics of place memory. *Political Research Quarterly* **64** (4): 723-735.

Friedman MT, Andrews DL, Silk ML. 2004. Sport and the façade of redevelopment in the post-industrial city. *Sociology of Sport Journal* **21**: 119-139.

Gammon S. 2002. Fantasy, nostalgia and the pursuit of what never was. In Gammon S, Kurtzman J. (eds) *Sport Tourism: Principles and Practice*. Eastbourne: LSA Publications; 61-71.

Gammon S. 2004. Secular pilgrimage and sport tourism. In Ritchie BR, Adair D. (eds) *Sport Tourism: Interrelationships, Impacts and Issues*. Clevedon: Channel View; 30-45.

Goulding C. 1999. An exploratory study of age related vicarious nostalgia and aesthetic consumption. *Advances in Consumer Research* **29** (1): 542-546.

Heritage Hockey Classic 2003. *Edmonton Oilers Toast their 25th Anniversary by Celebrating Hockey's Heritage*, June 3. http://www.heritagehockeyclassic.com/.

Holbrook MB, Schindler RM. 1991. Echoes of the dear departed past: Some work in progress on nostalgia. In Holman R, Soloman M. (eds) *Advances in Consumer Research*, Provo, UT: Association for Consumer Research; 330-333.

Holbrook MB, Schindler RM. 1994. Age, sex and attitude toward the past as predictors of consumer's aesthetic tastes for cultural products: *Journal of Marketing Research* **31** (3): 412-422.

Howell D. 2003. Edmonton's hockey wonderland. *The Edmonton Journal*, B1 & B3, November 23.

Hutcheon L. 1998. Irony, nostalgia, and the postmodern. University of Toronto English Library Criticism and Theory Resources http://www.library.utoronto.ca/utel/crticism.html; 1-18.

Lowenthal D. 1985. *The Past is a Foreign Country*. Cambridge: Cambridgeshire University Press.

Mapes J. 2001. Downtown ballparks offer taste of the past. *National Geographic News*. April 4. http://news.nationalgeographic.com/news/2001/04/0404_ballparks.html

Ramshaw G. 2005. Nostalgia, heritage and imaginative sports geographies: Sport and cultural landscapes. Paper presented at the forum UNESCO University and Heritage 10th International Seminar. *Cultural Landscapes in the 21st Century*, Newcastle-upon-Tyne.

Ramshaw G, Hinch T. 2006. Place identity and sport tourism: The case of the heritage classic ice hockey event. *Current Issues in Tourism* **5** (4&5): 399-418.

Ramshaw G, Gammon S. 2007. More than just nostalgia? Exploring the heritage/sport tourism nexus. In Gammon S, Ramshaw G. (eds) *Heritage, Sport and Tourism: Sporting Pasts – Tourist Futures*. London: Routledge; 9-22.

Redmond G. 1973. A plethora of shrines: Sport in the museum and the hall of fame. *Quest* **19**: 41-48.

Schlossberg H. 1996. *Sports Marketing*. Oxford: Blackwell.

Sedikides C, Wildschut T, Basen D. 2004. Nostalgia: Conceptual issues and existential functions. In Greenberg LS. (ed.) *Handbook of Experiential Existential Psychology*. New York: Gilford Publications; 200-214.

Seifried C, Meyer K. 2010. Nostalgia-related aspects of professional sport facilities: A facility audit of major league baseball and national football League strategies to evoke the past. *International Journal of Sport Management Recreation & Tourism* **5**: 51-76.

Simons P. 2003. Canada's national game repatriated and redeemed. *The Edmonton Journal*, B1-B2, November 22.

Snyder E. 1991. Sociology of nostalgia: Halls of fame and museums in America. *Sociology of Sport Journal* **8** (3): 228-238.

Stock C. 2003. From London to L.A. to Manning, Alta.: If you build it (a rink), they will come. *The Edmonton Journal*: C7, November 23.

Ancillary Student Material

Further Reading

Gammon S. 2011. Sports events: Typologies, people and place. In Page S, Connell J. (eds) *The Routledge Handbook of Events*. London: Routledge; 104-109.

Inglis S. 2004. *Played in Manchester: The Architectural Heritage of a City at Play*. London: English Heritage.

Kulczycki C, Hyatt C. 2005. Expanding the conceptualization of nostalgia sport tourism: Lessons learned from fans left behind after sport franchise relocation. *Journal of Sport & Tourism* **10** (4): 273-293.

Ramshaw G. 2011. The construction of sport heritage attractions. *Journal of Tourism Consumption and Practice* **3** (1): 1-25.

Schindler RM, Holbrook MB. 2003. Nostalgia for early experience as a determinant of consumer preferences. *Psychology and Marketing* **20** (4): 275-302.

Schuman H, Scott J. 1989. Generations and collective memories. *American Sociological Review* **54** (3): 359-381.

Wood J. 2005. Talking sport or talking balls? Realising the value of sports heritage. *Industrial Archaeology Review* **27** (1): 137-144.

Related websites

Aegon Masters Tennis: http://www.aegonmasterstennis.com/

Baseball Pilgrimages.com: http://www.baseballpilgrimages.com/index.html

Fantasy Baseball Camp Directory: http://www.baseballfantasycampdirectory.com/

National Baseball hall of Fame: http://baseballhall.org/

Legends UK: http://www.legendsuk.com/legends-events.html

Predas Cyclismo: http://www.prendas.co.uk/explorer.asp?page=1&selMFCPKID=0&selPRIPKID=0&selTEAPKID=0&selCOLPKID=101&selTYPPKID=0&selSortBy=2

Soccerex: http://www.soccerex.com/events/global/football-festival/

Mitchell & Ness (Nostalgia Co): http://www.mitchellandness.com/departments/jerseys.aspx

UK Soccer Shop: http://www.uksoccershop.com/retro-football-shirts.html

Self-test questions

Try to answer the following questions to test your knowledge and understanding of the case. If you are unsure of any answers, please re-read the case and refer to the references and further reading sources.

1 How has the meaning of the term nostalgia changed over the last 300 years?

2 What are the key characteristics of nostalgia?

3 Why are younger generations becoming more nostalgic?

4 Why are sport and nostalgia suited so well?

5 In what ways do sport halls of fame cater for the nostalgic fan?

6 Why might sports fans prefer to purchase retro shirts/jerseys?

Key themes and sub-themes

The key themes raised in this case study relate to the following:

Forms of nostalgia

♦ Personal nostalgia
♦ Collective nostalgia
♦ Commercial nostalgia
♦ Vicarious nostalgia

Sport nostalgia products and services

♦ Sport halls of fame
♦ Nostalgic sports events
♦ Sport fantasy camps
♦ Merchandising sports nostalgia

If you need to source any further information on any of the above themes and theories then, these headings could be used as key words to search for materials and case studies.

 Scan here to get the hyperlinks for this chapter.

11

Personal Mobility and Professional Movements

Monitoring the Motives of Modern Sports Migrants

Richard Keith Wright

Introduction

In October 2011, New Zealander Rangi Chase revealed his plans to represent England ('the Lions') in the 2011 Four Nations rugby league tournament. Six months later, James Tamou accepted an offer to play for Australia ('the Kangaroos') against New Zealand ('the Kiwis') in the 2012 ANZAC Day test match. These life-changing 'career decisions' dominated the online sports media discourse for several weeks, turning two relatively unknown athletes into household names and headline news within at least three different time zones. The purpose of this case study is to enable readers to revisit, perhaps re-ignite, the debates that divided members of the global rugby league community and overshadowed at least two international test matches. The study presents some of the conclusions drawn by a number of stakeholders, including players and coaches (past and present), agents and administrators, family and, most importantly, the two migrants themselves. It highlights a multitude of potential motivations simultaneously pushing and pulling professional athletes in multiple directions, but also demonstrates the varying degrees of empathy and apathy found within the public communities affected by these personal cases of elite athlete mobility. Finally, it raises questions regarding the continued creation of local loyalties, national identities and international eligibilities within today's truly global sports arena.

A global 'local' community

"With mobility comes encounter" (Robins, 1997: 18).

The reduction of boundaries associated with the globalisation process has opened up a world of potentially lucrative business encounters for both the producers and consumers of professional sport (Maguire and Falcous, 2011;

Spaaij, 2011; Woodward, 2012). Giulianotti and Robertson (2006) trace the links back to the 1870s, with the financial rewards of being able and willing to relocate having been highlighted on a number of occasions over the past decade (Magee and Sugden, 2002; McGovern, 2002; Falcous and Maguire, 2005; Cornelisson and Solberg, 2007; Higham and Hinch, 2009; Maguire and Falcous, 2011). Higham and Hinch (2009: 11) argue that "globalisation and contemporary mobility have brought enormous change to the values and reference points that once framed people's lives". They refer to contemporary mobility as being both "a cause and a consequence of globalization" (Higham and Hinch, 2009: 35) that "lies at the heart of place attachment" (Higham and Hinch, 2009: 263), suggesting that "[m]igration, return migration, transnationalism and diaspora represent different manifestations of the interface of activity, people and place" (Higham and Hinch, 2009: 177).

Figure 1 reveals one attempt to capture the complexities of contemporary sports mobility within a continually evolving spatial setting. The model incorporates a range of temporary/short-term and permanent/long-term sports-inspired movements, located locally, regionally, nationally, internationally and transcontinental/globally. It illustrates the existence of local and regional-scale excursions and seasonal-based activities that essentially feed or fuel the more time- and distance-consuming cross-border movements found at the other end of the scale. The acknowledgement of 'return migration' also supports evidence suggesting that modern sporting migrations are rarely permanent and almost always result in a significant number of trips 'back home' to visit friends and relatives (Maguire, 1999).

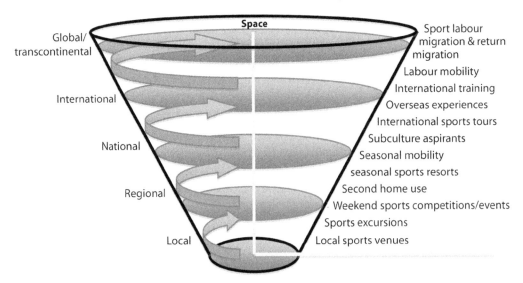

Figure 1: Manifestations of temporary mobility and circulation in sport. *Source:* Higham and Hinch (2009)

While the study of short- and long-distance mobility may not be considered as well advanced as some of the other sport-related research areas (Maguire, 2004), the concept of crossing national borders for sports-based employment is certainly not new. It has been estimated, for example, that around 2,000 Welsh rugby players migrated to the North of England between 1894 and 1994 in order to further their career, enhance their bank accounts and escape areas unable to provide them with the resources they required (Williams, 1994). One of the most recent contributions to the ever-expanding body of literature lists an impressive number of academic studies specifically addressing the issue of labour migration and athlete mobility (Love and Kim, 2011). This publication notes research on the sports of baseball, basketball, cricket, handball, ice hockey, rugby and soccer, as well as research conducted in Eastern Europe, Scandinavia, Finland, Africa and Latin American. Furthermore, the number of new authors contributing to Maguire and Falcous' (2011) impressive collection of global sports migration research, covering new issues in previously untouched areas of the professional sporting arena suggests that this is a highly relevant and rapidly expanding area of contemporary research.

Over the past 20 years, Maguire's extensive individual and collaborative research activity has not only examined the emergence of 'donor' regions and the establishment of sporting nurseries that satisfy the world's constant need for new sporting commodities, but also explored the various push and pull factors that motivate elite athletes to migrate (Maguire 1993, 1994, 1999, 2004, 2011; Maguire and Bale, 1994; Maguire and Stead, 1996, 1998; Stead and Maguire, 1998, 2000a, 2000b; Falcous and Maguire, 2005, 2011; Maguire and Pearton 2000a, 2000b; Maguire, Jarvie, Mansfield and Bradley, 2002; Maguire and Falcous, 2011). In 1999, Maguire produced one of his most influential contributions to the knowledge base, in which he claimed that the vast majority of sporting migrations were inspired by the desire to maximise their short-term earnings potential (Maguire, 1999).

By referring to athletes as commercially valuable commodities, who are bought, sold and transported all over the world in order to supply an ever-increasing demand for international sporting entertainment, Maguire (1999) effectively transferred the study of sports consumption and production away from the social sciences and into the world of international business management. Having explored the more mercenary aspects of sporting migrations (i.e. those who happily exchange their loyalties in return for a larger salary), Maguire also acknowledged the increasing number of 'nomadic cosmopolitans', which included athletes who spend most of their year away from their country of origin, checking in and out of hotel rooms and competing in ever-expanding seasonal 'world' tours (e.g. professional golfers and tennis players) (Maguire, 1999).

Magee and Sugden (2002) challenged Maguire's initial five migrant types (the Pioneer, the Mercenary, the Nomad, the Settler and the Returnee), highlighting the dangers and difficulties of 'pigeon-holing' athletes into certain categories based on their primary or secondary reasons for leaving 'home'. They focused on stories of 22 migrants plying their trade within England's top professional football leagues, concluding that money was merely one of many contributing factors pulling them away from their countries of origin (Magee and Sugden, 2002). They discarded Maguire's Pioneer and Returnee but identified three new reasons for sports labour migration. The 'Exile and Expelled' gave specific consideration to those forced out of their country of origin by political unrest, off-field 'personal' problems and/or public persecution by the 'local' press. The 'Ambitionist', which came in three different forms, acknowledged the influence of pre-established career aspirations, including a desire to compete among the best competitors, created prior to them turning professional (Magee and Sugden, 2002)

More recently, Love and Kim (2011) also adopted the typologies adopted and adapted by Maguire, Magee and Sugden, describing them as the most appropriate conceptual framework available for their analysis of labour migration within the US Collegiate Sport sector. Rather than change, challenge or critique the existing typologies, however, they opted to test their relevance at a semi-/non-professional level. Figure 2 not only lists the brief definitions and descriptions they offered their readers, but also provides a suitable platform for the author's own contribution to this growing area of research (Figure 3).

Figure 3 suggests that modern migrants are twice as likely to be drawn towards (pulled into) leaving 'home' (and creating new identities, loyalties and eligibilities) than they are to be pushed away by personal and professional circumstances situated their place of origin.

Migrant Types	Definition & Description (Love and Kim 2011: 92-93)
Ambitionist (Magee and Sugden, 2002)	Magee and Sugden (2002) describe three dimensions of the ambitionist category: (a) the desire to achieve a sport career anywhere, (b) the preference for playing in the certain location as compared to elsewhere, and (c) the desire to improve one's career by moving to a higher-quality league. In response to Magee and Sugden's typology, Maguire (2004) noted that, although research by himself and colleagues had found the ambition to play at a high level to be an important part of athletes' explanations for migrating, they believed that such ambition transcended several of the categories, rather than comprising a category of its own.
Exile and Ex-pelled (Magee and Sugden, 2002)	Magee and Sugden (2002: 432) describe the exile as "someone who, for football-related, personal, or political reasons (either voluntarily or through domestic threats to his career, his liberty, or his life), opts to leave his country of origin to play abroad", whereas the expelled is one who is "forced" to leave his/her country of origin.
The Mercenary (Maguire, 1999; Magee and Sugden, 2002)	Magee and Sugden (2002: 429) describe the mercenary as one "who is mo-tivated, above all else, by earning capacity," and who migrates for reasons of economic reward. Maguire (1999) employs a similar definition, adding that mercenaries are often motivated by "short-term gains" (p. 105).
Nomadic Cos-mopolitan (Maguire, 1999; Magee and Sug-den, 2002)	Magee and Sugden's (2002: 432) description of the nomadic cosmopolitan includes individuals who are "motivated by a desire to experience different nations and cultures". Maguire (1999: 105-106), meanwhile, describes "nomads" who are "motivated by a cosmopolitan engagement with migration" (p. 105). Such athletes, "embark on a quest in which they seek the experience of the 'other' and indeed of being the 'other' ".
Pioneers (Maguire, 1999)	Maguire (1999: 105) describes pioneers as individuals who possess "an almost evangelical zeal in extolling the virtues of 'their' sport". Further, the words and actions of pioneers "can be seen as a form of proselytizing by which they seek to convert the natives to their body habitus and sport culture".
Returnee (Maguire, 1999)	As Maguire (1999: 106) explains, "some cosmopolitans, along with pioneers, mercenaries and even long-term settlers, act as 'returnees' in the global process. The lure of 'home soil' can prove too strong".
Settler (Maguire, 1999; Magee and Sugden, 2002)	Magee and Sugden (2002: 431) describe the settler as "someone who has moved to English football and remained in England for a sustained period, of four or five seasons or more," and that "the most advanced settlers stay in England beyond the finish of their playing careers". Maguire (1999: 105) simply describes settlers as "sports migrants who subsequently stay and settle in the society where they perform their labor".

Figure 2: The multiple migrants of Maguire, Magee and Sugden. *Source:* Adapted from Love and Kim (2011)

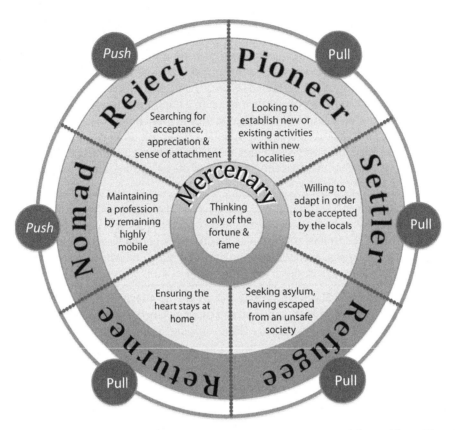

Figure 3: The multiple motives of modern-day sports migrants. *Source:* Adapted from Maguire (1999) and Magee and Sugden (2002)

Of all the migrant types identified, only the reject and nomad are actively encouraged to migrate and/or travel in search of regular sports-based employment. The mercenary migrant is placed at the heart of the model, supporting the belief that it remains the most visible of all the possible/potential motives publicly reported within the home and host nations affected. The decision to position it above the other six categories demonstrates the author's belief that the desire for financial gain is often, if not always, underpinned by (i.e. the result of) at least one of the other overlapping social factors affecting that particular athlete.

The justifications first introduced by Maguire (1999) have also been reduced from those discussed by Love and Kim (2011), to place further emphasis upon the core features that modern migrants may be searching for and/or trying to maintain. The author supports Maguire's (2004) rejection of the 'Ambitionist' sports migrant, a personal feature believed to be found within all professional athletes, and (re)packages Magee and Sugden's 'Exile' and 'Expelled' migrants as 'Refugees' and 'Rejects'. The inclusion of the these two additional categories encourages the reader to build upon Magee and Sugden's research and (re)consider the degree of asylum or rejection that athletes find within their various 'home' and 'host' environments. Rather than separate the seven categories, the model illustrates that player migration is unlikely to be influenced by any one isolated intention (Magee and Sugden, 2002; Maguire, 2004). Finally, the presence of (external) push and pull factors, surrounding the more private (internal) motives of the individual migrant, highlights the inevitable, if not increasing, influence of families, friends, agents and fellow athletes.

Figure 4 focuses on the various different issues and experiences that athletes are expected to encounter upon arrival in their new 'home' environments. Though some of Maguire's (1999) observations are presented as problems and potential barriers, others are seen as potential recruitment opportunities and alternative motivations. An athlete's right to work wherever they deem fit is considered particularly applicable to the following case study, as is Maguire's identification of off-field adjustment, dislocation and retention issues, as well as his acknowledgement of the various personal identities created by professional sports performers operating within an increasingly global local community (Maguire, 1999). The online media discourse presented within the following case study certainly touches upon some of the challenges found within this model. England and Australia's unexpected recruitment and retention of Maori migrants Rangi Chase and James Tamou also offers academics such as Maguire another contemporary case to (re)examine and (re)evaluate.

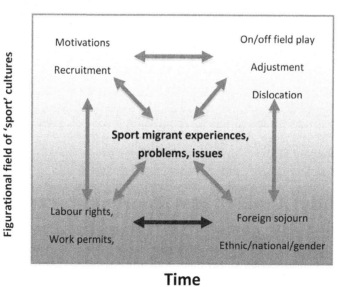

Figure 4: Sport migrant experiences, problems and issues. *Source:* Maguire (1999)

This following case study documents issues and experiences published on-line in England, Australia and New Zealand over an eight-month period, between October 2011 and May 2012. It starts with some of the background material published on the upbringing of Rangi Chase and James Tamou (see Figure 5), including a number of quotes extracted from one-to-one interviews conducted on both sides of the world by journalists trying to generate debate and dialogue among their followers. While some genuinely appeared interested in reporting the 'truth' behind these two professional athletes, others were content to redistribute the personal reactions and public responses captured in the buildup to the 2011 Four Nations Tournament in England and the 2012 ANZAC Day test match in New Zealand. The case study reveals the constructive and critical conclusions drawn by a number of players and coaches (past and present), having first identified the thoughts and feelings of the athletes, and their family. Finally, it highlights issues regarding the international eligibility laws that appear to embrace, if not encourage, elite-level athlete migration within the relatively localised sport of rugby league.

Figure 5: Two modern-day Maori migrants: Rangi Chase (left) and James Tamou (right). Images courtesy of Paddynapper (2012)

The case study: A tale of two Maori migrants

In September 2011, Rangi Chase was shortlisted for the English Super League's (ESL) Man of Steel having narrowly avoided a three-year prison sentence on the other side of the world (Clark, 2011). According to Price (2011, n.p.), "the athlete's good work in the English community and his position as a role model", was cited by the Australian magistrate, who also noted the fact that he [Chase] was "brought up in circumstances of extreme poverty and violence" and "...applauded him for turning his life around". Two months later, a story published online by an English newspaper delved a little deeper into the player's 'troubled' childhood. The headline read:

> "Rangi Chase: Grandad bashed my Nan's face so badly I couldn't recognise her': England rugby league star on overcoming the odds" (Parry, 2011: n.p.)

Rangi Chase was born in the small New Zealand settlement of Dannevirke on 11th April 1986 (Parry, 2011). He was raised by his grandparents, attended a Maori boarding school aged 13 (for a year) before being adopted by some distant relatives and migrating to Australia in the search of a professional rugby league contract. Chase moved to England in 2009 after spending three seasons trying and failing to establish a new life and livelihood playing in Australia. His fast-tracked UK residency application was approved in 2011, supported by the fact that his English Super League team, the Castleford Tigers, was willing to offer him a three-year contract extension (Wilson, 2011).

On the eve of playing against New Zealand for the first time, Chase publicly confessed to being:

> "...a really naughty kid. I was a nasty bully, getting into fights. I was feared by other kids ... We were so poor that I often went to school without shoes or anything to eat. So I would beat people, steal their lunch or steal from their bags ... I would skip school and go to parties. I was drinking at 13 and first smoked weed when I was 11 ... I had run-ins with the police all the time. I attacked people in the street. I was stealing, breaking into houses ..." (Chase, 2011, cited in Parry, 2011: n.p.)

The same article later concluded that:

> "... rugby has taken Rangi out of a life of poverty and crime and to the pinnacle of the game, preparing to line up for England in their Gillette Four Nations match against New Zealand in Hull tomorrow. Since his arrival in 2009, the skillful stand-off has been named [Castleford Tigers] Player of the Year in every season. This year he also won the coveted Man of Steel award, making him the Super League's best player" (Parry, 2011: n.p.).

Chase's personal movements were undoubtedly influenced by a perceived lack of professional opportunities in New Zealand and Australia. In November 2011, he was portrayed in the English online media as someone pushed away by his failure to settle or succeed on either side of the Tasman Sea. In New Zealand, however, he was labelled as a 'troubled' outcast (or reject), whose services were unlikely to be missed. According to Chase, England offered him asylum and a second chance (making him a refugee, as opposed to reject). When asked to explain his decision to the sporting press, Chase was cited as saying:

> "Growing up was hard, really hard, I was never really happy. This is the happiest I've been in my whole life. I have found a girl I love, I've got my self-confidence back and I've turned my back on my old life. Things have changed completely. England has given me the opportunity to make a life. I wish I could live my life over again, but I don't regret anything because it's made me the person I am. Rugby gave me discipline and patience. It gave me hope for my life. When I was a kid I had nothing, no money, no future, no one to guide me in the right direction … As a rugby player, when you're happy off the field you do well on it. This is why I want to stay here and that is why I call England home. I know I'm not English, I haven't got the English tongue, but I'm behind them 100%, I'd do anything for my team-mates. This is my home, what matters is that I've got the same intentions as my teammates" (Chase, 2011, cited in Parry, 2011: n.p.)

In comparison, James Tamou was born two years after Chase, on 13th December 1988, and had a much more settled childhood, growing up in a safe and stable family environment alongside his older brother (Richie Paul) and a younger brother (Zinzan) in the small New Zealand town of Levin (a short drive from where Chase was raised). He was 13 years old when his parents decided to move the entire family to Australia in search of a better life. Unlike Chase, Tamou's upbringing was almost totally ignored by the online media. The fact that he had been happily living in Australia for a decade was clearly deemed non-newsworthy and/or irrelevant. His mother, Pippa Tamou, clearly saw the value in sharing some stories of her son's past, however, and happily told an Australian reporter that he was Head Boy in his final year at Matraville Sports High School, having played local junior league rugby at every opportunity since their move (Jackson, 2012).

Despite spending all of his teenage years in Australia, James Tamou was not seen as a Settler. On the contrary, he was still predominantly portrayed within the online media discourse as being a Kiwi pulled in by the promise of bigger pay packets available in Australia (i.e. as a Mercenary). This narrative was arguably fuelled by a report which revealed how Tamou had told an Australian sports reporter at the start of April 2012 that he would be disappointed if he had not earned a place in the Kiwis' ANZAC Test squad (Jackson, 2012). Less than a fortnight later, however, the online rugby league community found themselves reading the following headlines:

"Kangaroos snare NZ-born Tamou for Anzac test" (Barclays, 2012a: n.p.)

"Aussies pick NZ-born Tamou for league Test" (Jancetic, 2012: n.p.)

Similarly, Chase stated in July 2011 that he was hoping his man-of-the-match performance for a team of Exiles, who had just beaten England in an international friendly match, would result in a call up for the Kiwis prior to the 2011 Four Nations tournament. Four months later he was a British resident, citing the "improbability of a Kiwi call-up" as a reason why he was making himself available to play for England (Chase, 2011 cited in Wilson, 2011a: n.p.). He told British reporters that he had "… never been given the chance to play for them [the Kiwis]" (Chase, 2011, cited in BBC 2011a: n.p.), and further justified his decision with the following ethnic identity-based conclusion:

> "I've played for the New Zealand Maoris, which is [sic] my native people. But I've never played for the New Zealand Test team – the coach has said I never will. So I can't see how I've turned my back on them – I'm just taking my opportunity to represent the place I call home. I don't want to play anywhere else. I have resurrected my life in England and feel more at ease here than anywhere else in the world. I spend all my time at home and don't go back to New Zealand in the off season. I have thought long and hard about the opportunity of playing for England after I became eligible to play. England, and in particular Castleford, is my home now and I want to lay my long-term roots here. Getting selected for England will be my greatest honour" (Chase, 2011, cited in BBC 2011a: n.p.)

While Chase spoke openly about his desire to settle down and create a new family in England, Tamou's opinions remained relatively private as he tried to avoid the media scrum caused by his unexpected, equally unpopular, decision. Though Rangi Chase and James Tamou had been teammates in the New Zealand Maori team, only the latter had represented the Kiwis at a junior level and been rewarded with a place within the Kiwi's elite training squad during their preparations for the 2011 Four Nations tournament. According to his family, Tamou's failure to secure a place in the final squad for that tournament generated the first approach from the Australian selectors (Jackson, 2012). While this offer was politely declined, Tamou's subsequent failure to secure a place in the 2012 Kiwis team triggered a second, much stronger, approach that also including the prospect of him competing in the 2012 State of Origin Series for his 'home' state of New South Wales (Massoud, 2012).

James Tamou's parent's made no attempt to hide their family's affiliation to New Zealand, or their son's aspirations and ambitions to play for his country, as opposed to his state, of origin. They also spoke publicly on several occasions about the circumstances that had pushed their son into making such an unpopular life-changing career decision. His mother told an Australian journalist; "I wanted to go up there [to Townsville]… I was really worried about him… There were phone calls at all hours, day and night" (Tamou, 2012, cited in Jackson, 2012: n.p.). She described the situation as "agonizing" and admitted;

> "He's always wanted to play for the Kiwis, even when he was a little lad over back in New Zealand … He hasn't turned his back … He's always going to be a Maori and he's always going to be a New Zealander. But New Zealand should have moved faster. It was a career decision and he's happy with it. He hadn't heard anything from the Kiwis [when Stuart called this year]. He had to make a decision" (Tamua, 2012, cited in Jackson, 2012: n.p.)

Pippa Tamou was later captured re-iterating her belief that her son falls into both 'the Settler' and 'the Reject' category of migrants, blaming the "hurtful snub" her son received prior to the Four Nations for driving him away from the Kiwis. She defended his choice, and revealed her anger at reports he had rejected the Kiwis, stressing that:

> "James never knew where he stood with New Zealand. Last year he made the train-on squad for the Four Nations, but they told him not to bother joining the rest of the team in Sydney. They just told him to keep training alone in Townsville. A few days later (New Zealand coach) Stephen Kearney called to say he didn't make the cut. They played mind games with him and James didn't know what he was supposed to do to get selected. Being told to stay in Townsville made him really confused. He was very disappointed … James had to stop and have a really good think about it. He spoke to so many people before making his decision [to make himself available to the Australian selectors] just before Easter [2012]. By the time Tony Kemp and Stephen Kearney called James, it was too late. He'd already made his decision. It was a really tough decision for James and he didn't take it lightly. He knew it was a decision that would affect the rest of his career. But in football that can be very short. You've got to take your chances when they come along and we couldn't be prouder of him' (Tamou, 2012, cited in Massoud, 2012: n.p.)

When asked about the negative reactions in Australia and New Zealand, his Mother felt her son would handle the pressure appropriately, describing him as "a very humble boy" who "doesn't really say a bad word about anybody", adding "On Facebook, a lot's been going on [about his decision], but James doesn't dwell on things like that. I said to him, You could go play for China, I don't care. As long as he's happy" (Tamou, 2012, cited in Jackson, 2012: n.p.). Tamou's older brother was equally vocal, claiming "I'm proud of him, eh, really proud of him. He's playing international football and that was his dream regardless of the colour of the jumper" (Paul, 2012, cited in Lawton, 2012: n.p.). He concluded that he was neither disappointed nor surprised by the negative public reactions, but displayed confidence that James would remain 'grounded' despite the attention, adding "Nah, man. We knew it was going to come. He knew it was going to come. But that's rugby league. He's really humble, eh. He's a typical Maori kid" (Paul, 2012, cited in Lawton, 2012: n.p.)[1].

Though James Tamou tried to remain out of the public spotlight, he was quoted talking about his personal (New Zealand) identity and professional (Australian) loyalties, saying: "Being born in New Zealand, New Zealand will always be my home but this is a career decision. I'm happy to be here to be picked this quickly for the green and gold. I'm happy, can't wipe the smile off my face" (Tamou, 2012, cited in Tulloch, 2012: n.p.). Unlike Chase, he opted against highlighting the fact he has represented his ethnic (Maori) identity on the international sporting stage, leaving that to his family. He was captured, however, commenting on the rough treatment he expected to receive during the ANZAC Day test itself. Tamou admitted that he was expecting "about five or six black jumpers rushing up on me", adding "I'm in the green and gold. I'm representing my country of choice. I'm happy to take it on. When I made this decision, I knew there would be a bit of backlash, and the Kiwi team would be the first people to let me know about it, so I'm expecting it" (Tamou, 2012, cited in Webster et al., 2012: n.p.).

Tamou claims that he had been congratulated by one of the Kiwi team, but knew that was "off the field" and that "… it will be a different story on the field when he and I come together" (Tamou, 2012, cited in Webster et al., 2012, n.p.). When questioned on the eve of his debut, James Tamou laughed off the claims that he was only interested in the money, saying: "I've heard it and I couldn't believe it. The excitement of State of Origin, it's one of the most viewed things on television, it's awesome and I want to one day hopefully be a part of it" (Tamou, 2012, cited in Webster, 2012c: n.p.). He appeared a lot

---

1   The article included a picture of Richie Paul wearing an Australian shirt, but revealed that their mother had been hospitalised the day before and was forced to miss the match. According to Paul, "All the stuff in the media and the nerves she had for Jim, I think, took its toll on her" (Paul, 2012, cited in Lawton, 2012, n.p.).

more serious when responding to those saying that he was pressured into making the change of allegiance, telling reporters:

> "I know I've made the right decision to pull on the green and gold. Last year, Ricky called me (about being eligible for NSW) and I said no. Then I went through the whole year ... I watched Origin, just thinking to myself that it could be me. That's where the flame ignited. As soon as Ricky Stuart gave me that second phone-call, I knew what I wanted to do" (Tamou, 2012, cited in Webster *et al.*, 2012c: n.p.)

Finally, on the issue of facing, as opposed to performing, the pre-match haka (see Figure 6) – something Rangi Chase had already publicly admitted to feeling 'strange' about (Walter, 2011: n.p.) – Tamou was said to be smiling when he told reporters that "It will be tough. But I know I've had this situation in my head, and I'll be ready to take it on" (Tamou, 2012, cited in Webster et al., 2012: n.p.). He told another Australian reporter that:

> "Right now, I'm an Aussie. Happy to be an Aussie. I play for Aussie. I'll pull on the green and gold and play my best football for it. I'll go against the Kiwis and play my best footy. Right now, I'm an Aussie" (Tamou, 2012, cited in Webster, 2012a: n.p.)

Having helped England defeat the Kiwi's in the 2011 Four Nations Tournament, Chase admitted that he had "struggled to maintain control after being heavily targeted by his countrymen"[2] (Walter, 2011: n.p.). He also revealed that he had visited the Kiwi's dressing room after the game and accepted the harsh treatment he had received on the field of play, including some illegal conduct by those who had publicly defended his decision during the pre-match build-up. He concluded that;

> "They [the Kiwis] are passionate people and as soon as I pledged my allegiance to England I knew this was going to happen. People were going to get fired up and want to have a go at me. In a way it is a good thing because they are trying to put me off my game and I respect them. What happens on the field stays on the field and if I had of reacted in a different way they probably would have got what they wanted' (Chase, 2011, cited in Walter, 2011: n.p.)

In comparison, having been asked whether he had any regrets about helping Australia beat New Zealand 20-12 in the 2012 ANZAC Test, James Tamou responded with the following statement:

> "Absolutely not ... I was sitting down and my legs wouldn't stop shaking. Once I got out there, I felt good ... I know a few of the (Kiwi) boys

---

2   Isaac Ross was later charged by the RFL and banned for two matches having confessed to trying to break Chase's leg during the ill-tempered 2011 Four Nation's fixture (Fox Sport, 2011).

and after the game, they said "Congratulations on your choice". It all went pretty well. This feeling is addictive and I want to keep it going. Hopefully, next step NSW. I am proud to put on the green and gold and I chose the winning side tonight. I am one from one. It was awesome - unreal. Still trying to soak it all in. But it was also a gut-churner, particularly during the haka. I think two thirds of the (Kiwi) team were staring straight at me, so I knew it was going to be on. I knew once we got out there, with the help from the boys, I'd go well. There was a fair bit (of niggle), but that's rugby league" (Tamou, 2012, cited in Read, 2012: n.p.).

The similarities to Chase's post-match reflection are somewhat obvious, in terms of his off-field expectations and the on-field experiences encountered. This final quotation also acts as a suitable bridge across to the following section, which reveals the public conclusions made by his fellow professionals (past and present).

Figure 6: Chase (wearing 7) performing the haka and confronting the opposition in 2008. Tamou (not pictured) was involved in the same game. Images courtesy of Paddynapper, 2012.

Meaningless mercenary, silly settler or rejected refugee?

While numerous comments and conclusions were published questioning the role the NZRL in James Tamou's decision, the press appeared less interested in finding answers about why (or how) Rangi Chase was never provided the opportunity to represent the Kiwis. Lawton (2011: n.p.) offered his support to Chase's decision to play for England, pointing out that – despite his "success in the Super League" – the sporting migrant "was always going to struggle to win selection for his native New Zealand". The journalist's opinion was subsequently proven correct by Kiwi's coach Stephen Kearney's announcement that, unlike James Tamou, Chase was never in contention for a place in the Four Nations squad (BBC 2011a) having only made it onto his list of potential players for the future. Having shared some of the online discourse produced by Chase and the Tamou family, the case study will look at some of the comments publicly provided by a number of past and present rugby league professionals located in England, Australia and New Zealand, including those involved in the off-field administration of the sport.

In November 2011, Andy Platt, a former British Lions representative who migrated to Australia after his retirement from Rugby League, defended Rangi Chase, telling a reporter that, "I'm sure if England had better players, then they wouldn't have to call him up" and "as long as he feels the passion to play, then I have nothing against him" (Platt, 2011 cited in The Age, 2011, n.p.). He supported the similar selection of Brisbane-based professional Jack Reed3, but showed concern about the increased number of English players migrating to Australia (The Age, 2011). Garry Schofield, one of his former international team mates still living in England, strongly disagreed with this view and used his social media account to tweet:

> "Speechless... What a f---ing joke!! ... It needs sorting out ... This is wrong. It may be in the rules but morally this is bull ... In July [2011] Chase was desperate to play for the Kiwis. How can ANYONE defend these rules?!" (Schofield, 2011, cited in Mascord, 2011, n.p.).

Six months later, back in Australia, former Kangaroos captain Gorden Tallis stated his belief that someone should have stepped in and forced James Tamou to honour the professional commitment he made in November 2011 when he accepted a place in the Kiwis' Four Nations training squad. Tallis told reporters that "It was a great opportunity for the [ARL] commission to stand up and be strong. It was the first chance for the game to get rid of the past and be strong on this subject. This is not a grey area, this is black and white and by black and white I mean New Zealand" (Tallis, 2012, cited in Balym, 2012: n.p.). Kevin Walters, another former Australian International, agreed wholeheartedly and stressed that: "It shouldn't come down to players nominating ... the [ARL] commission should take the issue out of the players' hands and take all responsibility for which players go where" (Walters, 2012, cited in Balym, 2012: n.p.).

Another former Australian representative, Greg Dowling, publicly questioned Tamou's motives, reminding reporters that:

> "Last year, he (Tamou) aligned himself with the Kiwis but spat the dummy after he got dumped ... and that's when the commission

---

3   Like Tamou, Reed's family migrated to Australia when he was a child, making him eligible to play for the both his state (Queensland) and his country (Australia).

should have taken a stance and stamped him as such. They're making a joke out of it. You can't change your mind every year. The [ARL] commission should have stepped in and said 'you're a Kiwi, you play for New Zealand' and taken the decision out of his hands. They need to do it now and not let this shambles go on any longer" (Dowling, 2012, cited in Balym, 2012: n.p.).

Interestingly, Paul Sironen, yet another former Australian player to speak publicly about James Tamou's switch of national allegiance, appeared more upset with the way the switch was been reported in the New Zealand media, claiming that:

"The Kiwis are kidding. They can hardly complain, they shouldn't be throwing stones from their glass house. I shake my head at a few blokes. One minute Brad Thorn (former Broncos forward) was playing for Queensland and Australia, and the next he's playing for the All Blacks in a World Cup. There needs to be a massive overhaul of the selection process. We need some clear defining guidelines because the whole thing is causing confusion" (Sironen, 2012, cited in Shannon, 2012, n.p.).

Overall, it proved harder to find similar criticism coming from former Kiwi representatives, although former Kiwis captain, Hugh McGahan, was cited saying, "It's crazy – it makes a joke of the game at international level. It's just plain silly for a bloke to go from being a Kiwi one year to an Aussie the next and a lot of people in the game must be wondering what's going on. I bet there are plenty of Aussie front rowers who aren't impressed either" (McGahan, 2012, cited in Hatton, 2012: n.p.). In comparison, former Kiwi's coach Graham Lowe was happy to share his support for James Tamou, telling a reporter:

"If the kid wants to play, if he is living in Australia, and he's made Australia home, I have no problem with him wanting to play for the Australians. Nathan Fien is as Australian as Ned Kelly and yet the Kiwis embraced him into the Test side so I don't see any difference. I don't think that we in New Zealand should be too up-tight about it. If he doesn't want to play for New Zealand well too bad, see you later" (Lowe, 2012, cited in Skipwith, 2012: n.p.)

Stephen Kearney, the coach of the 2011 and 2012 Kiwi team, appeared equally understanding of Tamou's choice, telling reporters that he "totally" respected the player's decision (Kearney, 2012, cited in Tulloch, 2012: n.p.). Six months earlier, Kearney had also publicly supported Rangi Chase, telling reporters, "[i]f that's the decision he wants to make, we wish him all the best. He wants to play international footy and at the moment there isn't really a position for him" (Kearney, 2011, cited in Lawton, 2011: n.p.). In November 2011, however, Kearney reminded English reporters that: "I'm sure if you ask Rangi he's still a Kiwi, he just chooses to play for England" (Kearney, 2011, cited in BBC, 2011b: n.p.), before offering his support to the English Coach, Steve McNamara, who had also selected Australian-born forward Chris Heighington within his 2011 Four Nations squad (BBC, 2011b). Finally, Kearney told a press conference full of reporters that most countries had a history of picking players born elsewhere and revealed that eight of his 22-man squad were either born or educated in Australia (Wilson, 2011), and later told the press that "it is up to the individual which country they should choose to play for" (Kearney, 2011, cited in Lawton, 2011: n.p.).

Though the movements of Rangi Chase and James Tamou received little public support from former rugby league professionals, the current crop of players seemed to accept, if not agree with, the justifications offered in November 2011 and April 2012. Thomas Leuluai, for example, saw nothing wrong with Chase's decision, but had some mixed feelings about the way it was done. The only English-based New Zealander representing the Kiwis in the 2011 Four Nations cited, "he [Chase] has played here [England] for a while and never really got a look in with the Kiwis so if he has a chance to play international football then why not ... obviously he made up his mind ... and you can't fault him for that" (Leuluai, 2011, cited in Lawton, 2011: n.p.). Kieran Foran also noted his "surprise", before concluding that "he [Chase] has to do what's best for his football" (Foran, 2011, cited in BBC, 2011b: n.p.).

During the buildup to the 2012 ANZAC Day test, Sydney-born Kiwi representative Nathan Fien was quoted as saying, "The way the rules are, Tamou hasn't done anything wrong. Every player has the right to choose what he wants to do and you have to respect that decision" (Fien, 2012, cited in ODT, 2012: n.p.). Another Australian-born Kiwi, Josh Hoffman, admitted that "there is a bit of bitterness in the [Kiwis] camp", before adding:

> "... I think the decision that he made is 100% his decision, and no one else can criticize what he's done ... If he [Tamou] decides he wants to play Origin that's his decision. Full credit to him. Players should have the right to choose what they want to do. I've had that pressure as well and my decision has stood with the Kiwis. His decision is to play for New South Wales and once we go out on that paddock he is just going to be treated as another Aussie. (Hoffman, 2012, cited in NZ Newswire, 2012: n.p.)[4].

---

4   Hoffman, who was making his Kiwis debut in the 2012 ANZAC Test Match, was born and raised in Australia but eligible for New Zealand through his father.

Benji Marshall, New Zealand's captain and a former Australian schoolboy representative, was particularly vocal in both his empathy for Rangi Chase and his apathy for James Tamou. In November 2011, he told the English media that he had jokingly called his former housemate "a dog" for being "a Kiwi playing for England!", but in reality "wish him all the best" (Marshall, 2011, cited in Wilson, 2011: n.p.). He reminded another reporter that:

> "Growing up as a kid, he had nothing – no money, very little family … for him [Chase] to turn that around and be where he is now is something I'm very proud of. It's great to see him doing well … I'm just proud of him – he's matured as a player and a person. He's definitely made the right move." (Marshall, 2011, cited in Carter, 2011: n.p.)

Though Marshall publicly stated that "Chase should not be lambasted" (Wilson, 2011: n.p.), he accused James Tamou of being only motivated by the money he could make in the State of Origin Series (Hatton, 2012; Honeysett, 2012; Jackson and Barclay, 2012; Shannon, 2012). He challenged one reporter to:

> "Just listen to him talk and listen to his accent and tell me he's Australian. … I've seen it happen before with guys. Maybe the thought of playing State of Origin got to him. At the end of the day, these guys are making 40-odd thousand [dollars] off playing State of Origin every year, whereas to play a test match, you probably get $3000. That money side of things might be luring him. If that's where his heart is, good luck to him. We don't want him" (Marshall, 2012, cited in Jackson and Barclay, 2012: n.p.).

When asked if Tamou had made himself a target for retribution, Marshall claimed that they [the Kiwis] had "got caught in that trap with Rangi Chase last year" (Marshall, 2012, cited in Jackson and Barclay, 2012: n.p.). Marshall's comments about the pull of the State of Origin series were repeated on several occasions by others offering their opinions to the world's sporting media. Nathan Fien, for example, told a reporter that:

> "Benji [Marshall] made a really good point about the carrot of playing Origin, where you can earn up to $50,000 in an Origin series as opposed to a test match can sway young Kiwi guys. It's something the NZRL are going to have to address and address really fast or we might see a bit of a drain on players, which is going to affect the international game. We have always been the little brother. We won the World Cup and have won the Four Nations but we don't want to see our young players drawn away to the bright lights of Origin" (Fien, 2012, cited in ODT, 2012, n.p.).

Unsurprisingly, the media were equally keen to record and redistribute the thoughts of the sports administrators and agents affected by these two incidents, especially the case of James Tamou. Tony Kemp, The NZRL's high performance manager, for example, was particularly vocal in his anger at the loss of a player he clearly felt was already a part of the New Zealand system. Kemp's comments were subsequently redistributed by a number of reporters covering the controversial story (Badel, 2012a; Shannon, 2012). He was cited acknowledging the complexities of assessing a player's international eligibility[5], but criticised the way the ARL had influenced Tamou's sudden change of heart (Shannon, 2012). Badel cited the following statement from the clearly apathetic NZRL representative:

> "This whole thing is ridiculous; it would be embarrassing for the game to see James Tamou running out in NSW and Australian jumpers. James is currently eligible for New Zealand, he's been in our system, and yet he could be picked for Australia (tonight) ... what a joke. As it stands, we could pick him (tonight), but the bottom line is we want players who want to play for New Zealand. If they tell us they don't want to play for New Zealand, we won't pick them. James is unfortunately a confused young man. I've seen other Kiwi kids face the haka and then they realise it doesn't feel right. I really believe James will regret not playing for New Zealand because he's a proud Maori, like I am, and I know what representing his country would mean to him. I actually feel sorry for James. It's not a good look for the game when James is in our train-on squad, embedded in our culture, and within months he is running around saying he wants to play for NSW. The whole eligibility issue has to be cleared up because this is embarrassing" (Kemp, 2012, cited in Badel, 2012a: n.p.)

Scott Carter, the Chairman of the Rugby League International Federation (RLIF), was much more pragmatic, arguing, "you can't blame athletes being brutally commercial. People will say: how can you value anything more than tradition, pride and amateurism? The reality is that, in the modern world, loyalty is not everything" (Carter, 2012 cited in Alderson, 2012: n.p.). Similarly, Jim Doyle, The New Zealand Rugby League chief executive, was also captured reminding the public that, "we've [New Zealand] got six or seven

---

5   Kemp stated: "Both my kids were born in England and were brought up there until the ages of six. That doesn't make them English" (Kemp, 2012, cited in Vannisselroy, 2012, n.p.). What makes Kemp's public opposition to this case particularly interesting is the fact that he not only played and coached professionally in England, Australia and New Zealand, but played a leading role in the easing of international trade restrictions, taking his current employers to court in 1989 and winning a legal challenge that allowed him to continue his career outside of New Zealand (NZRL, 2009).

guys in our side who were born in Australia ... it's not fair for us to say James Tamou should only be able to play for New Zealand when we are the recipient of Australian-born Kiwis. There's a lot of Kiwis in Australia... but there are guys like James Tamou who see themselves as more of an Aussie and that's their call" (Doyle, 2012, cited in Badel, 2012b: n.p.). In another interview, Doyle admitted that there was nothing New Zealand could do to compete with the financial packages available to Australian athletes. He revealed their desire to create a similar 'origin' fixture, but admitted that it was unlikely to draw the same amount of investment or support as the annual contest between NSW and Queensland (Webster, 2012a). He concluded that:

> "State of Origin has been around for 30 years and attracts 70,000 to each game as well as huge broadcasting dollars. Some of that money goes to the players. We are not in that position ... it will take a number of years to get to that sort of income. It really comes down to players wanting to play for the New Zealand because you are Kiwis. If players say they want to earn more money, then we are never going to compete with them" (Doyle, 2012 cited in Webster, 2012b: n.p.)

James Tamou's manager, Sammy Ayoub, remained surprisingly quiet during the aftermath of his client's announcement. A week later however it was reported within a story headlined "Tamou attacks are way off the money", that he was "furious" and "disgusted" at those questioning Tamou's personal and professional motives. He further told the reporter that:

> "For starters, there is only one representative bonus in his contract, and that is if he plays for New Zealand. There is not one bonus for playing for Australia or Origin. There certainly are no Origin bonuses in there at all. Not once has James called me asking about what this meant for him in terms of bonuses. It disgusts me to hear this claim that it's all about the money. It is so insanely wrong it's not funny" (Ayoub, 2012, cited in Webster, 2012c: n.p.).

Fixing the eligibility minefield

According to Anderson (2012), the issue of increased player migration has not only raised doubts regarding the validity of the existing guidelines, but also undermined their value in a global sport controlled by three dominant nations (England, New Zealand and Australia). He disagrees with those arguing that players should be given less freedom, suggesting that the guidelines are too restrictive and damaging the expansion of the game outside of the big three 'Tier 1' nations (Anderson, 2012). He proposes that elite-level athletes with dual eligibility should be allowed the opportunity to move back and forth between emerging and established nations (i.e. Tier 2 countries trying to develop the game and Tier 1 countries within which the professional game is already developed). Figure 7 illustrates this. Bernstein (2012) supports this idea, believing it could increase the potential talent pool, provide better competition and improve the global interest in rugby league.

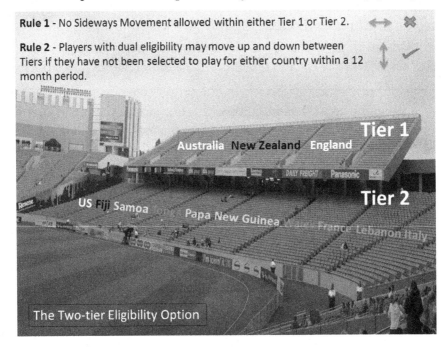

Rule 1 - No Sideways Movement allowed within either Tier 1 or Tier 2.

Rule 2 - Players with dual eligibility may move up and down between Tiers if they have not been selected to play for either country within a 12 month period.

Tier 1

Australia New Zealand England

Tier 2

US Fiji Samoa   Papa New Guinea   France Lebanon Italy

The Two-tier Eligibility Option

Figure 7: The two-tier option: Anderson's solution to the rugby league eligibility minefield. *Source:* Adapted from Anderson (2012)

In November 2011, Rangi Chase's change of eligibility was said to have "split rugby league in two" (Parry, 2011: n.p.). Five months later, Tamou's decision was labelled "a farce" (Ikin, 2012: n.p.), "crazy" (McGahan, 2012, cited in Hatton, 2012: n.p.), "a joke" (Kemp, 2012, cited in Shannon, 2012: n.p.), "embarrassing for the game" (Kemp, 2012, cited in Badel, 2012a: n.p.) and, more significantly, "a golden opportunity to rid the game of eligibility dramas" (Tallis, 2012, cited in Balym, 2012: n.p.). The rules for international rugby league eligibility are fundamentally similar to those found within most other professional sports, with the RLIF being responsible for their development and enforcement across an ever-expanding international arena (Alderson, 2012).

The aim of this final section is to contextualise the case of Rangi Chase and James Tamou within the global sporting world they have both chosen to make their profession. One of the Australian reporters, responsible for gathering 'expert' opinions on the authenticity of James Tamou's Australian eligibility concluded that:

> "While Tamou undoubtedly took advantage of the code's dual eligibility rules, the Kiwis have exploited the same guidelines to strengthen their stocks ahead of tonight's clash at Eden Park. Fullback Hoffman was born in Mackay. [Nathan] Fien hails from the mining town of Mt Isa. Nightingale grew up in Sydney and played for Renown United, the same junior club as former Dragons teammate Mark Gasnier. Pritchard emerged from Campbelltown in Sydney's west, Kenny-Dowall and Beale were born in Brisbane, and McKendry is a product of Perth" (2012c: n.p.).

Similarly, France (2012: n.p.) concluded that "Eligibility will never be straightforward, particularly in Australasia where various races from across the Pacific migrate to the bigger cities of Australia and New Zealand. Individuals with dual eligibility have the right to choose who they want to represent. That's not solely in league, but in life". Scott Carter, the RLIF chairman, responded to the criticism being published across a host of online forums, blogs and social networking sites, publicly defending the criteria used to determine an individual's international eligibility. Carter argued that increased player mobility is "reflective of the modern world" (Carter, 2012, cited in Alderson, 2012: n.p.) and that the movements and motives of all international players were carefully scrutinised. As the personal ultimately responsible for the modern-day management of international rugby league, his lengthy response to the question of monitoring and managing identities, loyalties and eligibilities of sporting migrant provides the perfect conclusion to this case study, providing a platform and plenty of scope for further discussion and debate. He identifies the frustrations of people situated within and outside the sport, acknowledges the multiple push and pull factors affecting player movements and, more importantly, attempts to place it into the context of our increasingly mobile contemporary society.

> "Eligibility still comes down to a player's right to choose. League has two main competitions [in Australia and Britain] that naturally draw talent from a lot of countries. The reality is no one will commute from Tonga to Leeds or Christchurch to Brisbane so its natural players will clock up a lot of time in those two countries and [the Kangaroos and Lions] will have access to a strong talent pool … People get frustrated when someone appears to have made their choice and changes their mind. But in the modern world people's circumstances change. If someone genuinely wants to play for Australia, and qualifies, there's no point standing in their way. For years Australia and New Zealand

have sucked people out of the islands to work in factories, go to university and become professionals. Those people also play sport and the natural path is for them to move countries. I don't think it's contentious. Society has changed, there has always been a flow between countries but these days it is more common, especially with professional athletes. It comes down to an individual's right to choose. Critics need to realise many players have numerous options. I've known players who are eligible for four nations … a player can have Samoan grandparents who move to New Zealand. The parents then move to Australia and have children. Those children might go and play in England for three years … We also need to decide whether eligibility rules apply to junior internationals. At the moment they don't. I believe there's a natural expectation they should … I don't believe we should complicate that rule by including age group teams or schoolboy sides. There are plenty of cases where people go overseas to work and their kids go to local schools. If they're talented they play representative sport for their temporary country … Look at the Tamou case. He'd played for New Zealand Maori and the Junior Kiwis" (Carter, 2012, cited in Alderson, 2012: n.p.).

Conclusion

Rangi Chase and James Tamou, like so many of their fellow professional athletes operating at the elite level, have found themselves in a position where their public movements through space and time have resulted in them being able to pick which national flag they wish to represent on the international field of play. The purpose of this case study is not to try and justify why Rangi Chase and James Tamou opted to play international rugby league for England and Australia, as opposed to their native New Zealand. The aim was to demonstrate the different responses these unexpected announcements received within the globally accessible online media. Both athletes were captured commenting on a feeling of rejection, claiming to have been pushed into changing their mind by their failure to be selected by the Kiwi management. Both also spoke openly about their desire to 'settle' in their countries of residence, showing no obvious degree of attachment or desire to return to their country of birth. Neither came across as being mercenaries, or motivated by anything other than their desire to be happy on and off the field. Rangi Chase was largely portrayed as someone searching for asylum and trying to escape a troubled past. James Tamou was portrayed by those closest to him as a humble individual pushed into the open arms of the country he calls home by the lack of faith shown within his country of origin. While these reasons were accepted by some commentators, they were rejected and rubbished by other.

Maguire's mercenary motive may be the catalyst for most modern day sporting migrations, but the responses captured within this case study support the author's suggestion that each case must be evaluated as an individual movement affected by a host of internal and external events. Though the majority of athletes are unlikely to admit it publicly (i.e. to the media), all professional sporting movements are going to affect, and be affected by, the potential financial rewards available. Life-changing 'career' decision that involve changing one's identity, loyalty and eligibility should come predominantly from the head (i.e. professional logic), as opposed to the heart (personal emotion). The extent to which the external factors are reported, revisited, reinterpreted and replayed within the public domain, however, appears dependent upon the athlete in question (i.e. the perceived importance of the migrant, the popularity of the migrant's sport and the nations affected by the migrant's movements). Clearly, the local loyalties of those observing from the outside are also a major factor in the degree of apathy or empathy reported within the online sporting press.

Arguably, one of the biggest issues to emerge from this case study relates to the suggestions that Australia's State of Origin series is thought to have greater pulling power than playing international rugby league, causing modern day migrants such as James Tamou to reconsider the traditional career pathways that push them towards playing for their country of birth. The findings appear to support the work of Giulianotti and Robertson (2006), which stresses the importance of developing and demonstrating local loyalties within an increasingly mobile 'global' community. Finally, the tales of these two Maori migrants reveal that sporting migrations do not have to involve individuals trying to seek the acceptance or approval of those who pay their wages (i.e. the public). In doing so, this case study offers some considerable scope for further sport management studies into the complex cultural connections that exist between personal mobility, local loyalty, national identity and professional eligibility. Furthermore, it also provides a suitable platform for similar case studies to be conducted within the context of other equally mobile international sporting communities.

References

Alderson A. 2012. League: A question of when residency begins. http://www.nzherald.co.nz/sport/news/article.cfm?c_id=4andobjectid=10800643

Anderson D. 2012. Fixing the eligibility minefield. www.abc.net.au/news/2012-04-19/finding-solutions-to-the-eligibility-minefield/3960712?section=sport

Badel P. 2012a. New Zealand hierarchy label Blues poaching of James Tamou as an 'embarrassment'. http://www.couriermail.com.au/sport/nrl/new-zealand-hierarchy-label-blues-poaching-of-james-tamou-as-an-embarrassment/story-e6frep5x-1226326568018

Badel P. 2012b. James Tamou is risking his representative career, says NZ chief Jim Doyle. http://www.heraldsun.com.au/sport/nrl/james-tamou-is-risking-his-representative-career-says-nz-chief-jim-doyle/story-e6frfgdf-1226335177304

Badel P. 2012c. Almost half of the New Zealand side to play Australia in ANZAC rugby league Test are from Australia. http://www.couriermail.com.au/sport/nrl/almost-half-of-the-new-zealand-side-to-play-australia-in-anzac-rugby-league-test-are-from-australia/story-e6frep5x-1226333622315

Badel P. 2012d. NRL is adamant new eligibility rules will provide more clarity. http://www.couriermail.com.au/sport/nrl/nrl-is-adamant-new-eligibility-rules-will-provide-more-clarity/story-e6frep5x-1226331997758

Balym T. 2012. James Tamou representative bonus in NRL contract based upon him playing for New Zealand. http://www.couriermail.com.au/sport/nrl/tamous-incentive-still-black-and-white/story-e6frep5x-1226328182224

Barclays C. 2012a. Kangaroos snare NZ-born Tamou for ANZAC test. www.stuff.co.nz/sport/league/6747356/Kangaroos-snare-NZ-born-Tamou-for-Anzac-test

Barclays C. 2012b. James Tamou ready for backlash from Kiwis. http://www.stuff.co.nz/sport/league/6753179/James-Tamou-ready-for-backlash-from-Kiwis

BBC. 2011a. Castleford's Rangi Chase called up to England squad. http://news.bbc.co.uk/sport2/hi/rugby_league/15151939.stm

BBC. 2011b. Four Nations 2011: England's Rangi Chase is a Kiwi, says Kearney. http://news.bbc.co.uk/sport2/hi/rugby_league/15666799.stm

Bernstein J. 2012. Anderson's international eligibility idea should be a stepping stone to expansion. http://www.loverugbyleague.com/blogpost_493-anderson--s-international-eligibility-idea-should-be-a-stepping-stone-to-expansion.html

Carter G. 2011. Benji Marshall backs Rangi Chase for England. http://www.thesun.co.uk/sol/homepage/sport/rugby_league/3895758/Benji-Marshall-backs-Rangi-Chase-for-England.html

Clark L. 2011. Kiwi in line for top UK rugby league award. http://wwos.ninemsn.com.au/article.aspx?id=8352671

Cornelissen S, Solberg E. 2007. Sport mobility and circuits of power: The dynamics of football migration in Africa and the 2010 World Cup *Politikon* **34** (3): 295-314.

Falcous M, Maguire J. 2005. Globetrotters and local heroes? Labor migration, basketball, and local identities, *Sociology of Sport Journal* **22** (2): 137-157.

Falcous M, Maguire J. 2011. Future directions: Sporting mobilities, immobilities and moorings. In Maguire J, Falcous M (eds) *Sport and Migration: Borders, Boundaries and Crossings*. Oxford: Routledge; 274-277.

France M. 2012. The Sin Bin: Marvin France's take on the NRL. www.7daysindubai. com/Sin-Bin-Marvin-France-s-NRL/story-15839588-detail/story.html

Fox Sport. 2011. I tried to break Rangi Chase's leg because he turned his back on New Zealand, Issac Luke admits. http://www.foxsports.com.au/league/i-tried-to-break-rangi-chases-leg-because-he-turned-his-back-on-new-zealand-issac-luke

Giulianotti R, Robertson R. 2006. Supporters in North America glocalization, globalization and migration: The case of Scottish Football *International Sociology* **21** (2): 171-198.

Hatton S. Ex-Kiwi slams Tamou selection. 2012 http://www.loverugbyleague.com/news_8805-ex-kiwi-slams-tamou-selection.html

Higham J, Hinch T. 2009. *Sport and Tourism: Globalisation, Mobility and Identity*. Oxford: Butterworth-Heinemann.

Honeysett S. 2012. Tamou expects torrid Eden Park reception. http://www.theaustralian.com.au/sport/nrl/tamou-expects-torrid-eden-park-reception/story-fnca0von-1226328180970

Ikin B. 2012. Selection farce as Tamou picked ahead of Petero. http://www.stuff.co.nz/sport/opinion/6756287/Selection-farce-as-Tamou-picked-ahead-of-Petero

Jackson G. 2012. NZ should have moved faster - Tamou's mum. http://www.stuff.co.nz/sport/league/6756110/NZ-should-have-moved-faster-Tamous-mum

Jackson G, Barclay C. 2012. Benji Marshall slams Tamou allegiance switch. Confusing decision labelled 'joke'. http://www.stuff.co.nz/sport/league/6748405/Benji-Marshall-slams-Tamou-allegiance-switch

Jancetic S. 2012. Aussies pick NZ-born Tamou for league Test. http://news.smh.com.au/breaking-news-sport/aussies-pick-nzborn-tamou-for-league-test-20120415-1x1ah.html

Kim A, Love S. 2011. Sport labor migration and collegiate sport in the United States: A typology of migrant athletes *Journal of Issues in Intercollegiate Athletics* **4**, 90-104.

Lawton A. 2011. Rangi Chase picks England for top honours. http://www.stuff.co.nz/sport/league/5874017/Rangi-Chase-picks-England-for-top-honours

Lawton A. 2012. Kiwi Mum misses out on rookie Roo's debut. http://www.stuff.co.nz/sport/league/6786252/Kiwi-Mum-misses-out-on-rookie-Roos-debut

Love A, Kim S. 2011. Sport labor migration and collegiate sport in the United States: A typology of migrant athletes. *Journal of Issues in Intercollegiate Athletics* 4: 90-104.

Magee J, Sugden J. 2002. 'The World at their Feet': Professional football and international labor migration. *Journal of Sport and Social Issues* 26 (4): 421-437.

Maguire J. 1993. Globalization, sport and national identities: The empire strikes back? *Society and Leisure* 16, 293-323.

Maguire J. 1994. Preliminary observations on globalization and the migration of sport labour. *Sociological Review* 42 (3): 452-480.

Maguire J. 1999. *Global Sport: Identities, Societies, Civilizations.* Cambridge: Polity Press.

Maguire J. 2004. Sport labor migration research revisited. *Journal of Sport and Social Issues* 28 (4): 477-482.

Maguire J. 2011. Preliminary observations on globalization and the migration of sport labour. In Maguire J, Falcous M (eds) *Sport and Migration: Borders, Boundaries and Crossings.* Oxford: Routledge; 73-87.

Maguire J, Bale J. 1994. Introduction: Sports Labour Migration in the Global Arena. In Bale J, Maguire J. (eds) *The Global Sports Arena: Athletic Talent Migration in an Interdependent World.* Portland, OR: Frank Cass; 1-22.

Maguire J, Falcous M. 2011. Introduction: borders, boundaries and crossings: Sport, migration and identities. In Maguire J, Falcous M (eds) *Sport and Migration: Borders, Boundaries and Crossings.* Oxford: Routledge; 1-12.

Maguire J, Pearton R. 2000a. Global sport and the migration patterns of France 98 World Cup Final players: Some preliminary observations. *Soccer and Society* 1 (1), 175-189.

Maguire J, Pearton R. 2000b. The impact of elite labor migration on the identification, selection and development of European soccer players. *Journal of Sports Sciences* 18 (9): 759-769.

Maguire J, Stead D. 1996. Far pavilions? Cricket migrants, foreign sojourns and contested identities. *International Review for the Sociology of Sport* 31 (1): 1-24.

Maguire J, Stead D. 1998. Border crossings: Soccer labor force migration and the European Union. *International Review for the Sociology of Sport* 33 (1): 59-73.

Maguire J, Jarvie G, Mansfield L, Bradley J. 2002. *Sports Worlds: A Sociological Perspective.* Champaign, Il: Human Kinetics.

Mascord S. 2011. On the Road: Drama over international selections. http://www.nrl.com/on-the-road-drama-over-international-selections/tabid/10874/newsid/65118/default.aspx

Massoud J. 2012. Parents blame 'mind games' for switch. http://www.heraldsun.com.au/sport/nrl/parents-blame-mind-games-for-switch/story-e6frfgbo-1226328230543

McGovern P. 2002. Globalization or internationalization? Foreign footballers in the English League, 1946-1995. *Sociology* **36** (1): 23-42.

New Zealand Rugby League. 2009. *Rugby League – Contributing to New Zealand's Future*. Report of the Independent Review Committee, February 2009.

NZ Newswire. 2012. Kiwis won't be targeting turncoat Tamou. http://sport.msn.co.nz/sportnews/rugbyleague/8452749/kiwis-wont-be-targeting-turncoat-tamou

Otago Daily Times 2012. League: Fien says more Tamous will be lost to Aussie. http://www.odt.co.nz/sport/league/205817/league-fien-says-more-tamous-will-be-lost-aussie

Parry R. 2011. Rangi Chase: Grandad bashed my Nan's face so badly I couldn't recognise her - England rugby league star on overcoming the odds. http://www.mirror.co.uk/news/top-stories/2011/11/11/rangi-chase-grandad-bashed-my-nan-s-face-so-badly-i-couldn-t-recognise-her-england-rugby-league-star-on-overcoming-the-odds-115875-23553054/#ixzz1jHRXdkng

Pierce J. 2011. League player Rangi Chase gets suspended sentence for breaking man's jaw in Gold Coast pub fight.: http://www.couriermail.com.au/sport/nrl/league-player-rangi-chase-pleads-guilty-to-breaking-mans-jaw-in-gold-coast-pub-fight/story-e6frep66-1226112349337?from=public_rss

Radio NZ. 2012. Dowling says Tamou shouldn't be allowed to play for Kangaroos. http://www.radionz.co.nz/news/sport/103653/dowling-says-tamou-shouldn%27t-be-allowed-to-play-for-kangaroos

Read B. 2012. Tamou has last laugh in glare of spotlight. http://www.theaustralian.com.au/sport/nrl/tamou-has-last-laugh-in-glare-of-spotlight/story-fnca0von-1226334843307

Robins K. 1997. What in the world is going on?. In Du Gay P. (ed.) *Production of Culture/Cultures of Production*. London: Sage; 11-67.

Shannon K. 2012. Sparks fly over Tamou's switch. http://www.thechronicle.com.au/story/2012/04/17/sparks-fly-over-tamous-switch-to-kangaroos/

Skipwith D. 2012. Kiwis in 'glass house' over Tamou – Lowe. http://tvnz.co.nz/rugby-league-news/kiwis-in-glass-house-over-tamou-lowe-4835505

Stead D, Maguire J. 1998. Cricket's global finishing school: The migration of overseas cricketers into English county cricket. *European Physical Education Review* **4** (1): 54-69.

Stead D, Maguire, J. 2000a. No boundaries to ambition: Soccer labour migration and the case of Nordic/Scandinavian players in England. In Bangsbo J. (ed.), *Soccer and Science in an Interdisciplinary Perspective*. Copenhagen: University of Copenhagen Press; 35-55.

Stead D, Maguire J. 2000b. Rite de passage or passage to riches? The motivation and objectives of Nordic/Scandinavian players in English League Soccer. *Journal of Sport and Social Issues* **24** (1): 36-60.

Spaaij R. 2011. *Sport and Social Mobility: Crossing Boundaries.* New York: Routledge.

The Age. 2011. Platt backs England's decision to select Chase. http://www.theage. com.au/rugby-league/league-news/platt-backs-englands-decision-to-select-chase-20111014-1los0.html#ixzz1jHgNSyAH

Tulloch A. 2012. Aussies part of Kiwis squad and vice versa. http://www.3news. co.nz/Aussies-part-of-Kiwis-squad-and-vice-versa/tabid/415/articleID/250634/ Default.aspx

Vannisselroy B. 2012. Kemp not happy with Tamou's Aussie selection. http://www. newstalkzb.co.nz/auckland/news/spleg/1600981952-Kemp-not-happy-with-Tamau-s-Aussie-selection

Walter B. 2011. Kiwi defector Chase cops a verbal barrage but shines as England reach decider. http://www.smh.com.au/rugby-league/league-news/kiwi-defector-chase-cops-a-verbal-barrage-but-shines-as-england-reach-decider-20111113-1ndv5.html#ixzz1jHac6isi

Webster A. 2012a. I still call Australia home ... for now. http://www.heraldsun.com. au/sport/nrl/i-still-call-australia-home-for-now/story-e6frfgbo-1226328230750

Webster A. 2012b. Kiwis consider Origin as a strategy to retain talent. http://www. heraldsun.com.au/sport/nrl/kiwis-consider-origin-as-a-strategy-to-retain-talent/ story-e6frfgbo-1226330701787

Webster A. 2012c. Tamou attacks are way off the money. http://www.dailytelegraph. com.au/sport/tamou-attacks-are-way-off-the-money/story-e6freye0-1226334737901?from=public_rss

Webster A, Balym T, Hamilton A. 2012. James Tamou happy with his decision to opt to play for Kangaroos but ready for retribution from New Zealand. http:// www.dailytelegraph.com.au/sport/nrl/james-tamou-happy-with-his-decision-to-opt-to-play-for-kangaroos-but-ready-for-retribution-from-new-zealand/story-e6frexnr-1226328230477

Williams G. 1994. The Road to Wigan Pier Revisited: The Migrations of Welsh Rugby Talent since 1918, In Bale J, Maguire J. (eds), *The Global Sports Arena: Athletic Talent Migration in an Interdependent World.* Portland: Frank Cass; 25-38.

Wilson A. 2011. Kiwi captain Benji Marshall backs Rangi Chase's switch to England. http://www.guardian.co.uk/sport/2011/oct/27/benji-marshall-rangi-chase-england?INTCMP=ILCNETTXT3487

Woodward K. 2012. *Planet Sport.* Oxford: Routledge.

Ancillary Student Material

Further reading

Agergaard S. 2008. Elite athletes as migrants in Danish women's handball. *International Review for the Sociology of Sport* 43 (1): 5-19.

Andreff W. 2011. Why tax international athlete migration? The 'Coubertobin' tax in a context of financial crisis. In Maguire J, Falcous M (eds) *Sport and Migration: Borders, Boundaries and Crossings*. Oxford: Routledge; 31-45.

Brock D. 2012. Why Tamou should play for NZ and NSW. www.bigpondsport.com/why-tamou-should-play-for-nz-nsw/tabid/91/newsid/86984/default.aspx

Chepyator-Thomson J. 2003. Kenyan scholar-runners in the United States: Their thirst for education and intercollegiate experiences. *AVANTE* **9**: 31-39.

Elliott R, Maguire J. 2008. Getting caught in the net: Examining the recruitment of Canadian players in British professional ice hockey. *Journal of Sport and Social Issues* **32** (2): 158-176.

Heming W. 2012. Clarity sought on league eligibility. http://news.smh.com.au/breaking-news-sport/clarity-sought-on-league-eligibility-20120417-1x54d.html

Lanfranchi P, Taylor M. 2001. *Moving with the Ball: The Migration of Professional Footballers*. Oxford: Berg.

Miller T, Lawrence G, McKay J, Rowe D. 2001. *Globalization and Sport: Playing the World*. London: Sage.

Rattue C. 2012. Turncoat Tamou sells his skills to highest bidder. http://www.nzherald.co.nz/sport/news/article.cfm?c_id=4andobjectid=10799586

Takahashi Y, Horne J. 2011. Moving with the bat and the ball: The migration of Japanese baseball labour, 1912-2009. In Maguire J, Falcous M (eds) *Sport and Migration: Borders, Boundaries and Crossings*. Oxford: Routledge; 46-55.

Thorpe H. 2011. 'Have board, will travel': Global physical youth cultures and transnational mobility. In Maguire J, Falcous M (eds) *Sport and Migration: Borders, Boundaries and Crossings*. Oxford: Routledge; 112-125

Related websites

The National Rugby League: http://www.nrl.com/

The New Zealand Rugby Football League: http://www.nzrl.co.nz/

The Rugby Football League: http://www.therfl.co.uk/

The Rugby League International Federation: http://www.rlif.com/

Self-test questions

Try to answer the following questions to test your knowledge and understanding. If you are not sure of the answers, please re-read the case and refer to the references and further reading sources.

1   Read the two Australian blog entries (below) and discuss how the opinions raised by these fans could be used to support the movements of Rangi Chase and James Tamou.

    International-rugby-league-eligibility:
    http://www.theroar.com.au/2011/10/28/international-rugby-league-eligibility/?utm_source=feedburner&utm_medium=feed&utm_campaign=Feed%3A+theroar+%28The+Roar%29

    Tighter-eligibility-laws-better-for-international-league:
    http://www.theroar.com.au/2012/04/20/tighter-eligibility-laws-better-for-international-league/

2   Based on the case study material and the opinions raised in the two additional blogs introduced above, discuss why traditional "donor" nations might choose to fight a rule stating that elite athletes can only represent one nation during their professional career.

3   Based on his online opinion piece (below), develop three strategies which could 'save' James Tamou and 'the game' from further 'humiliation'.

Rattue's Rant

The best that can be said about his nation-hopping disgrace is that it has added an explosive element to Friday night's test at Eden Park. The current rules are good enough considering league's limited international standing. They respect the individual's right to decide his allegiance based on heritage and residency and have enabled the small Pacific Island sides to use top players who can later join the big guns when their careers blossom. We all know that there are tricky eligibility situations in sport and difficulties in framing rules. But he made that choice when accepting a place in the Kiwi train-on squad last year and declaring it would be an honour to wear the black and white. A 23-year-old with definite Kiwi loyalties and prospects, plus a history in the junior system, has not suddenly decided he is Australian. A player on the verge of Kiwi test selection has allowed someone to persuade him that he is Australian via a State of Origin carrot, or an element of vice-versa. The Aussies are hypocrites, using the rigidity of their state eligibility rules which involve national loyalty to recruit international players whose hearts, in truth, lie elsewhere. Like vultures, the Aussies are preying on the weakness of New Zealand's domestic game, which can't provide an Origin alternative or pay packet. Ultimately, these decisions rest with the players and unlike many others I regard [Nathan] Fien as an equal villain in that scandal alongside the administration and team management. Fien had to virtually deny the existence of his real grandmother in order to relocate his great-grandmother in the lineage chain. What a way to treat your granny.! (Rattue, 2012)

4 Using the following State of Origin (SoO) eligibility criteria, develop a new/improved strategy that could be adopted by other nations looking to develop similar domestic competitions in order to attract new migrants and/or retain the loyalties of local talent.

State of Origin

Australia's State of Origin Series has been referred to as 'the pinnacle' and 'the biggest challenge' in modern day rugby league (Brock, 2012). According to Brock, the Queensland (Maroons) versus New South Wales (NSW Blues) fixtures are "played ar a higher standard and a greater intensity than internationals", and "is also an annual three-match blockbuster that pays much better than one-off Test matches".

In November 2-11 the Australian Rugby League Commission simplified the eligibility criteria, asking players to answer the following five questions:

1. In which State were you born?

2. In which State did you play junior rugby league (aged 6-18 inclusive)?

3. In which State did you spend the majority of your school years (aged 6-15 inclusive)?

4. In which State did you first play rugby league in a State-run Junior Rep competition aged 15 years or above?

5. For which State did you first play rugby league at a School Representative level?

5 Identify five more modern sporting migrants, place them within the relevant sections of the following model (based on their internal motives and external influencers) and provide a brief justification to support your case.

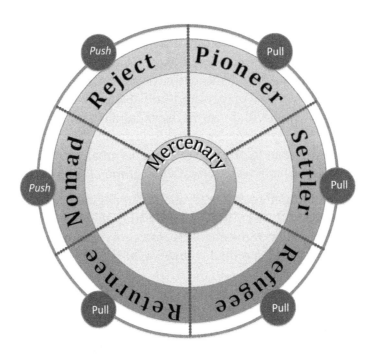

Key themes and messages

The key themes raised in this case study relate to the following areas:

Globalisation

Mobility

♦   Temporary / Short-term

♦   Permanent / Long-term

Place Attachment

Migration

♦   Return Migration

♦   Transnationalism

Elite Sport

Messages arising from the above are as follows:

♦   Sport and border-crossing movements have a long and well-established relationship, dating back over 100 years. Contemporary globalization processes have merely made the links more obvious, if not acceptable, to sports performers and, to a lesser extent, the general public.

♦   Led primarily by Joseph Maguire, sport labour migration has established an ever-growing body of knowledge, which has moved beyond the who, when and why to look at the experiences and issues faced by various migrants playing a variety of sports in a number of different locations.

♦   Modern migrants can be pulled in by a variety of private and public promises, but are also pushed away by personal and professional rejections encountered in their home communities.

♦   Professional 'business-like' decisions that impact upon the construction and consumption of local loyalties, national identities and international eligibilities are influenced by both the head and the heart. They are often reported to the public, however, as coming from one or the other (not both), which can have consequences on the degree of empathy and apathy received.

♦   Chase's professional eligibility was overlooked due to his personal identity, and the empathy generated by his career choice was fuelled by the media discourse portraying him predominantly as a (social) reject. Tamou's professional eligibility was questioned by numerous stakeholders, and the apathy generated was fuelled by the media's decision to portray him as a mercenary migrant.

 Scan here to get the hyperlinks for this chapter.

Abbreviations

A$	Australian dollars
ANZAC	Australian and New Zealand Army Corps
ARL	Australian Rugby League
BBC	British Broadcasting Corporation
BMX	Bicycle Motor Cross
BOBICO	Beijing 2008 Olympic Games Bid Committee
BOCOG	Beijing Organising Committee of the Games
BODA	Beijing Olympic City Development Association
CAN$	Canadian dollars
CBA	Cost-Benefit Analysis
CBD	Central Business District
CC	Corporate Citizenship
CDR	Canadian Death Race
CGE	Ccomputable General Equilibrium (modelling)
CSR	Corporate Social Responsibility
DCMS	Department of Culture Media and Sport
DDF	Dirt-jump, downhill and freeride
DFB	German Football Association
ESL	English Super League
FA	Football Association
FC	Football Club
FIFA	Fédération Internationale de Football Association
HOC	House of Commons
GDP	Gross Domestic Product
GVA	Gross Value Added
IOC	International Olympic Committee
I-O	Input-Output (modelling)
LOCOG	London Organising Committee of the Olympic and Paralympic Games
OPCY	Oriole Park at Camden Yards
NHL	National Hockey League

NSW	New South Wales
NZRL	New Zealand Rugby League
OECD	Organisation for Economic Cooperation and Development
R	Rand
RLIF	Rugby League International Federation
SED	State Electoral District
UNWTO	United Nations World Tourism Organization
US$	United States dollars
WAG	Welsh Assembly Government
WTO	World Trade Organization

Index